THE

GUIDE TO COPING
WITH PANIC DISORDER

Dear Reader,

Panic disorder is often considered a serious concern because it can lead to a loss of productivity and large medical expenditures to treat panic attacks in hospitals and clinics. However, no one is more distressed over panic disorder than the people who suffer from it. Panic attacks are so upsetting that they often significantly alter people's lives. Panic disorder imprisons a person with feelings of fear and impotence.

There is no need to let this disorder take control. The anxiety disorders, of which panic disorder is one, constitute the largest class of psychological disorders, but interestingly, a large number of people with anxiety disorders do not receive treatment despite the number of empirically validated treatment approaches available.

No one should suffer with panic disorder. The reason I wrote this book is to offer people with panic disorder as much basic information as they need in order to make an informed decision about how to approach their issues. It is my hope that reading this book can help just one person gain control over his or her panic attacks and panic disorder. If that happens, then all of the effort put into this book will be well worth it.

Rudolph C. Hatfield, PhD

Welcome to the EVERYTHING. Series!

These handy, accessible books give you all you need to tackle a difficult project, gain a new hobby, comprehend a fascinating topic, prepare for an exam, or even brush up on something you learned back in school but have since forgotten.

You can choose to read an Everything® book from cover to cover or just pick out the information you want from our four useful boxes: e-questions, e-facts, e-alerts, and e-ssentials.

We give you everything you need to know on the subject, but throw in a lot of fun stuff along the way, too.

We now have more than 400 Everything® books in print, spanning such wide-ranging categories as weddings, pregnancy, cooking, music instruction, foreign language, crafts, pets, New Age, and so much more. When you're done reading them all, you can finally say you know Everything®!

QUESTION

Answers to
common questions

FACT

Important snippets
of information

ALERT

Urgent
warnings

ESSENTIAL

Quick
handy tips

PUBLISHER Karen Cooper

MANAGING EDITOR, EVERYTHING® SERIES Lisa Laing

COPY CHIEF Casey Ebert

ASSISTANT PRODUCTION EDITOR Alex Guarco

ACQUISITIONS EDITOR Eileen Mullan

DEVELOPMENT EDITOR Eileen Mullan

EVERYTHING® SERIES COVER DESIGNER Erin Alexander

Visit the entire Everything® series at *www.everything.com*

THE
EVERYTHING®
GUIDE TO COPING
WITH PANIC DISORDER

Learn how to take control of your panic
and live a healthier, happier life

Rudolph C. Hatfield, PhD

Adams media
Avon, Massachusetts

To my family, who have put up with all my antics over the years.

An Everything® Series Book.
Everything® and everything.com® are registered trademarks of F+W Media, Inc.

Published by Adams Media, a division of F+W Media, Inc.
57 Littlefield Street, Avon, MA 02322 U.S.A.
www.adamsmedia.com

ISBN 10: 1-4405-6964-9
ISBN 13: 978-1-4405-6964-7
eISBN 10: 1-4405-6965-7
eISBN 13: 978-1-4405-6965-4

Printed in the United States of America.

10 9 8 7 6 5 4 3 2 1

Library of Congress Cataloging-in-Publication Data
Hatfield, Rudolph C.
The everything guide to coping with panic disorder / Rudolph C. Hatfield, PhD.
pages cm
Includes bibliographical references and index.
ISBN-13: 978-1-4405-6964-7 (pbk. : alk. paper)
ISBN-10: 1-4405-6964-9 (pbk. : alk. paper)
ISBN-13: 978-1-4405-6965-4 (ebook)
ISBN-10: 1-4405-6965-7 (ebook)
1. Panic disorders. 2. Psychotherapy. I. Title.
RC535.H38 2013
616.85'223--dc23

2013031067

This book is available at quantity discounts for bulk purchases.
For information, please call 1-800-289-0963.

Contents

10 Medications Commonly Used in Treating Panic Disorder / 133

A Brief History of Medication Use for Anxiety Disorders **134**

Antidepressant Medications and Panic Disorder **135**

Antianxiety Medications and Panic Disorder **138**

Beta-Blockers and Panic Disorder **142**

Other Medications Used to Treat Panic Disorder **142**

Nonresponders to Medications **143**

Are Psychotropic Medications Effective? **144**

11 Psychotherapy and Panic Disorder / 147

Major Psychotherapy Schools **148**

Psychodynamic Therapy for Panic Disorder **152**

Behavioral Therapy for Panic Disorder **153**

Cognitive-Behavioral Therapy for Panic Disorder **154**

Relaxation Training **158**

Other Psychological Treatments for Panic Disorder **159**

12 Group Psychotherapy for Panic Disorder / 161

The History of Group Psychotherapy **162**

Types of Group Psychotherapy for Panic Disorder **164**

Support Groups for Panic Disorder **166**

Is Psychotherapy Effective in Treating Panic Disorder? **167**

13 Natural Remedies for Panic Disorder / 171

Warning about Natural Remedies for Panic Disorder **172**

Inositol **173**

Valerian Root **175**

Kava **177**

GABA **180**

Panic Disorder and pH Levels **181**

Other Herbs and Vitamins **184**

The Bottom Line **186**

14 Alternative Treatments for Panic Disorder / 189

Warning Regarding These Alternative Treatments **190**

Hypnotherapy **190**

Acupuncture **192**

Biofeedback Training **194**

Eye Movement Desensitization and Reprocessing (EMDR) **197**

Diet/Lifestyle **199**

Acknowledgments

As always, I would like to acknowledge all my professors at the University of Michigan and Wayne State University for their wonderful teaching and their patience with me as a student so long ago. However, I really need to thank the thousands of patients whom I have assessed or treated over the years. It is from you that I have learned more than I ever could have learned in the classroom. God bless you all.

The Top 10 Facts about Panic Disorder

1. Panic disorder is classified as an anxiety disorder. This is a class of psychiatric disorders where the major symptom is anxiety.

2. Having recurrent unexpected panic attacks is the major symptom, but not the only symptom, of panic disorder.

3. Panic attacks are periods of sudden intense anxiety that can also occur as a part of other psychiatric disorders, as a result of a medical or medication issue, and in people who do not have psychological of medical disorders.

4. There are a number of theories regarding the cause of panic disorder that incorporate both biological and psychological contributions.

5. The most often implicated biological cause of panic disorder is a disruption of the "fight-or-flight" mechanism.

6. Agoraphobia, the fear of being in places where one cannot escape, used to be exclusively associated with panic disorder but is now considered a separate anxiety disorder.

7. The vast majority of people who are diagnosed with panic disorder will also be diagnosed with another psychiatric disorder, most often with depression.

8. Medications commonly used for treating panic disorder include a class of antidepressants and the minor tranquilizers (benzodiazepines).

9. The form of treatment most often recommended for panic disorder is cognitive behavioral psychotherapy, but several alternative and complementary treatments may also be helpful.

10. At one time panic disorder was considered only to occur in adults, but it is now recognized that panic disorder can occur in children and adolescents as well.

Introduction

PEOPLE WHO HAVE PANIC DISORDER experience sudden and repeated attacks of severe anxiety or fear that can last for several minutes or longer. These episodes are more commonly known as panic attacks. The feelings experienced during a panic attack are so intense and so alarming to people that they often feel that they are about to experience another disaster, or that they are going to lose control even in situations when there is no such danger. Panic attacks can be so powerful that they can mimic heart attacks or other very serious medical conditions.

These attacks can occur at any time, and therefore, people with panic disorder tend to worry about them so much that it affects every aspect of their lives. This disorder is so overwhelming that people often become discouraged and feel ashamed because they find it difficult to carry out normal activities or perform normal routines like going to the grocery store, going out in public, driving, going to work, or going to social events. Does this sound like something you've experienced before? You are not alone.

Psychiatric disorders like panic disorder tend to run in families; however, at the present time it is not known why certain people develop panic disorder and other people do not. Heredity does not fully explain the disorder, and having an occasional panic attack is actually a common event affecting nearly one-fifth of the population in the United States. Panic disorder is not nearly as prevalent (the American Psychological Association reports that about one in seventy-five people will develop it). Research into panic disorder has indicated the potential involvement of several different brain neurotransmitters, several potential changes that occur in different parts of the brain, and other factors that are associated with getting panic attacks and developing panic disorder. Nonetheless, no one knows what the cause of panic disorder is.

The typical case of panic disorder is a person who presents with anxiety and anticipation of his next panic attack, limits his activities in anticipation of potential panic attacks, and lets this fear and anxiety dictate his life. If you share these symptoms, don't worry. The outlook should not be this bleak.

Anxiety is a fact of life; however, suffering from a disabling anxiety disorder like panic disorder does not have to be. Many people who suffer from repeated panic attacks but do not have panic disorder have medical issues that can be treated. People with panic disorder require special methods to address their particular issues. The potential for effective treatments is very real, and there are many options for everyone who suffers from panic disorder to explore. There are also a number of so-called treatments for panic disorder that are not effective. It is extremely important for anyone suffering from any type of psychological or psychiatric disorder to be able to ascertain what types of treatment options are potentially effective and what treatment options are not. This may sound complicated; however, it only requires a very basic understanding of what to look for.

No one who has panic disorder should be a prisoner of this anxiety disorder. This book discusses the relevant issues of anxiety, panic attacks, and panic disorder and outlines the empirical evidence for the majority of treatment options available for anyone who suffers with panic disorder. This information arms you with the necessary means to combat this condition and change your situation. With *The Everything® Guide to Coping with Panic Disorder*, you'll learn how to gain control over your panic and anxiety using a variety of easy-to-understand techniques.

CHAPTER 1

The Nature of Psychological/ Psychiatric Disorders

What is a psychological or psychiatric disorder? Surprisingly, most people do not understand the difference between common, everyday emotional experiences like feeling down or depressed and an actual psychological/psychiatric disorder. For instance, everyone feels nervous or anxious at one time or another; however, having a type of anxiety disorder is much more severe and disabling than normal anxiety. This chapter discusses what a psychiatric disorder or mental illness actually is, how these differ from normal experiences, how these are conceptualized, and how mental health professionals diagnose them.

ALERT

It is quite easy to get caught up in trying to figure out the different designations of psychological disorders. To avoid any confusion, the terms *psychological disorder*, *psychiatric disorder*, *mental illness*, and *mental disorder* generally refer to the same thing; therefore, these terms will be used interchangeably throughout this book.

The DSM Defined

Believe it or not, the definition of what comprises a mental disorder is not as clear as you may think. In the United States, mental health workers refer to the most current version of the DSM series to define and diagnose mental disorders (DSM stands for *Diagnostic and Statistical Manual of Mental Disorders*). At the time of this writing, the current upgrade to the DSM is the DSM-5, which was formerly released in May of 2013. A thorough explanation of the development of the DSM is beyond the scope of this book; however, in order to understand how psychiatric disorders are conceptualized, a brief history is in order.

History of the DSM

The origins of the DSM can be traced back to the 1800s when the United States government attempted to collect data on mental illness. The terms *idiocy* and *insanity* were used to describe various forms of mental illness at that time, but, of course, these were not only derogatory, they were not descriptive enough. Over time, mental health professionals increased the categories of diagnoses for mental illnesses, but there were no uniform designations across all the different mental hospitals, and therefore, different labels or diagnoses were used to describe the same behaviors. This led to quite a bit of confusion for both mental health workers and patients.

In the early 1900s, an organization then known as the Committee on Statistics of the American Medico-Psychological Association helped develop a series of manuals identifying different classes of mental illnesses for use in hospitals (this organization eventually became the American Psychiatric Association). However, there were still many different diagnostic symptoms for the same mental disorders, and the classification of mental illnesses remained confusing. It became clear in the 1950s that there was a real need to develop a set of common diagnostic criteria and diagnostic terms for psychological disorders so that mental health professionals could communicate with one another and so that a diagnostic label would have some utility.

ESSENTIAL

Psychiatrists are medical doctors specializing in the diagnosis and treatment of mental disorders. Psychiatrists most often prescribe medication, and do not perform psychotherapy. Clinical psychologists are not medical doctors, but specialize in the diagnosis and treatment of mental illness (with therapy); in most states they cannot prescribe medications. Counselors, social workers, etc., also receive training in treating psychological problems.

To fulfill this need, the first DSM (DSM-I) was created in 1952. The first DSM featured 106 different psychiatric disorders, but the descriptions were very general and were framed in Freudian terms (Sigmund Freud was the father of psychoanalysis—Freudian thought dominated clinical psychology and psychiatry in the 1950s).

Given the limitations of the first DSM, the DSM-II was released in 1968. However, that edition also consisted primarily of generalized descriptions and still retained a Freudian slant. In 1980, a major shift was made by the American Psychiatric Association (APA) when the DSM-III was released. At that time, the field of psychiatry was moving toward a medical viewpoint and more empirically based evidence (evidence based on research), and away from psychological explanations of behavior disorders and Freudian notions.

The major reason for the shift was that there had been suspicion surrounding the validity of psychiatry in America during this time. Psychiatric diagnoses were often formed on the basis of opinion instead of research, which was in direct opposition to how the rest of the medical field approached diagnosing different types of illnesses and diseases. The reliability of the psychiatric diagnosis from the earlier DSM manuals was quite poor (in this context the term *reliability* means "consistency of the actual diagnosis given to a patient from one psychiatrist to another"). However, even though the emphasis was put on reliability, this did not necessarily translate to greater validity of the diagnosis (*validity* refers to the actual truth or accuracy of the diagnosis). In addition, by this time, the number of psychiatric disorders had jumped to 264.

The trend of attempting to increase reliability continued throughout subsequent versions of the DSM. In addition to attempting to increase the reliability of the diagnostic process for mental illnesses or psychiatric disorders, the number of diagnoses increased from the DSM-III to the DSM-IV. In fact, the transition from the DSM-III-R to the DSM-IV did not involve a major shift in the approach, only an increase in the number of diagnostic categories. The change from the DSM-IV to the DSM-IV-TR saw a change in the demographic information for each diagnosis (male-female ratio, age of onset, etc.) but no change in diagnostic criteria.

FACT

Interestingly, the title of the current DSM, the DSM-5, may lead you to believe that there have been five versions of the DSM over the years. There have actually been seven versions, counting all of the revisions. The third and fourth versions of the DSM were revised, leading to the DSM-III, the DSM-III-R, the DSM-IV, and the DSM-IV-TR.

The DSM-5

The DSM-5 represents another major paradigm shift in how psychological disorders are conceptualized and diagnosed. This shift has been so dramatic that there has been quite a bit of controversy surrounding it. Not only have certain classes of disorders that have appeared in all of the previous DSMs, such as anxiety disorders, been totally overhauled (with some older disorders eliminated or moved to different classes); the diagnostic criteria for many childhood disorders have been completely changed as well. Nonetheless, the new DSM will eventually set the tone for how psychological disorders are conceptualized by mental health professionals in the United States.

In other countries, including many in Europe, psychological disorders are more often diagnosed using the International Statistical Classification of Diseases and Related Health Problems (ICD) diagnostic criteria. Interestingly, as will be discussed later in this chapter, the vast majority of psychiatric disorders are not defined by any type of medical tests or medical criteria.

The DSM series has traditionally provided criteria for mental health professionals to follow when determining the diagnosis of individuals with a suspected psychiatric disorder. These diagnostic criteria are also coded and accepted by insurance organizations (at least most of them) to provide reimbursement for the diagnostics and treatment of psychiatric conditions. The diagnostic criteria provided by the DSM allow mental health professionals to consistently categorize, understand, communicate about, and treat these various disorders. However, there is quite a bit of controversy and subjectivity still involved in this process. Again, it is beyond the scope of this book to discuss all of these controversies, but the current DSM-5 has caused quite an uproar, and many prominent psychiatrists and psychologists are condemning it. For those diagnosed with mental disorders, the new changes may eventually result in reclassifications and some confusion surrounding their diagnosis. In addition, several categories of psychiatric disorders may see increases in the number of people diagnosed with them such as ADHD or even cognitive disorders.

Why the DSM?

You might be asking yourself, why is the DSM-5 relevant to this book? Well, the diagnosis of a panic disorder will only be considered appropriate if an individual's symptoms satisfy the DSM-5 diagnostic criteria, since these are the criteria that mental health professionals will most likely be using. Fortunately, there is little difference in the diagnostic criteria for panic disorder from the DSM-IV-TR (the previous version of the DSM) to the DSM-5 (the current version of the DSM). The diagnostic criteria in the DSM-5 differentiate what actually defines a panic disorder from what the APA considers normal or common manifestations of anxiety and panic.

What Is a Mental Disorder?

The distinction between a disease and a disorder is admittedly a fine one. A disease can be defined as a type of disorder of structure or function within a person that produces specific signs or symptoms affecting a specific area of the body. Disorders are considered more general problems with behavior or functioning, but cannot be diagnosed by medical tests.

When pondering the notion of what constitutes a mental disorder, clinicians must consider what constitutes "normal" versus "abnormal" behavior. This is actually a much more complicated question than you might think. Whole books have been written on what should define the departure of normality in human behavior. The late Dr. Thomas Szasz, a distinguished psychiatrist but also a lifelong critic of psychiatry, often noted that a medical model defines abnormal behavior in terms of the result of some physical problem (e.g., a cellular derangement, a chemical imbalance, or a genetic issue) that causes the behavior to be abnormal; however, there are no physical markers for the vast majority of the diagnoses in the DSM-5, and there are no medical tests to diagnose psychiatric disorders in the same way that cancer is diagnosed. For example, one legal definition of insanity, based on psychiatric definitions, is that abnormal behavior occurs when the individual is unable to distinguish between right and wrong. This definition is far too extreme to be practical. For instance, most rapists realize that their behavior is wrong by societal standards, and yet rape is absolutely considered by most people to be an abnormal (and criminal) action.

Normality

The four commonly held criteria for distinguishing normal from abnormal behavior include:

1. *A statistical infrequency model*, which states that abnormal behavior falls on either of the extreme ends of a normal distribution. The problem here is that someone with an extremely high IQ or some other trait, such as being quite tall, would be defined as abnormal by this criterion.
2. The *disability or dysfunction model* states that behavior somehow results in a change in what would be considered "normal" functioning in some area. This is really a Catch-22 because it relies on the designation of "normal" behavior in its definition, which is akin to using a word in its own definition. "What is normal functioning?" is essentially the same question as "What is abnormal functioning?"

3. *Personal distress* notions of abnormality claim that the behavior leads to suffering or misery in the person. The issue here is that many obvious features of certain abnormal behaviors, such as personality disorders or drug abuse, often do not lead to personal distress in the individual, while many accepted "normal" behaviors do lead to suffering (e.g., cigarette smoking).

4. The *violation of social norms definition* is related to the notion that the behavior is a departure from the accepted norms in the person's peer group. There are several issues here: Cultural contexts can be hard to assess; they change frequently (look at all the piercings and tattoos young people sport today that ten years ago would have been considered extreme); some specific cultural behaviors, such as certain religious behaviors, cruelty to animals, or certain fertility rites, would not be tolerated in the overall mainstream society regardless of their specific cultural values; and certain culturally accepted behaviors may reflect misunderstandings of serious medical conditions, such as epilepsy.

Therefore, any one of these four definitions alone would be lacking as a qualifier of what constitutes "abnormal behavior," but used together, they can provide useful guidelines as to what qualifies as abnormal. This is essentially the approach of the APA when developing the diagnostic criteria for the DSM series. This means is that the distinction between "normal" and "abnormal" behavior is not as clear-cut as you may believe. The same behavior could be defined as "normal" or "abnormal" depending on the context in which it occurs and on how flexible the person who is behaving is. For instance, consider the type of behavior that often occurs from spectators at a professional wrestling match. That behavior would be considered quite abnormal in most churches.

ALERT

No matter how a mental disorder is defined, it always retains aspects of what is considered socially or culturally acceptable behavior. Therefore, any conceptualization of abnormal behavior or mental illness will be socially constructed and will be based on the norms of that particular culture or society. There is no universally accepted definition of normal behavior.

The DSM Definition of a Mental Disorder

Abnormal behavior is defined in terms of its departure from statistical and social norms and also by its "maladaptiveness (the DSM uses this term to mean that the behavior is harmful; that the behavior leads to negative social, physical, legal, occupational, and/or personal results). Thus, the DSM understands mental disorders to be conditions associated with harm. This harm is categorized as either distress or disability, or a risk of an adverse outcome. Other qualifications narrow this notion so that not all conditions associated with harm can be considered mental disorders. For example, a mental disorder has to involve a personal dysfunction (not just a deviation from social standards), and the condition cannot be an expectable culturally sanctioned response to an event, such as grieving over the death of someone. Mental disorders as defined by the DSM combine the four aforementioned criteria to distinguish normal behavior from abnormal behavior. In the current context, this suggests that someone who experiences an occasional anxiety attack may not have an actual mental disorder, as many people have occasional experiences of anxiety.

FACT

Most of the psychiatric disorders listed in the DSM will typically involve some personal distress for the individual. This distress is noted to lead to problems in daily functioning for the individual, such as affecting her social, occupational, educational, or physical functioning. Panic disorder often severely affects all of these areas of functioning in the individual.

Differences Between a Disorder and a Disease

Many psychiatrists (who are medical doctors), along with many in the pharmaceutical industry, often attempt to present psychiatric disorders as diseases similar to cancer, diabetes, and heart disease. For these individuals, there is no distinction between the notion of the psychiatric disorder and a physical disease. However (and fortunately), many others challenge this concept and point to the fact that the major reason for this belief is that the pharmaceutical industry makes billions of dollars by promoting this false notion. Many opponents reason that medical diseases like cancer involve an identifiable cellular derangement (a physical alteration of bodily tissues), have specific medical diagnostic tests to identify this cellular derangement, and can only be successfully treated by means of some medical intervention, such as medication, surgery, or some other medical treatment. On the other hand, psychiatric disorders (at least the vast majority of them) have no identifiable cellular derangement, cannot be reliably diagnosed by any medical procedure, and are often successfully treated by nonmedical means, such as psychotherapy (in fact, twelve-step groups for addictions have similar success rates to almost all other forms of treatment for addictions, and twelve-step groups are neither medical treatments nor psychotherapy). There are no empirically supported nonmedical treatments for cancer (in this context *empirically supported* means "supported by research methods").

ESSENTIAL

The medical model views psychological disorders as physical diseases like cancer. This model has become widely accepted by psychiatrists, the pharmaceutical industry, and some other mental health workers. However, opponents of the medical model point out the inconsistencies of this view with reality. Most of these opponents are not proponents of solely using medical treatments for psychiatric disorders.

The disease/disorder controversy has been going on for quite some time and will most likely not readily be resolved anytime soon. For purposes of this book, panic disorder will not be considered a physical disease in the same way that cancer is a disease. Thus, this book will accept the argument by medical model opponents that there is a difference between a disease and a disorder.

The Disease/Disorder Distinction

The distinction between a disease and a disorder is admittedly hazy. This book will follow the reasoning that there is a difference between a disease and a disorder. You may think of this as simply a semantic difference that has no meaning; however, given the current understanding of psychiatric disorders, this distinction is not purely semantic. For purposes of this book, a *disease* is defined as "a condition that is directly caused by some identifiable physical derangement." This physical derangement can be the result of a number of factors, including an infection, physical mechanical damage to the system, genetic factors, etc. These physical diseases can only reliably be identified or their presence confirmed via medical testing.

ALERT

You may be thinking that psychiatric disorders are the result of neurotransmitter imbalances in the brain. In fact, there are no reliable empirically identified neurotransmitter imbalances associated with any psychiatric disorder. The idea that psychiatric disorders result from neurotransmitter imbalances is based on speculation of how some medications work and not on identified brain chemical imbalances.

This book will consider something to be a disorder if it has no consistent identifiable physical derangement of cells and cannot be diagnosed via medical testing. Moreover, the majority of diseases can only be treated via medical procedures, such as medication, surgery, etc. Disorders may respond to medical treatments (but so do conditions that are not diseases, like occasional headaches); however, nonmedical treatments have also been empirically shown to be effective in the resolution of disorders (and in most cases these are equally as effective as medical treatments, if not more effective than medical treatments).

This distinction does not imply that diseases are more severe than disorders or that people with disorders are insane or that the disorder is "all in your head." There is no way to satisfy everyone with this distinction. Definitions of the terms *disease*, *disorder*, and *illness* will be flawed depending on the paradigm of the observer. This book uses the distinction to clarify the fact that panic disorder cannot be diagnosed in the same way that diseases like cancer, diabetes, heart disease, etc., are diagnosed.

ESSENTIAL

It is important to understand that subjective severity of the condition has no bearing on whether it is a disease or disorder. People with panic disorder often feel like they are going to die of a heart attack during their panic attacks; however, unless they have a cardiovascular condition, they do not have heart disease. If panic disorder were a real disease, then only a medical doctor would be qualified to treat it.

How Are Psychological/Psychiatric Disorders Discovered?

Because there are no medical tests that can be used to reliably or definitively diagnose the vast majority of the psychiatric disorders in the DSM, there must be another way to determine the diagnostic criteria for these disorders, right? The process by which these disorders are defined and their diagnostic criteria developed may surprise you.

A psychiatric disorder is considered to be a type of syndrome. A syndrome consists of a group of symptoms that hang together and define a specific type of abnormality, illness, disease, or disorder (e.g., panic disorder). In order to identify a syndrome, there has to be quite a bit of research done on a number of different people who have the same set of symptoms. This research can help to validate that a particular syndrome indeed does exist in enough people to define it as a psychiatric disorder. The following discussion on how this process takes place is intended to be very general.

How the Disorders in the DSM Are Defined

Essentially what happens is that, periodically, the APA assigns various task forces/committees to meet and determine how these syndromes should be identified for diagnostic purposes. A task committee may consist of any combination of psychiatrists, psychologists, or even social workers. These task committees are assigned to discuss the research findings that apply to a specific type of disorder (e.g., panic disorder). The APA chooses task committee members with expertise on the particular topic in question, and the committee meets to discuss how a particular psychiatric disorder will be conceptualized and diagnosed. The committee votes on the various diagnostic criteria and associated features that go with each psychological disorder.

In the past, this process was heavily criticized because many of the members of these various task committees had strong affiliations with pharmaceutical companies. Having a vested interest in a pharmaceutical company would obviously influence a person's vote as to what symptoms/criteria should be included in a specific type of psychiatric diagnosis or what specific psychiatric diagnoses should be in the DSM. The DSM-5 committees were designed so that the committee members did not have ties to pharmaceutical companies or other vested interests (at least according to the APA).

What happens in these committees usually takes quite a bit of time. Many years typically pass from one version of the DSM to the next. During this time, the committee members have to consider the research on the various disorders that has been performed and come to an agreement on the diagnostic criteria for existing disorders, any changes in diagnostic criteria for existing orders, whether or not to keep certain disorders in the DSM, and what diagnostic criteria should be applied to new disorders. When the diagnostic criteria for a specific disorder are finalized, it means that the committee voted on what criteria should be used to diagnose a specific disorder and came to some type of agreement as to what constitutes a specific disorder.

The diagnostic criteria for the disorders in the DSM are behavioral symptoms: symptoms that the person displays through his behavior and his actions. The committees are unable to identify any reliable medical tests that can differentiate psychological disorders from normal behavior (because at this time none exist), and so there is a large amount of subjectivity involved in how the disorders in the DSM are conceptualized. There is also a certain amount of subjectivity when any single individual is given a specific DSM diagnosis. This is a criticism of the DSM; however, there is some form of subjectivity involved in diagnosing even the most hardcore of medical diseases. The goal of the DSM criteria has been to try to maximize the reliability of the diagnostic process (in this case *reliability* means "the consistency of the diagnosis given to an individual by different clinicians"). Reliability is extremely important in diagnosing any type of disorder or medical condition, but it is not the only consideration. Most of the diagnoses in the DSM have acceptable reliability. (The term "acceptable reliability" is not universally acknowledged. The DSM adheres to a set of research standards that many have claimed may not be adequate for clinical purposes, even though they are "adequate" for certain research studies.)

FACT

The DSM has had a large number of critics since its conceptualization. Despite its faults, the DSM is still the standard used to diagnose psychological disorders in the United States. However, an untrained individual cannot buy a DSM and diagnose a psychiatric disorder in anyone. Only a trained and licensed clinician is authorized to diagnose psychological disorders in people.

How Do You Know If You Have a Psychiatric Disorder?

The simple answer to this question is, unless a person has a formal assessment from a psychologist, psychiatrist, or other qualified mental health care worker, the person does not definitively know if she has a psychiatric disorder. It is important to repeat over and over that this book is *not* a manual to help you self-diagnose.

You might be suspicious that you have a psychological disorder if:

1. You are experiencing quite a bit of discomfort from symptoms of anxiety or depression that interfere with your normal routine.
2. You are engaging in behaviors that interfere with your ability to do your job or relate to your family, such avoiding responses due to the fear of having an anxiety attack.
3. You keep repeating behaviors that cause extreme discomfort or legal issues (however, repeated criminal activities do not guarantee one has a psychological disorder). In these cases, you should seek out a licensed clinician for an assessment.

One thing that people often hear on the news is that 50 percent (or some large percentage) of Americans have mental health disorders. Some disagree with this number because many of the symptoms of the mental disorders in the DSM are experiences that most people have at one time or another, such as feeling depressed, getting anxious, doing something that gets one into trouble, etc. The difference between a normal manifestation of a behavior and having a psychological disorder is both a matter of quality and quantity. Everyone gets depressed or down at one time or another, and some have good reasons to be depressed. Losing one's job, breaking up with a girlfriend or boyfriend, doing poorly in school or at work, or any number of other occurrences in life will result in most people feeling sad and down. The difference between feeling sad and down due to life circumstances and a clinically significant psychiatric disorder can only be reliably determined by someone who is trained to understand and spot these differences. (The key here, of course, is the term *reliably determined*. Such a statement does not imply that people cannot recognize that they are in distress or have a problem; however, in order to determine the clinical significance of the problem, one must be trained formally to understand the difference between a clinical disorder and a problem that is associated with relatively normal aspects of living and experience). Therefore, if you have not had a formal assessment but think you might suffer from panic disorder or any other psychological disorder, seek out a formal consultation with a licensed mental health professional.

Diagnosing Psychological/Psychiatric Disorders

These disorders are diagnosed by a mental health professional. However, it might be useful to explain just how the diagnostic process typically works. First, different mental health professionals will approach the diagnostic process a little bit differently depending on their background. A psychiatrist is a medical doctor who is qualified to actually perform a medical evaluation of a particular person, whereas psychologists, social workers, and other mental health professionals must use secondary sources if they want a medical evaluation.

You may wonder why a medical evaluation is necessary given that there are no medical tests available to determine the presence of psychological disorders. The reason for this is quite simple: There are many medical conditions that can either mimic specific psychiatric disorders or have tertiary effects that mimic psychiatric symptoms. For instance, someone with a thyroid condition may often experience depression or extreme elation, depending on the nature of their condition. If the thyroid condition is addressed, these psychiatric symptoms will often dissipate. This means that the person did not have a psychiatric disorder, but instead had a medical condition that produced symptoms seen in psychiatric disorders. Therefore, a good medical evaluation can rule out the presence of some type of a physical or medical condition that is mimicking a psychological disorder. So no matter who does the diagnosis (e.g., psychiatrist, psychologist, social worker, etc.), it is often very important to order a medical evaluation of the patient.

A competent psychologist or other mental health worker will take a complete medical history of the person before considering any psychological/psychiatric issues and may require a medical evaluation of the individual or request to talk to the person's physician before making a specific diagnosis.

Psychological Tests

Some mental health professionals will administer psychological tests to individuals in order to help them with their diagnosis. Most often, tests for psychological/psychiatric issues are hand-written tests, fill in the blank, pick the best answer, etc. Psychological tests are not invasive; they do not require the person to be stuck with needles, shocked, or anything of that nature. In addition, many of these tests have built-in methods of determining whether the person is responding in a forthright manner. It is important when taking any of these tests to answer them as honestly as possible, because if there is a hint that a person is either trying to exaggerate symptoms or engage in some other dishonest means to present himself, the mental health professional often has no other choice but to view the assessment as invalid. Like the DSM, these psychological tests can only be administered and interpreted by a trained individual. Many of the tests that you see in bookstores or online are not psychometrically valid and cannot be used for diagnostic purposes.

FACT

Psychological tests can often assist in the diagnosis of a disorder; however, the results of a psychological test alone do not make a diagnostic decision. This is one of the reasons why only trained individuals should administer and interpret these tests. The potential for their misuse is quite large, and misinterpretation of the results by unqualified individuals is quite common.

The Interview

All of the different types of mental health professionals should perform a lengthy interview with the person in order to make a specific diagnosis. In the past, many diagnostic decisions were made after the first evaluation of the person; however, the DSM-5 criteria discourage making diagnostic decisions after only one evaluation (because only so much information can be gathered in a single assessment session). There are pros and cons to this approach, the biggest pro being that diagnostic decisions are more reliable if more information is gathered. The major downside to this approach is that it is more expensive both in terms of time and money to have to go through several different assessment sessions to get a diagnosis.

The types of questions usually asked in an interview are questions about the person's background, job, relationships, etc., and, of course, an in-depth evaluation of the person's presenting complaints, where and when the symptoms or complaints occur, how they affect the person and others, etc. Some clinicians will use a standardized interview with predetermined questions; others may be less structured; and some will use a combination of both the standardized (structured) interview and the more casual approach. Standardized interviews tend to have better results in empirical studies of the diagnostic process, so the clinician should use some form of standardized assessment tool, but he should also use his judgment and get information not solely covered on the questionnaire.

The assessment process can be complicated, and the clinician may have to integrate quite a bit of data before making a final diagnosis. There are certain emergency instances that require an immediate action. For example, the assessment of a suicidal person would require immediate measures to protect the person. These situations tend to be rare. A good clinician will review the information gathered in the assessment sessions and rule out potential issues, as opposed to simply trying to confirm something. It is important that the clinician withhold her initial opinion until all the information that is necessary to make a diagnosis can be gathered. Once the clinician is satisfied that a psychological disorder is present, the diagnosis is made and the appropriate steps can be taken to help the person.

CHAPTER 2

Anxiety and Anxiety Disorders

Panic disorder is classified as an anxiety disorder. Not surprisingly, anxiety disorders have anxiety as their primary symptom. This chapter discusses the difference between anxiety and fear, normal anxiety, anxiety disorders in general, the recent changes to their classification, and who these disorders affect. There are similarities in how normal anxiety is expressed and how anxiety that occurs in anxiety disorders is expressed. Understanding the general nature of anxiety and when it is dysfunctional is important before discussing the issues surrounding panic disorder. Don't be nervous. Read on . . .

The Role of Anxiety in Your Life

It is safe to say that everyone experiences anxiety at one time or another. Anxiety is a sense of apprehension that is often accompanied by physical symptoms such as perspiration, restlessness, feeling jittery, palpitations, headache, and other symptoms. The specific type of physical symptoms that a person experiences related to anxiety vary. Anxiety is an alert; it warns the person of some impending danger and allows him to deal with a threatening situation.

Fear is similar to anxiety, but most psychologists and psychiatrists define fear as a response to a known, definite, external threat, whereas anxiety is a response to an unknown or vague threat, or a threat that is expected to occur in the future (although this distinction is not always made). Fear is often thought to be more intense than anxiety; however, anyone suffering from an anxiety disorder might disagree with that designation. Like anxiety, the emotion of fear is also a signal to be prepared for a threat. When one considers that fear and anxiety are both alerting signals, the lines separating the definitions of anxiety and fear become very hazy.

As a warning mechanism, anxiety is adaptive. Anxiety allows the person to make preparations to prevent the threat or lessen the consequences of the threat. For example, anxiety about an upcoming class examination may prompt the person to study hard. The anxiety associated with having to walk a long distance may prompt the person to run after a commuter train that is leaving the station. In this way, anxiety has an adaptive function that prevents potential damage/discomfort by alerting the individual to carry out certain acts to avoid a particular threatening or dangerous consequence. Thus, the unpleasant experience of anxiety often serves a useful function for everyone.

FACT

The central nervous system (CNS) consists of the brain and spinal cord. The CNS controls the peripheral nervous system (outside the CNS), which consists of the somatic nervous system (under voluntary control) and the autonomic nervous system (which is not considered to be under voluntary control). The symptoms one experiences from anxiety result from the autonomic nervous system and CNS.

Three Components of Anxiety

The experience of anxiety, functional or dysfunctional, consists of three components: a cognitive component, a physiological component, and a behavioral component. The cognitive component consists of thoughts associated with an anxiety-provoking situation. The physiological component consists of the actual physical sensations associated with the anxiety. The behavioral component consists of the actions one takes in response to the anxiety. In the anxiety disorders, these three components are more rigid and extreme than in normal anxiety.

What Is an Anxiety Disorder?

Recall from the previous chapter that a psychological or psychiatric disorder consists of a set of symptoms that hang together (a syndrome). Many of these symptoms will consist of feelings that typically occur in people without the disorder (e.g., anxiety). Feelings of anxiety qualify as a disorder when they are qualitatively and quantitatively different from normal experiences of anxiety and result in difficulty in normal functioning.

Anxiety disorders are a group of specific types of psychological disorders that are characterized by excessive or prolonged anxiety that occurs in situations where most people would not experience excessive anxiety or fear (the key here is the notion of *excessive* or *prolonged* feelings of anxiety). The anxiety associated with an actual anxiety disorder is not like the relatively mild, short-lived type of anxiety that most people experience as a result of a stressful event or some upcoming situation, such as going on a first date with someone, performing in front of someone or a crowd, going to the dentist, public speaking, etc. It is normal to experience some anxiety in these and many other situations.

The notion that the anxiety in an anxiety disorder is excessive can be determined by statistical, cultural, and social comparisons. Such a consideration often requires quite a bit of experience on the clinician's part. The duration of the experience of anxiety that occurs in an anxiety disorder is a little more clear-cut. Anxiety disorders typically need to have been present for at least six months before they are diagnosed and will worsen if the person does not get some type of treatment for them.

A well-known observation about all of the psychological/psychiatric disorders is that they are almost always associated with some level of anxiety and also with some level of depression. This co-occurrence of anxiety with nearly every other type of psychological/psychiatric disorder in the DSM often results in individuals getting diagnosed with a particular psychiatric disorder and then an additional anxiety disorder (when a person has two or more different types of psychological/psychiatric disorders, clinicians refer to these disorders as being *comorbid*, or occurring in the same person at the same time). However, in some cases this may not be the appropriate way to view an anxiety disorder.

FACT

Even though anxiety disorders are often thought of as relatively mild psychological disorders compared to others, these disorders account for nearly one-third of the total economic costs of psychiatric disorders in the United States. These include a significant number of emergency room visits and medical tests for those individuals suffering from anxiety disorder symptoms such as a panic attack.

An anxiety disorder is a psychiatric disorder where the *primary symptom* is anxiety. A person can technically only be diagnosed with an anxiety disorder when the anxiety is the primary symptom of the disorder and is not a symptom related to some other psychiatric disorder or medical condition. People certainly can be diagnosed with one type of psychiatric disorder and with an anxiety disorder at the same time (in fact, this is common); however, the anxiety disorder would have to be a separate manifestation of anxiety that is different from any other anxiety related to the comorbid psychiatric disorder. For example, it would not be uncommon for someone with an anxiety disorder to also be very depressed. If the symptoms of depression the person experiences satisfy the diagnostic criteria for depression as a disorder, the individual could receive two diagnoses.

ALERT

Stressful events depend on a person's perception of stress. Perceived stress has a very important relationship with the manifestation of anxiety. However, to say that stress causes anxiety disorders would be inaccurate, as there are many other factors. Everyone experiences stressful events; not everyone will be diagnosed with an anxiety disorder.

The Historical Perspective of Anxiety Disorders

The history of how the anxiety disorders were conceptualized by psychologists, psychiatrists, and others is quite long and complicated. It is beyond the scope of this book to discuss this history in detail. However, three of the basic schools of thought have made major contributions to how anxiety and anxiety disorders have been understood throughout the last century. These three schools of thought include the Freudian or psychodynamic school, the behaviorist or learning theory school (along with the cognitive school), and the biological paradigm.

The Freudian Conceptualization of Anxiety

Sigmund Freud is typically the starting point when discussing the clinical interpretation of psychological issues related to anxiety. Freud used the term *anxiety neurosis* to describe a physiological increase in sexual tension that leads to a blocked libido because of the prevention of the direct release of sexual energy or sexual expression. Early in his thinking, Freud believed that anxiety was a "toxic transformation" of undischarged sexual energy (libido). The failure to discharge this energy could come from unsatisfactory sexual actions (Freud termed the anxiety associated with this as *realistic anxiety*). Realistic anxiety led to anxiety neuroses or actual neuroses.

Freud also believed that the failure to discharge sexual energy could come from repression, which was a psychological defense mechanism whereby the person unconsciously buried forbidden impulses or traumatic experiences deep into her unconscious mind. These impulses would be consciously repressed (e.g., forgotten), but they would still be active in the unconscious part of the mind. Anxiety results when these impulses try to surface. This led to what Freud called *psychoneuroses* like obsessions and hysteria. *Hysteria* in Freud's time was the name for disorders that appeared to be neurological in origin, but had no apparent neurological or physical bases to them (psychological blindness or paralysis). Freud believed that these disorders were due to repressed anxiety regarding some unconscious threatening impulse or past experience.

Freud initially developed a rather elaborate map of the mind that included conscious and unconscious elements and stressed the importance of unconscious drives as being responsible for behavior. Later Freud revised his ideas about anxiety. He abandoned the notions of neurotic and realistic anxiety, his idea that repression causes anxiety, and several of his other earlier ideas.

Freud distinguished between a reality-oriented anxiety that resulted when someone was overwhelmed by a traumatic event or threat, and a neurotic or secondary type of anxiety, where the person remembers or reappraises these situations, thereby setting up a defensive process. The reality-oriented or automatic type of anxiety was a reaction to the helplessness one experiences during a traumatic event (the prototype for this type of experience is the process of being born, thus the term *birth trauma*). The second form of anxiety was psychological and was termed *signal anxiety* by Freud. Here, one would re-experience past traumatic events in one's mind or would associate events in reality with the experience of some original trauma.

When Freud re-evaluated his conceptualization of anxiety's role in forming psychological defense mechanisms, he set the stage for several modern conceptualizations of anxiety. Several of Freud's notions have been substantiated by neuroscientists and are still relevant in certain types of psychological disorders, such as posttraumatic stress disorder.

Freud developed an elaborate model of the mind and of human personality. Essentially Freud saw the mind as consisting of three basic components: the conscious mind (containing things/thoughts that we are immediately aware of), the preconscious or subconscious mind (containing things that we are not aware of at the moment but that we can bring to awareness at any time), and the unconscious mind (thoughts/events that we cannot be aware of consciously).

Sigmund Freud's role in understanding and treating people with psychological issues cannot be understated. Nearly every student of psychology or psychiatry is exposed to basic Freudian theory. While it has become quite fashionable to write off Freudian thought, many of Freud's basic principles have gone on to form the basis for other theories regarding thinking, feeling, and the human mind, and have formed the basis for much of psychotherapy theory. It is true that Freud was wrong about many of his assumptions, but many of his basic principles have stood the test of time and still receive support, albeit in a different form and with markedly different terminologies involved.

ESSENTIAL

Many of Freud's basic principles remain popular today. A few are: childhood experiences can affect development and adult behavior; human behavior often occurs without conscious awareness; people often develop defense mechanisms to help them cope with their feelings and behaviors; and talking to a trained professional about one's problems can help one understand and solve those problems.

Behavioral Notions of Anxiety

Behaviorism and the learning theories of anxiety became popular as an alternative to Freudian thought when the Freudian viewpoint dominated psychology (behavioral theories in psychology refer to how behavior is learned; therefore, the terms *behavioral theory* and *learning theory* are considered to be equivalent). These theories have been responsible for some of the most effective treatments for the anxiety disorders. According to behavioral theories, anxiety is a learned response to a specific environmental event or to the anticipation of a stimulus or event. The two most well-known learning theories are classical conditioning and operant conditioning.

Classical Conditioning

Classical conditioning was first described by the Russian pathologist Ivan Pavlov. Classical conditioning is a type of learning in which an environmental event or stimulus is associated with a particular reflex action. For example, Pavlov noticed that the dogs he used in studying digestion began to salivate when they saw the white lab coats of his laboratory assistants. These assistants brought meat to the dogs, and the dogs had learned (unconsciously) to associate the white lab coat with the presence of meat (which automatically leads to salivation in dogs). Thus, when they saw the white lab coat, they automatically began salivating (a reflex that occurs when dogs see or smell meat).

According to classical conditioning theory, anxiety is conceptualized as a type of reflex reaction to a perceived or actual threat that is learned through the association of the event and some type of physical reaction or physical damage. For example, a child may experience pain when they go to the dentist. The child automatically associates the dentist with pain. Even telling the child that they will be seeing the dentist elicits anxiety related to this association. Children (and adults) will also generalize similar threats. For example, a child who fears going to the doctor after getting a shot may experience anxiety whenever confronted with anyone in a white lab coat.

Operant Conditioning

Arguably the most popular and influential of the learning theories is operant learning theory. This is the school of learning that the famous psychologist B.F. Skinner endorsed. Operant conditioning (learning) depends on the notion of reinforcement and punishment. Reinforcement (positive or negative) is always associated with an increased probability that a behavior will be repeated; punishment always decreases the probability that the behavior will be repeated (the key term here is *probability*). In operant learning techniques, the behavior is typically followed by reinforcer or punisher for optimal learning, as opposed to classical conditioning, where something is paired together before a reflex action occurs.

Reinforcement is believed to be more effective in learning new behaviors than punishment, but organisms can learn from either. Operant conditioning theories associate anxiety as a learned reaction to punishment (or the anticipation of punishment). When severely punished for an action (or when an action results in or is followed by severe consequences that are threatening or damaging), the person associates the severe consequences with the action. It is also important to note here that these severe consequences can be anticipated consequences as opposed to actual consequences. What this means is that a person can either actually experience some type of physical punishment or severe physical consequence as a result of an action, or the person can believe that severe consequences will occur if the person does something or is put in a specific situation. Anxiety serves as a warning to the person not to perform that particular action again or not to place oneself in a specific situation again.

Modeling

One other type of learning that is important to mention briefly is modeling. People can learn just by observing the actions of others. For example, watching someone get into a car accident would certainly be enough to produce anxiety in a person who has to drive every day. Modeling is considered to be learning, without being reinforced or punished, through seeing the consequences of a particular behavior in someone else.

FACT

Classical conditioning, operant conditioning, and modeling have all been empirically demonstrated to be valid types of learning that occur under different contexts. No single theory of learning is more valid or more accepted by learning theorists than another theory. All of these operate in specific contexts and are associated with different systems of learning and memory in the brain.

The Biological Paradigm

With the advent of biological psychiatry and biological psychology, the neurobiological correlates of anxiety were studied in greater depth. Understanding how certain brain structures and certain neurotransmitters (chemicals in the brain that allow neurons of the brain to communicate) are associated with the experience of anxiety resulted in researchers and clinicians trying to identify the biological substrates of anxiety and anxiety disorders. While some of the biological correlates of anxiety have been determined, the relationship of any behavior or psychiatric disorder to brain functioning, genetics, and biology has turned out to be a lot more complex and elusive than researchers originally conceived.

The basic premise behind the biological paradigm as an explanation for human behavior is quite simple: Human beings are biological organisms, and therefore all behavior can be reduced to biology. Again, this premise is simple and logical; however, after years and years of research, very few specific biological markers for psychiatric disorders have been discovered (in fact, there are no reliable biological tests or biological markers that can identify the psychiatric disorders in the DSM). Even as the understanding of how the brain is related to behavior and to psychological disorders continues to improve, it will be some time before the neurobiology of any psychiatric disorder is mapped and understood.

ESSENTIAL

One of the issues with purely biological explanations of behavior is that they often attempt to limit notions of free will and choice. The emphasis on understanding the biological and chemical substrates of behavior often lead researchers to assume a more deterministic view of behavior. Does one choose to try and get better or does one's biology determine this action?

Part of the issue in trying to conceptualize psychiatric disorders as biological disorders is related to the attitude that psychological disorders are diseases and the biology of psychological disorders is the *only* or *most important* factor in understanding and treating these diseases. As discussed earlier, the evidence that psychiatric/psychological disorders are diseases is scant. While it is true that everyone is a biological organism, there are also numerous other factors that need to be considered when trying to explain human behavior, such as past experience, goals and motivations, beliefs and attitudes, etc. It is wrong to say that one factor is dominant or more important than another. There is a large amount of variance in human behavior, and this variance cannot be fully explained by genes, neurobiology, or environmental experiences alone. It is clear that there is quite a significant and complex interaction of many factors that contribute to human behavior and to the manifestation of psychological/psychiatric disorders.

Nonetheless, treatment for anxiety disorders that is based on biological principles does have some effectiveness. Certain medications can successfully be used in the treatment of anxiety disorders like panic disorder even though it is not well understood how the neurobiology of anxiety contributes to psychiatric disorders.

Current Perspective Concerning Anxiety Disorders

The DSM makes no claims as to the origin or cause of most of the disorders it classifies. Neither does it make claims regarding effective treatments or interventions. The current DSM perspective is that anxiety disorders have anxiety as their primary symptom and that this anxiety is out of proportion to what would be considered a normal reaction to the different types of situations each anxiety disorder is concerned with. For example, a fear of snakes is not considered to be irrational, but an adult running away and hiding from a toy snake when he or she knows that it is a toy, is irrational.

Anxiety disorders persist beyond developmentally appropriate periods (e.g., separation anxiety is normal in infants, but not in adolescents). Anxiety disorders are not transient and typically must be occurring for at least six months. An anxiety disorder cannot be the result of substance or medication use and cannot be caused by a medical condition (although there is a diagnostic label for this). An anxiety disorder cannot be diagnosed if the anxiety experienced by the person is due to another psychiatric disorder.

Different Types of Anxiety Disorders

The DSM-5 recognizes several different types of anxiety disorders. Each of them presents with a different manifestation of anxiety, but remember that anxiety is the major component associated with each disorder. The following list of anxiety disorders is not intended to serve as a diagnostic tool for any reader, but is intended to serve as a general description of the major anxiety disorders:

1. *Panic Disorder* is characterized by panic attacks, which can strike without warning. However, the occurrence of panic attacks alone does not qualify for the disorder. Panic attacks are sudden experiences or feelings of terror that strike repeatedly. Since panic disorder is the subject of this book, we will move on to a brief description of the other anxiety disorders and discuss panic disorder later.

2. *Agoraphobia* has traditionally been associated with panic disorder, but in the DSM-5, it is now treated as a separate diagnosis. Agoraphobia is a marked fear or anxiety that is triggered by exposure (real or anticipated) to being in open spaces or away from what is considered a safe place. There will be a separate discussion of agoraphobia later in this book.

3. *Phobias* are disabling and unrealistic fears of objects or situations that possess little or no danger in most instances. These fears can be very disabling and often lead to the avoidance of objects or events that may trigger them.

4. *Social Anxiety Disorder* (Social Phobia) is an intense fear of social situations that results in the person experiencing problems with her personal, occupational, or social relationships. Often people with this disorder have an irrational fear of being humiliated in public. The extreme anxiety associated with social situations leads these individuals to avoid being in these situations at all costs. Social anxiety disorder is not the same thing as a fear of public speaking (which could qualify as a phobia if severe and disabling enough or could be part of a social anxiety disorder).

5. *Generalized Anxiety Disorder* consists of chronic, severe, and irrational worries about everyday events. This chronic and consistent worry lasts for at least six months and inhibits people from carrying out their routine activities, but anxiety levels experienced here are not the intense anxiety experienced in panic disorder or in phobias. It is more chronic and pervasive, but not intense. These people often have physical symptoms that are associated with their chronic generalized feelings of anxiety.

6. *Separation Anxiety Disorder* is a developmentally inappropriate or excessive fear or anxiety of being separated from home or from primary caregivers, such as parents or other individuals to whom the person is attached. Separation anxiety is quite common in infants; however, after the infant reaches the age of one year to eighteen months, separation

anxiety tends to dissipate. The diagnosis of separation anxiety in very young children requires a more subjective opinion than the diagnosis of separation anxiety in someone over the age of three or four years old.

7. *Selective Mutism* occurs in individuals (usually children) who do not initiate speech or reciprocate speech when spoken to by others. Often these children will speak at home or to familiar relatives but will not speak to anyone outside a very small group of individuals. This lack of speech interferes with their social and educational development.

Other anxiety disorders in the DSM-5 include anxiety due to medical conditions, substance/medication-induced anxiety disorders, and unspecified anxiety disorder.

Reclassified Disorders

Several other disorders that have traditionally been categorized as anxiety disorders have been reclassified. These are:

- *Obsessive-Compulsive Disorder* (OCD) is a severe disorder that consists of intrusive, repetitive, irrational, and unwanted thoughts (these are termed *obsessions*) and ritualistic behaviors that individuals pursue to avoid these thoughts (*compulsions*). The compulsions often seem impossible to control for sufferers. These individuals believe they must perform these rituals multiple times a day to avoid the anxiety associated with the repetitive sessions. This disorder now has its own category.

- *Posttraumatic Stress Disorder* (PTSD) occurs after a person experiences or witnesses a very traumatic event, such as a natural disaster, physical or sexual abuse, extreme violence, etc. Not everyone develops a psychiatric disorder following the experience of a traumatic event, but people with PTSD have recurrent flashbacks, nightmares, heightened startle responses, or feel numb and apathetic. Sometimes these symptoms can take months or longer to manifest. This is now in the Trauma and Stressor–Related Disorders category along with a shorter, related disorder that was previously classified as an anxiety disorder, *Acute Stress Disorder.*

ALERT

The recent reclassification of two very prominent disorders that were previously classified as anxiety disorders is an example of why the DSM is often criticized. Many of the categories reflect subjective viewpoints and opinion as opposed to empirically validated diagnostic testing methods, the use of physical markers to identify a disorder (e.g., a brain scan), and scientifically based categorization methods.

Who Gets Anxiety Disorders?

Anxiety disorders are the most common types of psychiatric disorders diagnosed in the United States. Estimates suggest that anxiety disorders affect nearly 40 million adults in the United States (an adult being defined as someone eighteen years of age or older). This means that approximately 18 percent of the U.S. population is diagnosed with an anxiety disorder in any given year. The lifetime prevalence of anxiety disorders (the proportion of the U.S. population that will experience an anxiety disorder during their life) is estimated at about 29 percent. So as far as psychiatric/psychological disorders go, anxiety disorders are quite commonly diagnosed. In any given year, about 4 percent of the people that are diagnosed with an anxiety disorder are considered to have a severe anxiety disorder. There is also evidence that the average age of onset for anxiety disorder is quite young (some sources say as young as seven years old).

Women are more often diagnosed with an anxiety disorder than men are. Caucasians are more likely to be diagnosed with an anxiety disorder than other ethnic groups are over the course of their lifetime. As with any psychological disorder, there are significant genetic contributions to the manifestation of an anxiety disorder. These genetic contributions represent risk factors for most of the psychological disorders in the DSM and are not direct causes. A risk factor is some element, biological or environmental, that increases the probability that someone will develop a disorder or disease. The presence of a risk factor does not guarantee that someone has a disorder or disease or will even get one; it only increases the probability that they will get or develop a disorder or disease. This means that genetic factors are not directly causal with regard to psychiatric disorders; genetic factors do not *cause* an anxiety disorder, but instead contribute to the probability that one may develop an anxiety disorder if other elements are present. It is quite possible to have several risk factors for a particular disorder, but never get the disorder. On the other hand, many diseases do have direct causes, such as smallpox and polio.

ESSENTIAL

The demographic information collected on psychological/psychiatric disorders helps researchers understand the distribution and the risk factors involved in developing one of these disorders. This information alone does not infer any type of cause-and-effect relationship. Being a certain age or from a certain ethnic background does not cause one to develop a specific psychiatric/psychological disorder.

Some risk factors have been noted to be very influential are often thought of as causal, such as the link between cigarette smoking and lung cancer; however, risk factors are not direct causes. Instead, they interact with other factors to increase the probability that someone will get the disorder or the disease in question. For example, not everyone who smokes cigarettes gets lung cancer. Depending on the figures you look at, only about ten percent or so of smokers develop lung cancer (this percentage varies slightly depending on a number of factors and the study involved, but the percentage reported in studies is typically is right around 10 percent). Therefore, it is clear that there is more to getting lung cancer than just smoking cigarettes alone. Consequently, we cannot technically say that smoking *causes* lung cancer because only a relatively small proportion of smokers get lung cancer and there are many people who get lung cancer who do not smoke; however, smoking certainly dramatically increases *the risk* of developing lung cancer by interacting with a number of other factors. The increased risk of developing lung cancer by smoking is so dramatic that it is recognized as being very significant and there are warnings on cigarette packages explaining the risk. Likewise, being female or being Caucasian does not cause one to have an anxiety disorder.

Given the nature of risk factors, probability, etc., it is nearly impossible to predict if a specific individual will develop an anxiety disorder, even if the person has several specific risk factors. However, anxiety disorders are more common in people who have first-degree relatives that have been diagnosed with an anxiety disorder and are more common in people that experience significant stressors. Nonetheless, it would not be advisable (or ethical) to give someone who does not present with the symptoms of an anxiety disorder medication to treat the disorder just because one or both of his parents suffered from an anxiety disorder.

FACT

Anxiety disorders respond well to a number of specific treatments; however, it has been estimated that only a little over a third of people with them get treatment. This means that understanding the nature of and the available treatment options for an anxiety disorder such as panic disorder is important to help people who have anxiety disorders deal with them.

CHAPTER 3

Panic Disorder

The previous chapter covered the difference between a disorder and a disease and what comprises an anxiety disorder. Now it is time to take the next step and focus on panic attacks and panic disorder. There has been very little change in the diagnostic criteria for panic attacks and panic disorder in the DSM-5 compared to the previous versions. However, there has been a major change regarding agoraphobia in relation to panic disorder. In this chapter, the specific components of panic disorder are discussed as well as some of the changes in the diagnosis of panic disorder.

What Is a Panic Attack?

Panic attacks are intense periods of anxiety or fear that develop abruptly and often peak within ten minutes of onset. Many subjective descriptions of panic attacks often describe them as unexpected periods of increased anxiety or fear; however, panic attacks can be expected or unexpected.

Unexpected panic attacks can occur any time or anywhere. They are not associated with any particular situation or stimulus. But panic attacks do not have to be unexpected. Panic attacks occur in individuals that have social anxiety or specific phobias, and these attacks are usually *expected* and occur in response to a specific situation or a specific stimulus. For example, someone with a snake phobia would anticipate having a panic attack when their best friend suddenly tells them that they are about to meet the person's pet boa constrictor. Someone with panic disorder cannot readily predict their panic attacks in this manner.

Some people experience panic attacks that do not easily qualify as expected or unexpected panic attacks. Clinicians sometimes refer to these types of panic attacks as situationally disposed panic attacks. Such panic attacks may or may not occur when the person is exposed to a specific situation, and they may occur either immediately after a situation or after a considerable time following exposure to a situation.

Panic Attack Symptoms

The DSM treats a panic attack as a symptom (or a cluster of symptoms) and not as a specific psychological/psychiatric disorder by itself. The DSM describes a panic attack as a period of intense fear or discomfort that consists of four or more specific symptoms that develop abruptly and peak within ten minutes. These symptoms include:

1. Sweating
2. Palpitations or accelerated heart rates
3. Sensations of being smothered or shortness of breath
4. Trembling (or shaking)
5. Chest pain or discomfort in the chest
6. Feeling like choking
7. Dizziness, lightheadedness, or feeling faint

8. Feeling like one is losing control or going crazy
9. De-realization (the feeling that things are not real) or depersonalization (feeling one is not oneself)
10. Feeling like one is dying or having the fear of dying
11. Chills or hot flashes
12. Nausea or abdominal distress
13. Numbness or tingling sensations (called paresthesias)

In order to qualify as a panic attack according to the DSM-5, the person must experience four or more of these symptoms at the same time, the symptoms must develop abruptly, and they must peak within ten minutes of onset.

FACT

The large number of potential combinations of symptoms that could qualify as a panic attack indicates there is a lot of variability in the experience of a panic attack. There are sixty-five different four-cluster combinations of thirteen total symptoms possible. Of course someone could have five, six, or up to all thirteen symptoms together, making for even more potential combinations.

One patient described a panic attack as "feeling like you are skydiving and realizing you have no parachute." Another individual described a panic attack as "feeling like a combination of having a heart attack and suffocating at the same time." The intense feelings of anxiety or fear that people who suffer from panic attacks experience are captured by these two quotes; however, panic attacks are events that cannot be fully appreciated until a person has actually experienced one.

In a typical panic attack, the person will feel sweaty, dizzy, or faint, experience tingling or numbness in her hands, and may feel flush or even chilled. It is not uncommon for individuals to feel discomfort in the chest or feel as if they are being smothered. People often have a severe sense of impending doom or a loss of control. The most common analogies people use when describing their panic attacks are that it feels like they are having a heart attack, are losing their mind, or are on the verge of dying.

ALERT

Two commonly heard terms are *nervous breakdown* (mental breakdown) and *anxiety attack*. A nervous breakdown is a period of intense anxiety and depression that is time limited and can be associated with any mental disorder, including an anxiety disorder. An anxiety attack is simply a panic attack.

In some rare cases, panic attacks have been known to last for longer, even an hour or more. There have been attempts to classify panic attacks and panic disorder by the symptom profile of the panic attacks (e.g., cardiac type, respiratory type, etc.), but the research has never fully supported such subtypes and the DSM-5 does not recognize them.

Panic Attacks versus Panic Disorder

The difference between having a panic attack and having panic disorder is much like the difference between feeling sad and having clinical depression. Everyone feels sad at one time or another, and people often say "I'm depressed" when they feel sadness. However, the difference between a normal feeling and a psychiatric/psychological disorder is quite significant. Feelings come and go, but disorders are clusters of emotions, thoughts, or behaviors that hang together; often represent lingering and rigid methods of coping, feeling, and behaving; and interrupt a person's ability to function normally.

Panic attacks are clusters of symptoms that cause the person some very intense but brief distress (remember that, according to the DSM-5, the symptoms peak within ten minutes). A panic attack does not represent a disorder, but instead represents a sudden onrush of anxiety and fear. In order for one to have a disorder, the clusters of symptoms one experiences need to last longer, occur regularly, and have more lingering effects on the person's functioning. Again, consider how the difference between having a panic disorder and just having a panic attack is much like the difference between having clinical depression and just feeling really sad. One is a feeling that lasts for a while and eventually goes away, whereas the other is a cluster of feelings and symptoms that hang together, linger for a specified period of time, and lead to difficulties in the person's normal functioning. So while having panic attacks is essential in order to be diagnosed with panic disorder, having panic attacks is not the same thing as having a panic disorder, as some sources have suggested. Panic attacks occur in several other psychiatric disorders, and many people who do not have a psychiatric disorder will have a panic attack at least once in their lives.

ALERT

Diagnosing panic attacks and panic disorder should only be performed by qualified mental health providers. Despite the attempt of this book to explain what these entities are in simplistic terms, reading this or any other book alone does not qualify someone to diagnose symptoms or to determine the presence of a mental disorder in anyone.

What Is Panic Disorder?

There have been quite a few research studies that have indicated that panic attacks are actually relatively common occurrences. A major issue when developing the specific criteria to diagnose panic disorder was trying to determine the number or frequency of panic attacks that would merit a diagnosis of panic disorder. If this particular diagnostic parameter was set too low, it could result in a diagnosis of a psychological/psychiatric disorder (panic disorder) in people who do not have significant impairment from an occasional panic attack. Setting the number of panic attacks to qualify as a panic disorder too high would result in a situation where individuals who are experiencing significant distress from their panic attacks are not being properly recognized. The panic attacks that occur in panic disorder must be unexpected panic attacks. If someone only experiences expected panic attacks, they cannot be diagnosed with panic disorder.

QUESTION

How do the three components of anxiety present in panic disorder?
The cognitive component of panic disorder includes the symptoms of feeling like one is going to die, is going crazy, and is worried. The physiological components include sweating, chest pain, choking, etc. The behavioral components include avoidance of situations thought to provoke panic attacks.

Panic Disorder According to the DSM-5

According to the DSM-5, there are three major diagnostic criteria that are used in the diagnosis of panic disorder. The DSM specifies that a person who qualifies for diagnosis of panic disorder experiences recurrent unexpected panic attacks, and that at least one of the attacks is followed by at least one month of persistent concern about having more panic attacks and/or consistent worry or concern about the implications of having another panic attack (the panic attack's consequences). The additional criteria of persistent concern must also lead to a significant change in the person's behavior related to the panic attacks.

The DSM criteria do not specify a specific number of panic attacks that must occur in order for the person to qualify for a diagnosis of panic disorder, but instead focus on the person's reaction to having recurrent unexpected panic attacks, and how this reaction interferes with the person's normal level of functioning. An example follows:

There has been a subset of individuals with panic disorder who experience nocturnal panic attacks. These panic attacks occur when the person wakes up from sleeping in a state of panic that is quite similar to the panic attacks people experience when awake. A nocturnal panic attack is not the same thing as waking up and then feeling anxious or having a nightmare that causes one to wake up in a state of anxiety or fear. In individuals with nocturnal panic attacks, there is often severe sleep avoidance and chronic sleep deprivation, which, in turn, makes one even more prone to further panic attacks. This is one example of how the worry associated with future panic attacks or with their consequences leads to a significant change in behavior that is dysfunctional for the person.

Individuals with recurrent daytime panic attacks often spend a considerable amount of time worrying about having another panic attack to the point of not being able to function in their personal, social, or occupational duties. It is the addition of this concern and behavioral change that distinguishes panic disorder from just having a panic attack.

Again, the diagnosis of panic disorder must include the verifiable presence of recurrent unexpected panic attacks and a persistent worry about having additional panic attacks and/or persistent worry about the consequences of the panic attacks. The worrying over recurring panic attacks or their consequences must lead to significant changes in the behavior of the person that affect the person's normal functioning.

ESSENTIAL

An additional consideration in the diagnosis of panic disorder is the determination that the panic attacks are not caused by the person's use of drugs or medications or by some physiological process such as a medical condition or disease. The panic attacks cannot be better accounted for by another psychological/psychiatric disorder, such as a specific phobia or an obsessive-compulsive disorder.

What Is Agoraphobia?

Agoraphobia has been conceptually linked with panic disorder in previous editions of the DSM. In fact, readers of this book who have been diagnosed with panic disorder previously may have been diagnosed with panic disorder either with or without agoraphobia. However, in the new DSM-5, agoraphobia has become a separate psychological disorder.

The essential feature of agoraphobia is severe anxiety concerning being in places or situations from which the individual might not be able to escape. Traditionally agoraphobia was viewed as an essential feature of panic disorder, and individuals with agoraphobia often were afraid to be in public because they might have a panic attack. However, in the new DSM-5, this distinction is no longer made.

The anxiety in agoraphobia usually involves being in situations outside the home, being in a crowd, being in a public place (e.g., standing in line), being on a bridge, or traveling in some form of motorized vehicle, such as a bus, a train, or a car. An individual who is diagnosed with agoraphobia typically goes to great lengths to avoid these situations. If they have to travel or go outside the home, they experience severe distress and significant anxiety (often to the point of experiencing a panic attack).

Getting Diagnosed with Agoraphobia

The key feature of agoraphobia is that it is generalized in its presentation. What this means is that the anxiety cannot be directed to or at a specific situation, such as an elevator or airplane, but instead is generalized to a number of different "unsafe" situations. Someone who experiences extreme anxiety when getting on an elevator but not in other situations would most likely be diagnosed with a specific phobia. Agoraphobia, then, is not situational but applies to being in a number of different situations where the person feels unsafe or where escape seems impossible and the person is fearful of being exposed.

People with agoraphobia will often venture out with a friend or family member and insist that they be accompanied every time they leave the house. People with severe cases of agoraphobia may not leave their homes for weeks, months, or even years at a time. Their behavior often results in significant marital discord. Those who suffer from agoraphobia are often brought into treatment for marital problems or relationship problems.

FACT

Prior to the DSM-5, panic disorder was diagnosed with or without agoraphobia. Back then, the fear of having a panic attack in public was viewed as a major correlate of agoraphobia. Now these disorders are diagnosed separately, making for two distinct disorders. One can still have panic disorder with agoraphobia, but these are now two separate psychiatric disorders.

In order to be diagnosed with agoraphobia, a person must have this generalized avoidance and anxiety for six months, and unlike in previous editions of the DSM, the person must not recognize that his anxiety is out of proportion to the actual danger involved (in previous editions, the person with agoraphobia had to have recognized that his anxiety was out of proportion to the actual danger involved; however, now the clinician is the sole judge of whether the anxiety a person experiences is out of proportion to the actual danger the person might be exposing himself to).

A person cannot be diagnosed with agoraphobia if his or her anxiety can be accounted for by another psychological/psychiatric disorder, is due to the effects of medications or drugs, or is due to some type of general medical condition.

How Does Panic Disorder Differ from Other Psychological Disorders?

At the risk of being repetitive, it is important to summarize the difference between panic disorder and other psychiatric/psychological disorders. Panic disorder is an anxiety disorder in which the major defining symptoms are:

1. Recurrent unexpected panic attacks
2. Excessive anxiety, worry, or avoidance that is concerned with experiencing additional panic attacks
3. Significant changes in one's behavior associated with the panic attacks or excessive concern with them

In between panic attacks, the person is excessively worried and concerned about having another panic attack, and her behavior or functioning is significantly affected. These features together define what panic disorder is and set it apart from any other psychological/psychiatric disorder. Experiencing anxiety or even having an occasional panic attack is a common manifestation of what the DSM defines as "normal" experience. This certainly does not mean that someone who has occasional panic attacks, but does not suffer from excessive worry or experience a change in her behavior, cannot be treated for her panic attacks. What it does mean is that such a person probably does not have panic disorder. Having recurrent panic attacks and having excessive anxiety or worry concerning future panic attacks that leads to problems in one's functioning or severe distress defines how recurrent panic attacks are conceptualized as a psychiatric/psychological disorder.

ALERT

Panic attacks commonly occur in other psychological disorders, such as PTSD, phobias, personality disorders, and schizophrenia. Panic attacks are also relatively common in people who do not meet the diagnostic criteria for a mental disorder. However, panic attacks are not formal symptoms of any psychiatric disorder except for panic disorder.

Comorbid Psychiatric Disorders

Other psychological disorders will inevitably be associated with some anxiety, and people who are diagnosed with other psychiatric disorders may also experience panic attacks. In addition, it is not uncommon for someone to be diagnosed with another psychiatric disorder, such as obsessive-compulsive disorder, and also be diagnosed with panic disorder. When these comorbid diagnoses are present, they both stand on their own. Whenever a person has panic disorder and it is diagnosed with another psychiatric disorder, both of the disorders meet the separate diagnostic criteria designed to diagnose them individually.

A useful analogy here is the analogy of the experience of depression. Clinical depression is a separate psychological disorder with its own specific set of criteria. However, it is not uncommon for someone with panic disorder to feel depressed over the limitations that his panic disorder has imposed upon him. If the depressive symptoms the person is experiencing do not meet the diagnostic criteria for clinical depression, the person is not diagnosed with a depressive disorder and the depression he is experiencing is considered to be part of his reaction to his panic disorder. On the other hand, it is not uncommon for a person to be diagnosed with clinical depression and panic disorder together. In this case, both of the diagnoses are made separately based on separate diagnostic criteria.

FACT

When more than one psychological disorder is diagnosed in the same person, these disorders are said to be *comorbid*. Comorbidity of psychological disorders is relatively common when using the DSM. This may be due to the way these disorders are conceptualized in the DSM.

As one would expect, the presence of two or more separate psychiatric disorders complicates things. Each disorder may require special treatment, may exacerbate the other(s), and sometimes comorbid disorders may not be diagnosed initially. Anxiety disorders and mood disorders often co-occur. This is why it is important to have a mental health professional assess these situations and for the patient to disclose their feelings candidly when being assessed.

CHAPTER 4

A Quick (Very Quick) Overview of Brain Functioning

Before going any further, it is important to discuss a little bit about brain functioning and the origins of disorders, normal behavior, etc. It would be hard to discuss any psychological/psychiatric disorder completely without discussing how different the neural circuits are related to the disorder. This chapter will provide a very brief overview of the brain, the contribution of genetics and environment to behavior, and a very general discussion on cause and effect regarding normal and abnormal behavior.

The Nervous System

Most sources divide the nervous system into the central nervous system (CNS) and the peripheral nervous system (PNS). The CNS consists of the brain and the spinal cord, whereas the PNS consists of all of the nerves outside of the brain and spinal cord. The CNS is the executive control center for nearly every function of an organism. There are certain reflexive functions that occur without the involvement of the brain; however, this book will not consider these behaviors in the discussion of panic disorder.

The brain is the executive control organ that regulates, produces, and is responsible for nearly every behavior that we perform and nearly every sensation that we experience. The spinal cord is a complex network of neurons that connects the brain to the PNS. The spinal cord is protected by the spinal vertebrae, and the brain is protected by the skull. The CNS regulates and controls an organism's behavior. For example, a person may want to read a specific book that she sees on a shelf. The message to reach for the book begins in the brain, is transmitted through the spinal cord to the person's arm and hand, and then the person picks up the book.

Likewise, a person receives feedback from the body through the PNS, to the spinal cord, and to the brain. If a person's shoe is too tight, the nerves in the person's foot (PNS) transmit this information to the spinal cord, and the information travels up to the brain. The person evaluates a course of action designed to relieve the tightness, and the message is sent back through the spinal cord to the person's hand to loosen the shoe.

FACT

The dual process model recognizes two levels of cognition: an automatic mode and a controlled mode. Automatic behaviors are performed without much conscious awareness, whereas controlled behaviors require reflection, logic, and more energy. More efficiency occurs when behaviors can be performed automatically, but this can lead to problems, such as cognitive biases and even the behaviors of many mental disorders.

You are bombarded with countless stimuli at any given moment, and there are mechanisms that allow for relevant stimuli to be noticed and stimuli that are irrelevant to be ignored. For the most part, much of your day-to-day behavior occurs without conscious awareness, such as driving a car, walking, etc. Many of our actions become automatic because it would be inefficient to have to think about performing them (even though the brain continues to send and receive signals to direct them).

The PNS

The PNS is traditionally divided into the somatic nervous system (e.g., the nerves that move skeletal muscles and are generally considered to be under one's voluntary control) and the autonomic nervous system (e.g., nerves not normally considered to be under voluntary control, such as the nerves that control the heart, stomach, etc.). The autonomic nervous system is of special interest in any discussion of panic disorder because this system is traditionally divided into the sympathetic nervous system and parasympathetic nervous system. In general, the sympathetic nervous system consists of nerves that "speed up" one's bodily processes, and the parasympathetic nervous system "slows down" one's bodily processes (hence the famous "fight-or-flight" preparedness).

ALERT

Panic attacks may represent the activation of the sympathetic nervous system, but in the case of no external threat. The fight-or-flight response is designed to protect the organism in cases of concrete threats to the organism's safety. The unexpected panic attacks occurring in panic disorder suggest some type of faulty adaptation of the autonomic nervous system.

The Neuron

Neurons are the nerves in the brain that are responsible for your behaviors. There are other cells of the brain, called glial cells, that support the architecture of the brain, move out debris or invaders, and indirectly contribute to certain behaviors. However, neurons are still considered the main nerve cells in the brain that produce behavior. Glial cells are far more numerous than neurons and serve many important functions (and many new functions for glial cells are being discovered), but most sources that discuss the neurobiology of behavior concentrate on neurons. There are a number of different types of neurons in the brain, and these differ by function and location. This section will just generally review what a neuron does and how it contributes to behavior.

How Neurons Work

The typical neuron has several functional sections. *Dendrites* are the branches on the receiving end of the neuron that receive signals from other neurons. The *soma* or cell body of the neuron contains structures that perform all the basic maintenance regarding the health and upkeep of the neuron. The *axon* is the sending part of the neuron; it is responsible for sending an electrical signal down its length to facilitate the release of chemical substances/messengers known as *neurotransmitters*. Most neurons are separated by a very small space called the *synapse*.

When a neuron is sufficiently stimulated, it sends an electrical charge down the axon called an *action potential*. This action potential stimulates the release of neurotransmitters at the end of the axon into the synapse, where these chemicals attach to the dendrites of the relevant adjoining neurons. These neurotransmitters signal the receiving neuron to repeat the process. The messages transmitted by different neurotransmitters can excite the receiving neurons to fire, inhibit them from firing, or modulate the rate at which the receiving neurons will fire.

ESSENTIAL

The use of neurotransmitters by neurons for communication is an adaptive function that allows for much more variability in the types of messages that can be transmitted. If neurons communicated with each other by means of an electrical charge (as a small subset do), this would limit the number and types of messages that neurons could send.

There are a number of different neurotransmitters that are implicated in different functions in the brain. Neurons are specialized to use a specific neurotransmitter or type of neurotransmitter. The process of neural transmission, communication between neurons, and the results of these processes are obviously much more complex than is explained here. Check Appendix B for further resources.

The brain sections that most people are aware of, such as the frontal lobe, have been designated both by very general classes of functions and by their position in relation to the adjoining bones of the human skull. It is important to understand that the brain is an organ that functions on multiple levels; it is very rare that one section of the brain is entirely responsible for one type of behavior or one set of functions without receiving inputs from other brain areas. Likewise, the brain cannot function without the rest of the body. You are not your brain. You are an organism composed of a brain, a heart, lungs, glands, muscles, etc., as well as your past experiences, your motivations, your upbringing, and so on. Thus, while the brain is an executive control mechanism, it cannot do anything by itself. Any psychiatric disorder is a disorder of a *person* and not specifically a "brain disorder," as many sources claim.

Sections of the Brain

There are several different ways to look at the divisions of the human brain. The outer surface of the human brain, the surface that people see when they look at pictures of the brain, is the *cortex* (bark). The cortex is very thin and composed of gray matter, which consists of the cell bodies of the neurons. Underneath the cortex lie the *subcortical* areas of the brain. The distinction between gray matter and white matter is simply a difference between the cell bodies of the neurons and the axons, which are covered with a fatty sheath known as *myelin*. This fatty myelin sheath gives the axons their white color (white matter) and facilitates the passage of electrical charge down the axon of a neuron during an action potential.

FACT

In order to make a significant contribution to behavior, neurons must fire in groups. The brain is organized so that neurons that contribute to a similar behavioral function are grouped together; this is why certain areas of the brain are involved in specific functions. Any behavior consists of several different groups of neurons that work in conjunction with one another.

The Lobes of the Brain

Most people are aware of the different lobes of the brain. As stated earlier, the lobes of the brain are named after the area of the skull under which they lie. In addition, each lobe of the brain appears to be important in a specific set of behaviors and functions. For example, the most anterior portion of the brain is termed the *frontal lobe*. This section of the brain is more advanced in humans than in other animals and appears to be responsible for a number of different functions, such as abstraction, the ability to control oneself, movement, expressive language, and a number of behaviors and functions that are associated with being human.

The parietal lobe sits directly behind the posterior portion of the frontal lobe, but near the top of the brain. The parietal lobe is responsible for a number of functions, including the sensation of touch, visuospatial functions, locating where objects are in space, and many other functions. Right below the parietal lobe and behind the posterior end of the frontal lobe is the temporal lobe. The temporal lobe is important in hearing, understanding language, reading, memory, and a number of other important functions.

At the very posterior portion of the brain is the occipital lobe, which is extremely important in analyzing visual information. Right below the occipital lobe is a structure known as the cerebellum, which has numerous functions but is primarily concerned with movement.

The brainstem is the connecting piece between the brain and spinal cord and is important in a number of very basic survival functions, such as breathing, heart rate, etc.

Left and Right Brain

Another common distinction is between the left hemisphere (left half) and right hemisphere (right half) of the brain. The left hemisphere of the brain is involved in the use of logic, language, verbal functions, the control of the right side of the body, and other functions. The right hemisphere is generally more intuitive, considers things like syntax and humor, is more involved in nonverbal functions, controls the left side of the body, and performs other functions. The two hemispheres are connected by several bands of nerves, the largest and best-known being a band called the corpus callosum. While it is true that one hemisphere is specialized for certain functions (e.g., the left hemisphere is for verbal language), the common designation of being left-brained or right-brained is an artificial designation that has little validity or explanatory power. The brain is a holistic organism. There are constant processes of activation and inhibition that occur between the different hemispheres, different clusters of neurons, and different major brain structures that all go into producing behavior. The left and right hemispheres of the brain do not function separately or independently, but instead function together in order to produce your subjective experience of the world and your behavior. No person is totally "left-brained," unless of course they have no right hemisphere.

ESSENTIAL

Neuroplasticity is not some new science. This term refers to the inherent ability of the brain to change in response to environmental stimulation. This ability declines as we age; however, it never disappears. These changes in the brain can be permanent or temporary depending on the experience. The brain is constantly changing and rewiring itself as a result of experience.

General Brain Functioning

Brain functioning is shaped by a number of different factors. In terms of brain development, the human brain begins developing right after conception. All of the different types of cells in the brain (neurons and different types of glial cells) develop as a result of genetic programs. These cells develop and migrate to specific locations in the central nervous system based on pre-programmed genetic influences. However, environmental events occurring both inside and outside the womb can exert a significant influence on how these programs actually play out. For instance, it is generally understood that a pregnant woman drinking alcohol is at risk to produce a child with fetal alcohol syndrome. Alcohol is a toxin, and a fetus exposed to alcohol can have these developmental programs interrupted or altered. The result of this environmental toxin is an identifiable neurological disorder that disrupts normal development and normal brain function. Likewise, a pregnant woman who contracts certain diseases like measles or experiences some physical trauma is at risk of disrupting these inherent processes occurring in the fetus. The brain functions as a result of environment stimulation and genetic influences.

Your Brain Needs Genetic and Environmental Stimulation

The brain functions on a number of different levels. As mentioned previously, there are certain clusters of neurons that are genetically programmed to participate in specific functions, but these programs cannot operate to their potential without environmental stimulation. For instance, research has indicated that kittens reared in an environment where they only see vertical lines have trouble distinguishing horizontal lines as adults. Likewise, there have been instances where human children have been denied environmental stimulation by abusive caregivers. In many cases these children have been discovered after it is too late for them to learn very basic skills, such as proper language, self-regulation, and the understanding of social norms, even though these children are still relatively young. In some cases, there are critical periods for development such that the absence of environmental stimulation at a certain period of time results in a specific ability or function not developing at all. In other cases, there are sensitive periods of development during which depriving the individual of environmental stimulation results in some development of the function, but the function cannot fully develop or be expressed to its potential.

These unfortunate cases have highlighted the understanding that brain development and brain functioning occur on multiple levels. The development of any brain function is a combination of genetic (inherited) factors, environmental stimulation, and timing. What this means is that any particular ability, skill, or psychological attribute is not purely "genetic" or purely "learned." In some instances it may be accurate to say that something has a stronger genetic influence or a stronger environmental influence, but it is rarely accurate to entirely discount one over the other.

In terms of having a genetic propensity for some specific psychiatric disorder, it has been recognized that nearly every one of these disorders is associated with a significant genetic contribution. However, few of these disorders are entirely genetic (most studies find that genetic factors account for significantly less than 100 percent of the contribution to the differences in behaviors). Any particular psychiatric disorder is a complex combination of numerous genetic influences, environmental experiences, and specific timing. How these factors can be combined to predict or fully understand the development of most of the psychiatric disorders we recognize has not yet been discovered.

ESSENTIAL

Currently, it is probably most appropriate to label genetic influences as risk factors instead of as direct causes of most mental disorders. The more risk factors one has for a specific disorder, the higher the probability that one will develop it; however, risk factors do not cause disorders directly—they must interact with other factors.

Brain and Behavior

It is certainly true that there would be no human behavior if we did not have a brain. Anyone who argues otherwise is out of touch with reality. There have been and there continue to be major breakthroughs in the understanding of how the human brain works, genetic and brain contributions to behavior, and the understanding of how certain neural circuits and brain structures operate to produce thinking, feeling, and behavior. However, as this chapter has tried to point out, the brain cannot operate on its own. A disorder, such as panic disorder, is a disorder of a person. The brain is a part of that person. Despite what many materialistic scientists want you to believe regarding your behavior, you are not your brain (the term *materialistic* here refers to a scientific philosophy that claims the only important thing in the universe is matter [matter being material things made of atoms, such as the brain]).

For instance, a person who suffers from panic disorder experiences a specific set of conditions that informs him about his mental and behavioral life. Panic disorder will influence a person's television viewing, circle of friends, occupational behavior, shopping behavior, reading choices, etc. The person's feelings/beliefs regarding his panic disorder and his experience of his panic attacks are separate things. These experiences require the involvement of more than just a computational brain; they require the involvement of one's brain, one's body, one's experiences, and the world. Brains do not have panic disorder; people have panic disorder. Thus, it is important to remember that panic disorder is a disorder of the person and not just a disorder of the brain.

Diathesis-Stress Model

A model that has been around for quite a while is the diathesis-stress model. This model has evolved and is now known under several different names (e.g., differential susceptibility); however, the basic premise of the model is the same no matter what name or form it is given. Simply stated, this model suggests that individuals have some inherent diathesis or vulnerability and that environmental circumstances (e.g., stress, learning, witnessing something) interact with this inherent vulnerability, resulting in some particular expression of psychopathology (e.g., a psychiatric disorder). Updated versions of the model include protective factors that can inoculate a vulnerable individual and help him avoid or overcome development of a specific disorder.

While this model has excellent face validity (this means that it looks like a good explanation), it becomes much harder to make specific predictions as to who will develop what specific kind of disorder. For instance, even in people who have a certain genetic marker that has been identified in some individuals with panic disorder, it is still very hard to determine what type of stress will result in the expression of panic disorder in someone, or who will develop panic disorder (people with the genetic markers often never develop panic disorder, and those without the genetic markers can develop it). The research findings do not allow reliable predictability. Nonetheless, the theory is generally accepted as being a valid understanding of how certain psychiatric disorders might develop in certain people.

ALERT

The diathesis-stress model highlights why numerous findings of biological markers in individuals who have mental illnesses do not guarantee that a person will develop a mental illness. In these studies, not everyone with the marker develops the disorder; therefore, having the diathesis alone is not enough to develop a disorder. Likewise, not everyone who experiences the same environmental stress will develop a psychological disorder.

Some Classic Diatheses for Anxiety Disorders

One proposed diathesis is when a deficit in the mechanisms of the brain that regulate anxiety fails to produce enough of a neurotransmitter called *GABA*. GABA (gamma-aminobutyric acid) is the major inhibitory neurotransmitter in the brain. When this neurotransmitter is released, it depresses the firing of other neurons. A deficit in the release of GABA would lead to impairments or functional difficulties in the experience of anxiety. In addition, the person who experiences even a little anxiety theoretically would not experience the normal dissipation of anxiety over time. This could lead to autonomic hyperarousal (being over-aroused) and recurrent panic attacks.

An older theory explained a personality trait known as neuroticism as a potential diathesis. People with neuroticism have an innate tendency toward cortical over-arousal (think of their brains as hyperactive) and as a result have sensitive autonomic nervous systems. The personality trait of neuroticism is still considered to be a valid personality trait by modern theories of personality. One observation regarding this hypothesis is that there is a group of people with panic disorder who are overly sensitive to a number of different things and are often described as "emotional" or "nervous" or "high-strung."

Another proposed diathesis is related to neuroticism. This diathesis is explained as a heightened fear of experiencing the physical sensations of arousal produced by the autonomic nervous system. People with panic disorder quickly develop a fearful response to certain normally benign internal body sensations. These internal cues are paired with some environmental stimulus by means of classical conditioning. Thus, the relatively benign feelings that most of us have are paired with some other environmental situation in people who have heightened anxiety sensitivity (this is probably due to some biological phenomena), which causes these people to begin having panic attacks.

To list all the proposed vulnerability factors for panic disorder is beyond the scope of this book. However, one can see that certain inherent factors can predispose someone to develop a specific disorder. This predisposition is triggered by an environmental event or stressor. The diathesis-stress model does not propose that there is only one set of vulnerability factors or one set of stressors that can produce any particular disorder, and the actual number and combination of potential vulnerability factors and stressors might be quite high. For example, a person might score high on the personality trait of neuroticism and have deficits in their ability to produce or use the neurotransmitter GABA.

FACT

There appear to be a number of different diatheses and stressors that can interact in different ways to produce the same or very similar end results. For example, the physical symptoms of unexpected panic attacks in panic disorder could not easily be distinguished from the physical experiences of expected panic attacks that might occur in a phobia.

CHAPTER 5

The Brain and Panic Disorder

Quite a bit of research has been done on emotions and the brain, anxiety and the brain, and the physiology of panic disorder. Some aspects of brain functioning and emotional states are relatively well understood; however, no one fully understands the whole picture. This chapter briefly discusses emotions in the brain, anxiety in the brain, and the physiology of panic attacks and panic disorder. These topics are quite complex, and each topic could create a book of its own. Here you will find an outline of the basic terms of these relationships.

How the Brain Affects Emotions

The title of this section is a bit misleading because it works both ways; the brain affects emotions and emotions affect the brain. Emotions are not fully experienced in the brain. Certain physical states contribute to the feeling or experience of emotions. On the other hand, depending on which emotion you are feeling, your physical state is affected, as is your perception of the emotion.

Research using neuroimaging has indicated that there is not a specific brain center for each emotion that people have. Brain activity associated with human emotions results in activation of the brain, but not in any specific area. The areas of the brain that are consistently activated during the experience of emotions are the areas involved in movement and physical sensation, suggesting that emotions are felt in the brain and in the body. Research also suggests that the brain appears to respond in a similar manner when a person experiences an emotion and when a person views another person experiencing the same emotion.

Some Specific Brain Areas Linked to Emotions

An area in the more anterior, temporal, medial (middle) portion of the brain called the *limbic system* has been often cited as being critical for the experience of emotions. As suggested by its name, the limbic system is not one structure, but consists of several structures. Some of the main structures include:

1. The amygdala: A structure in the brain that has been known to be important in the perception of fear and avoidance behaviors.
2. The hippocampus: A structure in the brain that is known to be crucial in the formation of new memories.
3. The thalamus: A brain structure that acts as a processing and relay station for nearly all sensory information. The thalamus receives sensory information, then decodes it and transmits it to other areas of the brain for processing. The thalamus also processes certain information itself.
4. The hypothalamus: An important brain structure that sits below the thalamus, regulates hormone secretion, and is involved in a number of different behaviors.
5. The fornix: A bundle of fibers that send messages from the hippocampus to the hypothalamus.

6. The cingulate gyrus: An area of cortex in the middle part of the brain that is involved in motivation and other behaviors.

All of these structures interact with the brain stem and have multiple functions. They are also involved in other forms of processing, such as in memory and sensory processing in the case of the hippocampus and thalamus, and in fluid and temperature regulation in the case of the hypothalamus. The limbic system receives input from many different structures of the brain and sends its output to multiple areas of the brain, particularly to the frontal part of the brain. The anterior portion of the brain is important in motivation, determining the meaning of events, movement, and linking events with the specific context.

FACT

The limbic system appears to be very important, as it helps interpret emotionally charged experiences or stimuli. The components of the limbic system have multiple connections with each other and with other parts of the brain. The limbic system appears to be important in a number of emotional experiences, but particularly in the experience of fear and reward.

Anxiety and the Brain

There remains no definitive neurophysiological mechanism to determine how anxiety develops and how people experience anxiety in the brain. It is understood that several neurotransmitters are important in regard to how someone experiences anxiety. These include serotonin, norepinephrine and epinephrine, dopamine, and GABA.

It is believed that during an anxious state, the brain signals the autonomic nervous system to release norepinephrine and epinephrine to prepare the body for the fight-or-flight response. The activation of the fight-or-flight response is considered to be one key aspect of the experience of anxiety. The release of epinephrine (adrenaline) leads to increases in heart rate, respiratory rate, and other related physical changes that are associated with anxiety (norepinephrine release decreases these rates of functioning).

The hypothalamus signals the release of the hormones epinephrine and nor-epinephrine, depending on the context involved.

Fight-or-flight responses disrupt homeostasis (balance) in the body to facilitate rapid energy use to deal with a threat. Typically these responses are the physiological components of *stress*. As will be discussed later, chronic stress can be harmful, but having no stress at all is also not good. Chronic anxiety is believed to occur as a result of prolonged fight-or-flight activation. The amygdala transmits warnings when some perceived danger may be present; the hippocampus is responsible for encoding memories and works in conjunction with the rest of the limbic system. Memories associated with fear or anxiety are given specific contexts. The subjective experience of anxiety probably occurs as the result of the limbic system's influence on the cortical areas of physical sensation and movement. The cognitive component of anxiety results as an evaluation of multiple brain areas that consider context, current physiological states, memory, and problem solving.

ESSENTIAL

There have been many theories regarding what components of the CNS interact with the peripheral nervous system to produce the fight-or-flight response. The current conceptualization consists of two different brain pathways: one activated for short-term threats and one activated for perceived long-term threats. The most damaging physical effects of stress accrue with long-term activation.

Panic Attacks and Brain Functioning

There is a great deal of research investigating the biological basis of panic disorder. This research has produced quite a broad range of findings. For example, several studies have concluded that the symptoms of panic disorder (including panic attacks) are due to a number of abnormalities in brain structure and brain functioning. One proposed idea is that the dysregulation of noradrenergic systems in the brain may be involved in panic disorder (noradrenergic systems are responsible for the synthesis, storage, and release of the neurotransmitter norepinephrine).

Many studies point to both autonomic and central nervous system (ANS and CNS) dysregulation in people with panic disorder. The autonomic nervous systems of some patients with panic disorder have been reported to display increased sympathetic tone (increased rates of normal firing of nerves during relaxed states), to respond more intensely to stimuli, and to adapt slowly to repeated stimuli (normally when a novel stimulus is presented and maintained, the ANS of most people will initially respond quickly and then adapt over time and slow down). Thus, perhaps people with panic disorder have nervous systems that are a bit "high strung" during resting states, are a bit more reactive, and do not tone down their activity when aroused. The reason for the arousal goes away quickly when compared to people who do not develop panic disorder. Certain hormones are responsible for the triggering of the peripheral nervous system by the central nervous system; however, findings regarding hormonal levels in people with panic disorder have been inconsistent.

Neurotransmitters

The major neurotransmitter systems in the brain that are identified in panic disorder are epinephrine, norepinephrine, serotonin, and GABA. Dysfunction in the serotonergic systems (those that primarily use serotonin) has been demonstrated in research by using drugs that block or facilitate serotonin actions and noting increased rates of anxiety in the participants. One of the major theories regarding serotonin is that the serotonergic postsynaptic neurons (the ones receiving the messages) are hypersensitive in people with panic disorder. The research also suggests that the systems using GABA (an inhibitory neurotransmitter that would slow down rates of firing during panic attacks) are weakened in several important brain areas, including the amygdala, midbrain, and hypothalamus. Some research focuses on areas of the brain stem that use serotonin and norepinephrine (these areas include the locus coeruleus and the raphe nuclei), the prefrontal cortex (which would inhibit anxiety), and the limbic system (which may be involved in anticipatory anxiety). This means that certain disruptions in how several major neurotransmitters work may affect certain brain areas that trigger panic attacks in people with panic disorder.

Neuroimaging

There have been many studies using structural brain-imaging techniques, such as magnetic resonance imaging (MRI). Structural imaging looks at the changes in the structures of the brains of people with panic disorder, and studies have found changes in the temporal lobes of the brain, especially in the amygdala and hippocampus. Some studies find greater changes or abnormalities in the right temporal lobe as opposed to the left temporal lobe of these patients.

Functional brain-imaging studies (looking at changes in brain metabolism), such as positron emission tomography (PET) or functional MRI (fMRI) studies, have often found changes in cerebral blood flow in the brains of people with panic disorder. The overall findings suggest that panic attacks may be associated with vasoconstriction (constriction of blood vessels) in the brain, which could lead to symptoms like lightheadedness, dizziness, etc. This vasoconstriction in the brain can often be induced in panic disorder patients by having them hyperventilate.

Panic attacks can be induced in people sensitive to anxiety by giving them stimulants (such as caffeine), having them hyperventilate, or having them inhale CO_2. Carbon dioxide is a controlling force in respiration, and having increased levels of carbon dioxide in the system reduces oxygen, leads to hyperventilation, and evokes feelings of anxiety.

How the Body Affects the Brain

It is very tempting to think that panic disorder (or any psychiatric disorder) is a brain condition. Certainly, while the brain is the executor of all behavior the brain, it is also intimately connected to all bodily systems, which are intimately connected to the person's environment. Here are some other considerations regarding how the body affects the brain:

- *Fight or Flight:* The fight-or-flight response is designed to protect the organism. The fight-or-flight response occurs as a result of the brain signaling the sympathetic and parasympathetic nervous systems and those systems releasing hormones into the bloodstream that change or affect bodily structures. Bodily systems speed up or slow down. The presence of these hormones can increase or decrease the subject's perception of anxiety. The major divisions of the peripheral nervous system send feedback to the brain, which in turn signals the release of hormones to either dampen the fight-or-flight response or to maintain it. Thus, the fight-or-flight response is an interplay between the brain, the body, and the environment.

- *Cardiovascular Contributions:* Sympathetic nervous system activity leads to an increase in the functioning of bodily systems, such as the rate and strength of one's heartbeat. The increase in heart rate is designed to improve the delivery of oxygen and nutrients to the tissues and the removal of waste products in times of increased activity. However, people monitor their internal sensations. Increased heart rate or stronger heartbeat can be interpreted to mean different things depending on the context; a person prone to anxiety will interpret them as sensations of being anxious, whereas someone else may interpret them as being stimulated. Simply increasing the heartbeat of someone with panic disorder can induce a panic attack. Thus, feedback one receives from one's heart rate or pulse can affect the brain and trigger a fight-or-flight response in an individual with panic disorder.

- *Respiratory Issues:* A person with panic disorder can have a panic attack by hyperventilating, as discussed earlier. The increased respiration is a signal to the person that she is anxious, and someone with panic disorder may misinterpret these symptoms as the onset of a panic attack. This increased anxiety is the result of a cognitive appraisal and may lead the person to initiate the fight-or-flight response and actually produce a panic attack that otherwise would not occur in a person without panic disorder.

- *Other Contributions:* Remember that there are a number of physical disorders that can produce panic attacks in people, including thyroid problems, seizures, strokes, etc. Not all of these conditions are brain-based conditions. It is important to remember that a person is not just a brain; every person has a body, and that body interacts with an environment. Conditions of the body, environmental stimuli, or one's interpretations of events can all lead to a panic attack. Thus, there are a number of contributions from outside the central nervous system that are important in the presentation of panic disorder.

Heredity and Panic Disorder

The notion of some behavior being "inherited" is a bit misguided. Unfortunately, many people who are not trained in understanding behavior, including the behavior that occurs in psychiatric disorders, often perceive a genetic link to some behavior as meaning that you are born with it and destined to display it. There is evidence that suggests that a person is at a higher risk to develop panic disorder (or any psychiatric disorder) if people in her family have been diagnosed with it previously. The closer the relationship one has with a relative that has been diagnosed with panic disorder, the higher the risk that one will get panic disorder.

Risk factors are not causes. Risk factors interact with other risk factors in ways that are not well understood by researchers and clinicians. The type of genetic transmission that occurs with behaviors is not the same type of genetic transmission that appears to occur in many physical attributes, such as eye color, hair color, etc. In fact, there are studies that have demonstrated genetic relationships for many personality traits, attitudes, abilities that require a great deal of practice, such as playing the piano, and preferences, such as food preferences. Having a first-degree relative diagnosed with panic disorder does not ensure that you will develop panic disorder; it only means that the risk for developing panic disorder is higher in you than in someone who does not have the same lineage.

Trying to Understand Genetic Associations

Research has consistently determined that there is a significant genetic connection between people who experience panic attacks and those who develop panic disorder. There are a number of ways to determine these relationships. Family studies look at how some traits run in families; however, the studies do not provide strong evidence of a genetic component because family members learn behaviors from each other as well.

Twin studies often look at the association between some trait or behavior in monozygotic (identical) twins compared to dizygotic (fraternal) twins. Monozygotic twins are genetically identical, whereas dizygotic twins are genetically no more alike than any other siblings. The general finding in these twin studies is that monozygotic twins show higher genetic associations for traits and behaviors compared to dizygotic twins and nonrelated individuals. Of course, the twins could also receive similar environmental experiences, so studies that look at twins adopted away from their parents by separate families at birth or before the age of one year are stronger evidence of a genetic association.

Other types of research, such as linkage studies, sequencing, and other genetic research, can look at the presence of certain genetic markers in individuals with a specific psychological disorder compared to people who do not have the disorder. Typically, there are certain genetic components that are specific to many individuals with the disorder; however, it is rare that all people with the disorder have these genetic markers. Thus, while genetic associations for panic disorder are very viable, their presence alone does not appear to guarantee that anyone will develop panic disorder (this is true for most psychiatric disorders).

FACT

The understanding of how genetic factors contribute to behavior is still in its infancy. However, it is clear that genetic associations alone do not determine the presence of the majority of psychiatric disorders listed in the DSM-5. Moreover, genes require interactions with the environment in order to be activated to their fullest potential.

Putting It All Together

If a person has a family history that is positive for panic disorder, this places the person at a higher risk to develop panic disorder than individuals who do not have this family history. Nonetheless, it is not uncommon for someone with panic disorder to have no family history of that disorder.

Having a family history that is positive for any psychiatric disorder also increases the risk of developing panic disorder (or any psychiatric disorder). Of course this means that almost everyone is at some risk to develop some psychological disorder. The closer the relationship between you and the person who is positive for the psychological disorder, the higher the risk is that you will develop that psychological disorder.

Genetic influences on psychiatric disorders most likely operate on a number of different levels, including influencing how a person's brain processes or responds to sensory information. There are several research studies that suggest that people who have panic disorder have some differences in certain brain structures from people who do not have panic disorder; however, these differences are not always observed and not everyone with panic disorder has them.

People with panic disorder report higher numbers of life stressors than people who do not develop panic disorder; however, again this relationship is not always observed and is definitely not causal. People with a family history of panic disorder who experience major life stressors are at an even higher risk to develop panic disorder (or any psychiatric disorder), but not all of these people develop a psychiatric disorder.

What Does It All Mean?

In the final analysis, the diathesis-stress approach appears to have the greatest validity regarding the explanation of who gets a psychiatric disorder and how a psychological disorder develops in the person. Some of the possible diatheses have been identified, and some of the possible sources of stress have been identified. At this time, though, it is unclear how these interact and which ones are most important in contributing to panic disorder. Even though it must be true that certain aspects of brain functioning are strongly responsible for the development of panic disorder in an individual, it is also true that no individual is just her brain and no brain can act by itself. Panic disorder is a disorder of the person and not exclusively a *brain* disorder.

ESSENTIAL

Some disorders are entirely due to genetic disruptions or mutations, like Down syndrome or Huntington's disease. However, these disorders do not consist of subjective perceptions like sadness or anxiety. Most of the disorders in the DSM consist of subjective perceptions and feelings that cannot be quantified. Genetic influences are important, but they do not fully explain most of these disorders.

CHAPTER 6

Panic Attacks Are Not Always Associated with Panic Disorder

The major feature of panic disorder is having recurrent unexpected panic attacks; however, a person experiencing panic attacks does not necessarily have panic disorder. This chapter discusses the demographic data associated with the experience of panic attacks and takes a closer look at the prevalence of panic attacks, how panic attacks can occur in other mental disorders, and medications or conditions that often elicit panic attacks.

How Common Are Panic Attacks?

Believe it or not, information regarding the actual prevalence of some symptoms that are used to diagnose many of the psychiatric/psychological disorders in the DSM is lacking. There are several different estimates of the pervasiveness of panic attacks in the general population. One of the better estimates came from the U.S. National Comorbidity Survey Replication (NCS-R). The original survey was done in the 1990s and then the replication was completed in the years 2001–2003. The survey included a large number of participants (nearly 10,000 U.S. adults the age of eighteen or older), making it one of the most complete efforts to understand the epidemiology of various disorders in the United States. Because the survey was done in the early part of the century, the data was collected under the DSM-IV-TR diagnostic criteria; however, the data is still relevant in terms of the prevalence of panic attacks in the United States.

According to the NCS-R data, the lifetime prevalence for an isolated panic attack without experiencing agoraphobia in the United States is 22.7 percent. Let this statistic sink in for one second here before going further. What this statistic means is that, according to a large nationally conducted scientific survey, slightly over one-fifth of Americans may experience at least one panic attack in their lifetime. In other words, panic attacks are not uncommon experiences for Americans.

ALERT

It is important to understand that these findings regarding panic attacks do not imply any causal explanations for the high number of reported panic attacks in Americans. These attacks could be the result of a number of different factors, including medications, medical conditions, mental disorders, or just single spontaneous panic attacks.

Some of the other findings from this study regarding panic attacks and panic disorder are as follows:

- The percentage of people experiencing a panic attack with agoraphobia but without a diagnosis of panic disorder was 0.8 percent.

- The percentage of people experiencing panic disorder without agoraphobia was 3.7 percent.
- The percentage of people experiencing panic disorder with agoraphobia was 1.1 percent.

It is important to note that the current version of the DSM, the DSM-5, treats panic disorder and agoraphobia as two separate mental disorders, whereas these data were collected under the old DSM-IV-TR diagnostic criteria. This survey, taken under the previous diagnostic criteria, did not consider agoraphobia separate from panic disorder.

Interestingly, people in all of these different categories were also found to be at increased risk of developing some other psychological disorder in their lifetime. Other anxiety disorders (as depicted in the DSM-IV-TR), mood disorders such as depression, and substance abuse disorders were noted to be the three areas of psychological disorders most commonly occurring with panic attacks of any kind; however, people who experience panic attacks were observed to be at increased risk to develop any particular mental disorder.

FACT

Prior to the DSM-5, epidemiological studies reported the lifetime prevalence of agoraphobia as between 0.6 percent and 6 percent. The distribution of agoraphobia and panic disorder differed depending on whether the data came from clinical or community samples, with community samples having high rates of agoraphobia without a panic disorder diagnosis. Many of these cases occurred following a traumatic event.

The Structure of a Panic Attack

Many researchers have attempted to understand the general presentation of panic attacks by having people who experience panic attacks rank the specific symptoms during the attack in the order of their severity. When researchers perform these studies over relatively large numbers of individuals, they can develop a type of ranking system of the symptoms that people have during panic attacks. One reason for doing this is to try to identify if there are different categories of panic attacks that can be differentiated by the symptoms experienced by individuals who suffer from panic disorder (or from panic attacks in other disorders).

Some of the earlier research suggested that people who experience panic attacks experience some symptoms more often than others and some symptoms tend to be very intense, whereas others are less intense. Research ranking symptoms by intensity has tended to find a hierarchy of panic attack symptoms that occur in a fair number of individuals. Several of these studies have found an ordering of symptoms similar to the one depicted below from the most intense to the least intense symptom.

1. Fear of dying
2. Palpitations
3. Shakiness or trembling
4. Difficulty breathing (Dyspnea)
5. Dizziness
6. Hot or cold flashes
7. Feeling faint
8. Feeling as if things were not real (Derealization)
9. Sweating
10. Chest pains
11. Feeling as if one is choking
12. Feelings of burning or tingling, especially in the extremities (Paresthesias)

Of course, part of the problem with this type of research is that these rankings are based on the *subjective reports* of people. Nonetheless, these findings are interesting, appear to replicate to some extent, and have been used to develop elaborate models of panic disorder that may suggest that there are different subtypes of panic disorder.

Why would models of panic disorder that suggested that different subtypes of panic disorder could be determined based on panic attack symptoms be useful in a practical sense? Actually, there are several reasons. First, certain types of symptom profiles in panic attacks may be predictive of health issues later. Thus people who have primarily cardiac-related symptoms may be at risk for later heart attacks or other cardiac-related health problems (in fact there is research that suggests this is the case). Second, the understanding of different subcategories of panic disorder may lead to a better understanding of differential causes of panic disorder based on these particular subtypes. Perhaps part of the difficulty with understanding the cause of panic disorder is that different subtypes of panic attacks have different causes. Third, different subcategories of panic attacks may respond better to a specific type of treatment than other subcategories of panic attacks/panic disorder. If there are different subtypes of panic attacks and different subtypes of panic disorder, specialized treatments could be targeted at the most prevalent symptoms in the particular subtype. This may increase the effectiveness of treatment for those people who suffer from panic attacks and from panic disorder.

Possible Panic Attack Subtypes

There are several different types of sophisticated statistical techniques that are used in categorizing data. The most reliable of these are techniques related to structural equation modeling and those related to a statistical technique called factor analysis. These techniques are able to determine the relationships of variables to one another (in the case of panic attack, these variables are the symptoms people experience during panic attacks) and then categorize them in specific groupings based on how the variable or symptom is related to other symptoms and how the symptoms line up together. Because the ranking of symptoms or the experience of symptoms in a panic attack is a subjective experience, different models can often have some major or minor differences between them; however, when this research is repeated over different groups of people, certain patterns of relationships that occur in the symptoms of panic attacks could theoretically be determined.

In general this research has indicated that there are three possible different subtypes of panic attacks (however, some studies find only two types). One type of panic attack is a panic attack that has primarily cardiac-related symptoms (often this subcategory will include both cardiac and respiratory symptoms). The second general type of panic attack that appears to often occur in the studies is a panic attack that consists of other somatic or bodily symptoms such as dizziness, sweating, etc. The third subcategory of panic attack is one that appears to have primarily cognitive-related symptoms such as thinking one is going to die, feeling as if one cannot escape, etc. Studies that find two types of panic attacks typically separate the categories into those with primarily bodily or somatic-focused symptoms and those with primarily cognitive-focused symptoms.

At this time these subcategories of panic attacks have not been recognized as distinct clinical entities, and they are not depicted in diagnostic manuals such as the DSM-5. In addition, panic attacks occur in a number of other psychiatric disorders, such as PTSD, obsessive compulsive disorder, personality disorders, etc. It is unclear if the panic attacks occurring in other psychiatric disorders could be differentiated from those in panic disorder by the symptom type (if such a designation is valid). Nonetheless, this type of research continues, and eventually it may be possible to distinguish between different categories of panic attacks. This might result in some more effective and personalized treatment approaches for panic disorder.

Panic Attacks Occurring in Other Disorders

According to the DSM-5, the prevalence of panic disorder is higher in individuals with other psychological disorders, especially other anxiety disorders. Agoraphobia, interestingly, has the highest comorbidity with panic disorder. Major depression, bipolar disorder, and substance abuse disorders also have high comorbidities with panic disorder.

Panic attacks are associated with nearly all of the anxiety disorders. Having a diagnosis of depression, bipolar disorder, impulse control disorder, substance abuse disorder, obsessive-compulsive disorder, or posttraumatic stress disorder is also a risk factor for experiencing panic attacks. It is not unusual for individuals diagnosed with certain personality disorders to experience panic attacks, but not a comorbid panic disorder. Since anxiety is a common feature of nearly every psychological disorder listed in the DSM-5, it is not surprising to find that panic attacks have been recorded to occur in nearly every one of them.

There is some research that has tried to use the presence of panic attacks in individuals without a co-occurring psychological disorder to predict the development of future psychological disorders. For example, one recent study looked at a sample of New York City residents following the World Trade Center disaster. By looking at individuals who began experiencing panic attacks, it was possible to develop a model that predicted the development of posttraumatic stress disorder in the first year following the disaster, but not in the second year following the disaster. Of course this prediction was performed retrospectively; however, in the future it may be possible to use the experience of a panic attack to predict later outcomes such as health problems or the development of a psychological problem.

FACT

While all of these studies are interesting and show promise, it is important to understand that they are speculative. If someone has a panic attack, it does not necessarily mean that they will have some psychological issue or health issue in the future. If someone suddenly has a first-time panic attack, the best course of action for them to follow is to see their doctor.

Medical Conditions That Elicit Panic Attacks

A large number of medical conditions can produce panic attacks or symptoms that resemble panic attacks. As you may recall, a common description of the experience of a panic attack is "It feels like I'm having a heart attack." Whenever a person, regardless of his or her age or previous medical history, winds up in an emergency room in a hospital with symptoms that could signal a potentially fatal condition such as a heart attack, it is imperative that the person undergo a complete physical examination, including a medical history, standard laboratory procedures, a urinalysis, drug screens, and of course an electrocardiogram. If these extensive medical tests rule out the presence of a life-threatening condition or other medical condition that could explain the symptoms of a panic attack in the individual, it is then that a diagnosis of panic disorder can be considered.

Panic Disorder and Cardiovascular Disease

A person with some type of a cardiovascular disorder is at high risk to experience panic attack–like symptoms. This is because the general criteria for a panic attack include symptoms very similar to a heart attack, such as chest pain, chest discomfort, difficulty breathing, accelerated heart rate, etc. Thus, patients with anemia, congestive heart failure, angina, hypertension, mitral valve prolapse, paradoxical atrial tachycardia, or other cardiac-related disorders are at a higher risk to present with panic attack–like symptoms.

ALERT

There are many cases of individuals being diagnosed with panic disorder and undergoing many different types of treatment without successful results. This becomes very frustrating and can continue for some time. Often when these individuals are evaluated medically, it is found that they have some cardiac or pulmonary issue.

There has been some research that indicates that people under the age of fifty who have been diagnosed with panic disorder are at higher risk for having a later heart attack. (Actually, the research indicates that anyone diagnosed with panic disorder, regardless of age, has a higher risk of having a heart attack later, but this finding was most salient for those under fifty years of age.) Interestingly, the same study also found that the risk of dying from a heart attack was decreased in those who were previously diagnosed with panic disorder (perhaps due to the treatment or evaluation they received).

It is unclear if being diagnosed with panic disorder represents some early warning sign of a cardiovascular problem, if panic disorder is just a risk factor for the later development of heart disease, or if there are other possible explanations. Moreover, there is no way to determine the cause-and-effect attributions of this relationship; this type of research cannot make the claim that having a panic disorder causes one to later have a heart attack.

ESSENTIAL

One useful distinction between the symptoms of a panic attack and a heart attack is the presence of chest pain. Panic attacks *usually* do not cause pain. The feeling of anxiety accompanying a panic attack is most often interpreted as chest tightness, palpitation, and intense anxiety with breathlessness. In any event, any of these symptoms warrants immediate medical attention.

Pulmonary Disorders and Panic Attacks

Because the symptoms of a panic attack include difficulty breathing and tightness in the chest, pulmonary disorders have been known to produce panic attack–like symptoms. Any pulmonary disorder can theoretically produce symptoms mimicking a panic attack. Common pulmonary disorders associated with panic attacks include asthma, pulmonary embolus, and chronic obstructive pulmonary disease (COPD).

ALERT

One study found that the prevalence of panic disorder in people with COPD was ten times higher than the prevalence of panic disorder in the "normal" population. In addition, any situation that causes someone to hyperventilate can produce panic attack–like symptoms.

Neurological Diseases/Disorders and Panic Attacks

There are a number of different neurological conditions that have been associated with panic disorder–like symptoms or with panic disorder itself. These include disorders such as stroke, epilepsy, migraine headache, multiple sclerosis, Wilson's disease, brain tumors, and several others. Any disorder that affects brain functioning could potentially produce anxiety and panic attacks in an individual.

Endocrine Disorders and Panic Disorder

The endocrine system is a system of glands that release chemicals known as hormones into the bloodstream, where they travel to target locations and affect a number of different bodily functions. Any endocrine disorder or disease can theoretically lead to panic attack–like symptoms due to the dysregulation of the bodily processes involved. Endocrine diseases commonly cited as producing panic disorder–like symptoms are Addison's disease, Cushing syndrome, diabetes, hyperthyroidism, hypoglycemia, menopausal disorders, premenstrual syndrome, and several others.

Hormones are chemicals released in the bloodstream; neurotransmitters are released in the CNS. Hormones usually travel some distance, whereas neurotransmitters are released in the small synaptic space and do not travel very far at all. Several substances, such as epinephrine and norepinephrine, can act both as hormones and neurotransmitters depending on the context.

Other Potential Causes of Panic Disorder–Like Symptoms

Panic attacks are also associated with illicit drug use. Panic attacks can be associated with intoxication from caffeine, amphetamines, marijuana, nicotine, cocaine, hallucinogens, and any other class of recreational drugs. In addition, drug withdrawal often produces panic attacks in those experiencing withdrawal. Potentially any type of drug withdrawal could produce a panic attack.

Certain vitamin deficiencies (e.g., vitamin B_{12} deficiency), electrolyte disturbances, systemic infections, lupus, heavy metal poisoning, and many other conditions have also been associated with panic attacks in individuals.

The experience of anxiety can be attributed to a number of different medical conditions, dietary changes, medications, and a number of other factors. Likewise, there are a large number of conditions that can result in the experience of a panic attack. Due to the large number of potential causes for panic attacks, anyone experiencing recurrent panic attacks should have a physical examination.

Medications That Can Elicit Panic Attacks

Taking certain medications can elicit a panic attack. This can occur via the intended action of the medication or in the form of side effects. Therefore, understanding a few general classes of medications that can elicit anxiety and potential panic attack symptoms is important.

Any medication with stimulant properties can increase anxiety in some people and can lead to panic attack symptoms under the right conditions. Medications that contain caffeine, such as Excedrin, NoDoz, and some cough medicines, can cause anxiety and, in sufficient amounts, could trigger panic attack symptoms. Decongestants often have stimulant properties and can cause anxiety in individuals. Some medications for thyroid conditions have been known to create anxiety in certain people and in sufficient doses might lead to a panic attack.

Any prescription medications with amphetamine could conceivably cause a panic attack in someone, including Ritalin and Dexedrine. Certain medications for asthma, including albuterol and salmeterol, have been known to cause anxiety as a side effect and could conceivably lead to panic disorder by inducing panic attacks. Certain medications that control hypertension can cause anxiety and could lead to a panic attack. Steroid medications, such as cortisone or prednisone, have been known to cause anxiety in some individuals and could lead to a panic attack. Hormone replacement medications have also been known to cause anxiety and therefore could cause panic attacks in certain individuals. Finally, antidepressant medications cause anxiety in some people and as a side effect might elicit panic attack–like symptoms.

ESSENTIAL

A large number of medications besides those listed here could have anxiety as a side effect. If you suddenly experience odd symptoms that you have never experienced previously, like anxiety, look to recent changes in your medication regime or diet. However, never discontinue prescribed medications unless instructed to do so by a physician. Always discuss suspected side effects from any medication with a physician.

What Should You Do If You Think You Have Panic Disorder?

If you are experiencing recurrent panic attacks, the very first thing that you should do is to see your primary care physician and explain the symptoms you are experiencing. If you do not have a primary care physician, seek consultation with a licensed medical doctor either through a clinic or an emergency room visit (although unless one is experiencing severe symptoms currently, an emergency room visit may not be appropriate).

The reason you must get a consultation from a medical doctor is that the experience of panic attacks may represent some severe medical condition, such as cardiovascular disease, some neurological condition like a brain tumor, or some other serious medical disorder.

The diagnosis of panic disorder can only be made after all other potential causes of the panic attacks you are experiencing are ruled out, and these potential causes can only be ruled out by a medical doctor or a team of medical doctors who specialize in specific areas of medicine. In addition, the medical doctor will need to get a full medical history from you, including your use of medications, past and current drug use, etc., and be able to rule out potential causes of the panic attacks based on your medical history.

FACT

It most likely is not necessary to see every type of medical specialist when trying to ascertain the cause of panic attacks. A good medical doctor will recognize that there are a number of potential explanations for the panic attacks and order a full set of medical laboratory tests to rule out the major potential causes of the panic attacks.

CHAPTER 7

Psychological Explanations of Panic Disorder

Because panic disorder is considered a psychological disorder, it is important to discuss the possible causes. Panic disorder is not purely a psychological phenomenon, but represents the interplay between psychological and biological factors. While there is no formally stated cause for panic disorder, it is assumed that there are biological vulnerabilities and psychological reactions that combine to produce an identifiable disorder. In this section, the psychological contributions to previous biological explanations of panic attacks and panic disorder are discussed.

History of the Panic Disorder Diagnosis

Panic disorder has been traced by some to the concept of "irritable heart syndrome" or "soldier's heart syndrome" that was observed in soldiers during the American Civil War. The American physician Jacob Mendes Da Costa has often been credited with this particular diagnosis. Dr. Da Costa apparently noted a syndrome in soldiers that included many of the psychological and somatic symptoms that are currently included in the diagnostic criteria for panic disorder. The syndrome, sometimes called *Da Costa's syndrome*, was observed to mimic the symptoms of a heart attack, but without any detectable physiological abnormalities, thus suggesting a psychological cause. Nonetheless, it took some time before panic disorder assumed its own diagnostic status.

Panic disorder became recognized as a distinctive psychological disorder in the 1970s and was first included in the third edition of the DSM in 1980 (the DSM-III). Prior versions of the DSM did have diagnostic categories for recurrent panic attacks that included names like anxiety reaction, psychophysiological disorders, or anxiety neurosis. In addition, there was research to suggest that panic disorder may actually be some type of genetic or neurophysiological disorder instead of a purely psychological disorder. However, in the 1990s the popularity of cognitive psychological explanations for depression and anxiety led to panic disorder being explained more in terms of psychological mechanisms than purely physiological mechanisms. These explanations suggested that the severe anxiety in panic disorder escalated from catastrophic cognitive reactions to anxiety that spiraled into panic attacks.

At this point, it is probably safe to say that panic disorder is currently neither considered purely biological nor purely psychological in its origin. The increased understanding of the human brain and the contribution of genetic influences on behavior has helped to merge psychological and biological explanations into a more holistic understanding of behavior, even though there are still hardcore proponents of these particular paradigms who would argue for a singular explanation of many of the psychiatric disorders in the DSM.

As discussed previously, the DSM-5 contains most of the diagnostic criteria for panic disorder that was decided in the earlier editions, except that now agoraphobia is considered to be a separate disorder and not part of panic disorder. That aside, the current conceptualization of the diagnosis of panic disorder has not formally changed much over many years; however, inroads to understanding the neurobiology, genetics, and treatment of panic disorder continue.

FACT

Before panic disorder was described as a separate disorder, people who presented with panic disorder–like symptoms were treated for heart problems or *psychosomatic conditions*, physical conditions that manifest themselves as a result of psychological causes. Stress has been linked to increased vulnerability to developing real physical problems, but the notion of psychosomatic disorders has lost favor with many.

The Early Explanations of Anxiety and Panic Attacks

The earlier psychological explanations of panic attacks came from the psychoanalytic, or Freudian, school of thought. In this explanation, panic attacks were thought of as originating from someone being unable to fight off the impulses that provoke anxiety. At first these impulses elicit mild "signal anxiety," but as the person attempts to unconsciously repress these feelings of anxiety, they become overwhelming feelings of apprehension with physiological symptoms, such as chest tightness, difficulty breathing, feeling like one is going to die, etc.

Traumatic events experienced during childhood were believed to affect the child's developing nervous system in such a way that she became very susceptible to anxiety in adulthood. Thus, even those with a Freudian viewpoint believed that there might be a predisposing biological vulnerability that interacts with certain kinds of environmental situations to produce panic attacks in these individuals.

Many individuals who suffered from panic attacks described the attack as coming out of nowhere, and that there were no psychological factors involved in producing them. However, when these people underwent psychoanalysis, the therapists often found what they believed to be clear psychological triggers that led to the panic attacks. Moreover, there has been recent research that has indicated that people with panic disorder tend to report a higher incidence of stressful life events than those who do not have panic disorder. These stressful life events often included some form of loss that occurred within several months before the onset of the panic attacks. This was viewed as support for the psychodynamic explanation.

In addition, people with recurrent panic attacks were noted by psychodynamic-oriented psychiatrists and psychologists to experience greater distress about life events than do people without a history of panic attacks. Thus, the early signifiers of a panic attack (and panic disorder) involved some type of psychological vulnerability experienced at an early age, the ineffective attempt to repress anxiety-producing impulses, and other traumatic/stress-provoking events that could conceivably result in anxiety and panic attack in vulnerable individuals.

ESSENTIAL

The observations of the psychodynamic viewpoint remain relevant to individuals who suffer from panic disorder. These include a probable vulnerability to anxiety, being more reactive to bodily sensations, experiencing more events subjectively considered to be traumatic or stressful, and a tendency to experience more stressors around the time of the panic attacks.

Learning Theories of Panic Disorder

You've already learned about some of the learning (behavioral) theories associated with anxiety. The learning theories that explain panic disorder acknowledge that the experience of a panic attack is relatively common, and for most people, experiencing a panic attack rarely escalates to panic disorder. People who have panic disorder anticipate the next attack and perceive their panic attacks as uncontrollable and unpredictable.

The learning theory of panic disorder assumes that a panic attack is a sort of dysfunction of the flight-or-fight response mechanisms. A learning theory of panic disorder is therefore more effective if, like other theories, there is some assumed vulnerability to the effects of anxiety or fearful states. In this way, those vulnerable individuals are the ones who develop panic disorder. When considering whether you have panic disorder, it may help to try and determine whether you have a vulnerability or predisposition toward anxiety. Such inherent vulnerability leaves one open for experiencing an unexpected panic attack as more intense than someone without this inherent vulnerability.

If someone who is predisposed to anxiety experiences an unexpected, traumatic panic attack, she can become conditioned to recognize similar internal cues as a signal for the onset of another panic attack. Thus, the person experiences an unexpected panic attack (a dysfunction of the fight-or-flight system). This leads the individual to associate these normal sensations of anxiety with the onset of another panic attack. Often, there is also rumination and worry over future panic attacks in the light of what would normally be considered routine internal sensations. The triggering of actual panic attacks occurs as a conditioned or learned response to the experience of anxiety or fear that has elicited previous panic attacks. The repeated experience of having panic attacks in response to internal cues of anxiety reinforces the notion that experiencing any anxiety cumulates in a panic attack that is uncontrollable. The person then becomes even more sensitized to anxiety, more vigilant to internal cues, more apt to have unexpected panic attacks in response to internal cues, and more concerned with future attacks.

ESSENTIAL

Nearly all psychological theories agree that a panic attack is different than normal anxiety. A panic attack is more equivalent to a fearful response than a generalized anxious state. Most psychological theories of panic disorder assume some sort of predisposition or vulnerability to internal sensations of anxiety and/or fear interacting with experience as a model for panic disorder.

Cognitive Theories of Anxiety and Panic Attacks

The development of cognitive psychology came about as a reaction to the radical behaviorism (learning theories) that dominated much of psychological thought in the early and middle part of the twentieth century. The most famous proponent of radical behaviorism is B.F. Skinner. Radical behaviorism viewed the brain as a sort of "black box" that was inaccessible to researchers. According to the radical behaviorists, people or animals have cognitive events like thoughts and feelings that cannot be measured or observed. For the radical behaviorists, the only thing they could observe and measure were the antecedents of the behavior, behavior itself, and the consequences of the behavior. In that sense, behavior is a result of the conditions occurring before the behavior and the reinforcement or punishment following the behavior. Learning was a result of reinforcement or punishment.

However, a famous study by Edward C. Tolman demonstrated that rats could learn without being reinforced and that they were able to make "cognitive maps" of their environments and note where resources like food and water were so that they could return to these places later if the need arose. Research like this led to the field of cognitive psychology, which emphasizes how people interpret the events in their lives and how they process the events that occur in their experience.

Most of the cognitive theories of panic attacks focus on how a person interprets his bodily sensations. In these theories, a person may experience panic as a result of focusing on internal sensations, even if the sensations are not produced by anxious feelings. Here is an idea of how this works: Certain people will place a great deal of focus on their bodily sensations, leading to catastrophic thoughts about what the sensations may mean, such as "I am about to have a heart attack" or "I am going to die." These "catastrophic interpretations" of bodily sensations lead to the feeling of anxiety in the person. The anxiety produced by these catastrophic interpretations produces more internal bodily sensations (these sensations *are* anxiety-related), which provide more emphasis on additional catastrophic thoughts, leading to more anxiety. As this vicious cycle continues, the probability of experiencing a panic attack increases because the catastrophic interpretations lead to more internal anxiety-like sensations, and the result is like a snowball rolling down a hill that accumulates more and more snow. The anxiety produced by catastrophic interpretations snowballs into a full-blown panic attack.

For instance, a person with panic disorder might be feeling anxious about a presentation they must give at work that day (a normal expression of anxiety in most of us). The person focuses on these feelings and notices some tightness in their chest. They begin to think that they may be having the early signs of a heart attack. This thought leads more anxiety, which increases the feeling of tightness in their chest, which further increases their anxiety, etc.

The cognitive model of a panic attack has provided some information regarding how individuals with panic disorder interpret their internal sensations. However, a full cognitive explanation of panic disorder has a couple of glaring inaccuracies. First, there are a number of individuals who suffer from nocturnal panic attacks that occur in stage two or stage three sleep, where little or no dreaming occurs. It is clear that these nocturnal panic attacks are not the result of some catastrophic cognitive process and are for the most part unexpected and spontaneous.

ESSENTIAL

There are a number of reasons why successful treatments for psychological disorders may not explain the causes of the disorders. For instance, aspirin may successfully treat headaches, but that does not mean that headaches are caused by a lack of aspirin. Likewise, though antidepressant medications can treat depression, it does not mean depression is caused by a lack of neurotransmitters.

In addition, fully cognitive models are vague in specifying what "catastrophic misinterpretations" of internal body sensations actually are. Even though catastrophic cognitions may occur in people with panic disorder, it is not clear that they are a causal factor in creating panic disorder in an individual. The cognitive model of panic disorder might help explain how the disorder is maintained in an individual, but it is probably not a good explanation of how the disorder is caused.

Finally, cognitive models of panic disorder do not distinguish between the obvious differences between anxiety, panic, and fear. Nonetheless, the cognitive model of panic disorder does provide some important, empirically validated treatment methods that can assist people in overcoming their panic disorder. But just because the cognitive model can suggest some excellent treatment techniques does not mean the model is valid in explaining the causes of panic disorder. It appears that the cognitive model does explain a sensitivity and reaction many people with panic disorder have to their feelings, but this reaction is not a cause of the disorder.

Other Psychological Theories Relating to Panic Disorder and Anxiety

The famous psychologist and expert on panic disorder David H. Barlow has proposed a model of panic disorder that combines cognitive, behavioral, and even psychoanalytical contributions with biological contributions.

False Alarms and Panic Disorder

First, Barlow acknowledges that panic attacks are relatively common in the population, but that the majority of people who experience panic attacks do not develop panic disorder. The integrated model describes the first panic attack a person experiences as a sort of "false alarm" of fear or panic that occurs in the absence of some type of life-threatening event. In contrast, a "true alarm" would be a fearful state or a state of panic that occurs in the presence of a truly dangerous threat to the person, such as being attacked by a criminal with malicious intent.

Vulnerability

In this theory, individuals who develop panic disorder have some type of an inherent biological vulnerability that leaves them susceptible to responding to stress and negative events with exaggerated CNS responses. In the case of a false alarm, the exaggerated CNS response occurs because these individuals perceive what other people might experience as normal stressors as being life-threatening. For some of the people with this biological vulnerability, the first false alarm is associated with the internal bodily sensations that occur with anxiety by means of classical conditioning. Such an association can lead to the person developing what Barlow terms "learned alarms." In these situations, an individual can learn to become afraid of the bodily sensations of anxiety because he believes that the sensations signal another panic attack. Such individuals will become more and more apprehensive about having additional panic attacks in the future and as a result will develop panic disorder. Their inherent tendency to be focused on their internal bodily sensations gets even stronger as they focus more attention on themselves. As a result they become even more sensitive to false alarms than they were originally.

Other Factors

Because panic attacks are fairly common in the population and only a few people will develop panic disorder, the integrated model must account for this. Barlow has proposed that there are probably several factors that result in a person being inherently vulnerable to developing panic disorder, which include biological or genetic factors, certain personality traits or dispositions, certain patterns of cognition (thinking), and even a lack of good social support. Any one of these things, or several of these factors in combination, may lead to the person being more vulnerable to the effects of stress and the development of panic disorder.

There have been several empirical studies that support the notion that people with panic disorder may have certain types of inherent vulnerabilities to stress, may have a negative interpretation of bodily sensations, and even may experience more negative life events before their first panic attack. There have also been some studies that suggest that people with panic disorder do exhibit greater concern and fear over their internal bodily feelings than do individuals who were diagnosed with other types of psychological/psychiatric disorders. It is also clear from research that anxiety can be conditioned (or learned) in animals and humans in laboratory conditions.

ALERT

While most psychological models acknowledge that a biological predisposition exists in most people who develop a psychological disorder, at this time no one can specify exactly what the predisposition is. The most likely answer is that a combination of genetic influences interact to make you vulnerable to developing some specific set of behaviors.

CHAPTER 8

Panic Disorder and Depression

Any book discussing anxiety disorders would be remiss if it did not also discuss issues surrounding panic disorder in combination with other psychiatric/psychological disorders. This section will cover the comorbidity of panic disorder and depression. It is important to understand how depression and panic disorder might be related and how depression can affect the presentation, course, and treatment of panic disorder. Some other considerations about comorbidity are also discussed.

What Is Comorbidity?

The term *comorbidity* is used to refer to cases where more than one diagnosis occur in the same person at the same time. *Comorbidity* was a term introduced in the medical field in the 1970s by an epidemiologist to refer to the presence of more than one distinct different disease occurring in the same individual at the same time. Prior to understanding that physical diseases could be comorbid in the same individual, the medical field struggled with trying to understand how to treat a person who suffered from the symptoms of two or more diseases at the same time. The designation of diseases as comorbid helped physicians determine protocols to prioritize the treatment of such individuals and to understand how having one disease could make one vulnerable to certain other diseases/conditions.

Comorbidity in Mental Health

The term *comorbidity* has become very popular in the field of psychiatry because individuals with psychiatric/psychological disorders often present with many diverse symptoms at the same time. Anxiety disorders are the most common disorders diagnosed in people, and this class of disorders comprises a number of broad symptoms (of which anxiety is the major symptom). However, anxiety disorders have been observed to have comorbidities with many other psychiatric/psychological disorders. Part of the reason for this is that anxiety is a common symptom of nearly every psychological disorder. Likewise, nearly every mental disorder in the DSM can be associated with some level of depression as part of its symptomatology. Thus, diagnosing a psychiatric disorder in any individual requires a clinician to consider many symptoms that include depressive and anxiety issues before identifying a specific disorder.

The diagnosis of physical diseases is often done on the basis of objective medical test results, whereas the diagnosis of psychiatric/psychological disorders is done on the basis of subjective feelings, behavioral observations, and some conjecture. The term *comorbidity* was originally designed to denote the presence of separate but distinct identifiable disease conditions. The use of the term *comorbidity* in diagnosing people with mental disorders may not reflect the presence of distinct multiple disorders; instead, it may reflect the inadequacy of the DSM diagnostic criteria and the inability of the mental health field to apply a single diagnostic label to a psychiatric disorder that is comprised of many different symptoms.

FACT

Due to the many controversies surrounding the DSM-5 changes, there have been outcries from several organizations, including the National Institute of Mental Health (NIMH), regarding issues with the reliability and validity of the DSM-5. The NIMH has started a new research and development program to develop a more reliable and valid diagnostic approach to understanding mental disorders.

Issues with Comorbid Diagnoses in Mental Health

In terms of how mental disorders in the DSM are diagnosed, there are a large number of comorbid conditions being diagnosed in individuals with suspected psychiatric problems. The use of the term *comorbidity* by mental health professionals highlights the inadequacies of the current diagnostic system. Moreover, the diagnosing of several comorbid mental disorders in an individual often reflects a "symptom management" approach to diagnosis in clinical psychiatry and psychology, as opposed to trying to understand the overall picture and treating a person's full syndrome.

Nonetheless, it is extremely important to understand how depression affects those with anxiety disorders. The next section will look at the comorbidity of depression and panic disorder.

Comorbid Panic Disorder and Depression

Studies like the aforementioned National Comorbidity Survey Replication (NCS-R) have indicated that individuals who have been diagnosed with one psychiatric/psychological disorder are often diagnosed with a comorbid psychological/psychiatric disorder. These studies have found that 74 percent to 92 percent of individuals reporting that they have been diagnosed with a particular mental disorder have also been diagnosed with a comorbid mental disorder. While it is common for mental health professionals to label someone with the diagnosis of panic disorder and no other comorbid disorders as having *uncomplicated panic disorder*, this situation is actually not a common occurrence. A person having a diagnosis of panic disorder and one or more comorbid psychological disorders is actually a fairly common situation.

The Comorbidity of Panic Disorder and Depression

There have been several major studies that have reported the rates of comorbidity between clinical depression and anxiety disorders. While any single study cannot be used to emphatically state rates of comorbidity between symptoms and disorders, the National Comorbidity Survey Replication (NCS-R) will be used in this description due to its large sample size and large number of citations in other areas of academic and professional literature regarding the epidemiology of psychological/psychiatric disorders in the DSM. This widespread usage indicates that these data are accepted by many sources.

According to the NCS-R, symptoms associated with anxiety are similar to those that are associated with major depression. The NCS-R results suggest that large percentages of people diagnosed with major depression have significant symptoms also associated with anxiety disorders: 72 percent present with worry, 62 percent present with psychic anxiety, 42 percent have anxiety concerning bodily sensations, and 29 percent have panic attacks. Up to 60 percent of patients diagnosed with clinical depression by DSM standards have a diagnosed comorbid anxiety disorder.

The lifetime prevalence of those diagnosed with depression and then comorbid panic disorder was, in the original NCS, nearly 56 percent of the sample, whereas the lifetime prevalence of those diagnosed with panic disorder and then comorbid depression was around 12 percent. One way to look at these numbers is to say that of those people who were diagnosed with depression first, 56 percent were also diagnosed with panic disorder, and of those diagnosed with panic disorder first, 12 percent also met the criteria for major depression. Of course this percentage does not include those individuals with panic disorder who suffered from symptoms of depression but did not meet the diagnostic criteria for comorbid diagnosis of clinical depression. The findings from the NCS and the NCS-R suggest that depression and panic disorder concur more frequently than any other two psychological disorders in the DSM.

ALERT

Anyone experiencing symptoms of depression or symptoms of anxiety (or both) should not be afraid to report these symptoms to their physician and to ask for referral to a mental health professional if a psychological disorder is suspected. This is especially true if these symptoms are interfering with the person's normal everyday functioning. The sooner these problems are addressed, the more successful the intervention will be.

Some Representations of Depression and Panic Disorder

There are four general representations of concurring anxiety symptoms and depressive symptoms:

1. A person with an anxiety disorder can also present with depressive symptoms.
2. A person with a diagnosis of clinical depression can present with anxiety disorder symptoms (e.g., panic attacks).
3. A person can have a formal diagnosis of both an anxiety disorder (e.g., panic disorder) and clinical depression.
4. A person can have symptoms of an anxiety disorder (e.g., panic attacks) and symptoms of depression (e.g., feeling sad or blue).

The last of these presentations may be quite common in the general population and may be quite common in individuals undergoing normal life events such as grief and bereavement. You may even experience them yourself. It is interesting to note that patients who are subclinical in their presentation (they have some of the symptoms but not enough of them to be diagnosed with the disorder) have been found to have a level of functional disability very similar to the levels of functional disability in individuals diagnosed with an actual psychiatric disorder like clinical depression. While the previously mentioned hypotheses are useful areas of investigation for lay-persons, clinicians, and researchers to understand how depression and panic disorder co-occur, they offer little relief to the person suffering from them together. The point here is that even someone who does not meet the formal diagnostic criteria for depression can experience significant effects from sadness, loss of motivation, etc., that can affect their ability to address their panic disorder. It is important to recognize and identify such symptoms and get treatment for them regardless of how they are classified.

A General Description of the Presentation of Comorbid Depression and Panic Disorder

There are some difficulties faced by clinicians who are confronted with mixed symptoms. This can be especially problematic in primary care environments where a physician is not sufficiently trained in understanding and diagnosing mental health issues. Even though there is no such thing as a "typical" presentation for panic disorder in a primary care environment (e.g., with a family doctor), the following description can help to illustrate the difficulty that many physicians encounter in primary care settings when dealing with these presentations.

Often a patient will present with a complaint like a headache, tightness in the chest, or some other physical symptoms. When the physician inquires about symptoms of depression and/or anxiety, these complaints are typically intertwined with real-life problems, such as the loss of a job, marital or relationship issues, day-to-day struggles with finances or relationships, etc. When these symptoms are explained by patients in the context of living conditions, a physician not trained in the diagnosis and understanding of mental health issues may often simply attribute these complaints as normal reactions and take a symptom management approach (e.g., prescribing medication for depressive and anxiety symptoms without establishing a formal diagnosis by consulting a psychiatrist or a psychologist).

In addition, a person who experiences panic attacks may view any feelings of depression as reactions to these attacks and therefore may not consider them to be significant. Depression can interact with panic disorder so as to make the treatment of panic disorder difficult. It is important not to write these off as inconsequential or simple reactions to other circumstances.

Mental health professionals such as psychiatrists, clinical psychologists, social workers, etc., are trained to help untangle the mixed presentations that many people often display. A professionally trained mental health worker will attempt to ascertain whether the reaction or symptom is a normal reaction to a specific life event or if the symptoms represent something else. The problem with diagnosing a psychological disorder lies in determining the proper level of suspicion for the presence of significant anxiety or depression in the context of the person's bodily complaints and life issues. Thus, the diagnosis of clinically significant anxiety or depression should be left to licensed mental health professionals (e.g., psychiatrists, psychologists, etc.) who work with primary care physicians and other medical personnel to determine the relevance of both the somatic (bodily) complaints and the emotional/behavioral complaints. Unfortunately this is not the case most of the time, and the vast majority of antidepressant medications (used for the treatment of both depression and anxiety) are prescribed by primary care physicians. While a primary care physician might be your first stop regarding any feelings of panic or anxiety, it is best to seek out a trained mental health professional to handle all areas of your symptoms.

ALERT

A very real concern is the common failure of primary care physicians to recognize psychiatric disorders in their patients. Another concern is the use of screening tools by physicians to diagnose psychological disorders. Screening tools are aids to direct evaluations by an experienced mental health professional, but these tools are not designed to be the sole method of diagnosing a mental disorder.

How Depression Affects Treatment

People who are diagnosed with clinical depression, especially moderate or severe depression, are at risk for a number of different psychological, physical, and neurological disorders. Research has indicated that people with moderate to severe clinical depression are at a higher risk of developing Alzheimer's disease, other forms of dementia, stroke, heart disease, and various other diseases, and typically have poorer outcomes than individuals with the same disorders but no history of moderate or severe depression. Because there is an interface between the symptoms of anxiety disorders (e.g., panic disorder) and depression, this relationship affects the treatment and course for both conditions. Therefore, one concern for people with depression and another co-occurring psychological disorder such as panic disorder is that the depression places these individuals at risk to develop other health issues, which in turn makes both the diagnosis and the treatment of their panic disorder more complicated.

Secondly, people who have comorbid panic disorder and depressive symptoms or actual clinical depression will tend to have more severe symptoms and be more impaired in their functioning than individuals with uncomplicated panic disorder. Research has demonstrated that individuals with panic disorder and comorbid depression show slower responses to treatment, show poor responses to treatment, have a poorer prognosis, and have higher rates of suicide.

Some Things to Look For

When a person suffering from panic disorder also has significant symptoms of depression, even if that person does not qualify for a clinical diagnosis of depression, this can present some very special problems. There are several considerations to be aware of.

First, there are a couple of general guidelines to follow regarding recognizing depressive symptoms in people and there are often differences in the way the symptoms are often expressed differently in men, women, and adolescents or younger individuals. For instance, women are much more likely than men to express feelings of guilt, to overeat, to gain weight, and to sleep excessively when they are depressed (although men can certainly display these symptoms as well). Women are also more likely to directly express feeling hopeless or helpless than men. Typically they will express feelings of being worthless or that anything they try to do to change their situation (or think of trying) will be of no use.

Men with depression are more likely to complain about having problems going to sleep, being fatigued, having a loss of interest in things they used to enjoy doing, such as work or hobbies, and are more likely to be irritable than women. Men are also more likely to engage in aggressive acts and substance abuse as a expression of their depression (although women can also express these behaviors). Adolescents are more likely to display irritability, issues with their temper, and complaints of aches and pains or restlessness than are adults. Remember that these are general guidelines; in reality you

may find that some men are open about their depress
get irritable and aggressive. There are no absolutes here

Next, it is important to recognize that people who are
have significant depressive symptoms) often experience fe
ness or hopelessness. These feelings of helplessness or h
interfere with the person's desire or motivation to seek help
attacks and panic disorder. It is extremely important to rec
symptoms in oneself or someone else who is experiencing them
helplessness and hopelessness can be ascertained by discussing
outlook with them. When people begin to express very pessimistic
cal views, express the idea that they have little or no control over th
ation, or begin to question the meaning of their actions or their signif
in life to their family and friends; these can be signs that the person is b
ning to feel hopeless regarding their situation. These are definitely time
consider seeking professional help.

Finally, it is important to understand that feelings of depression are no
in any way signs of emotional weakness but represent reactions to one's perceived conditions. From time to time everyone experiences feelings of sadness, questions their worth, feels as if things will never get better, etc. When
these feelings last longer than a couple of days and/or begin to interfere with
a person's ability to function in their normal environment, it is important for
that person to get help. When a person has significant feelings of depression
in conjunction with a psychological disorder such as panic disorder, then
even if the depression is not clinically significant, these feelings can interfere
with a person's recovery. Often symptoms of depression will require special
treatment.

ESSENTIAL

People with panic disorder and depressive symptoms have increased anxiety and worry compared to individuals with panic disorder only. For example, people with mixed depressive symptoms and panic disorder have higher blood pressures and higher cardiac loads compared to patients with only panic disorder.

Complications

The presence of clinical depression, or even significant nonclinical depressive symptoms, with panic disorder can complicate the treatment for panic disorder. This is not only because the presence of depression is associated with more intense ANS arousal, but also because depression can interfere with treatment motivation, how a person interprets his treatment progress, and a person's outlook on his recovery or potential for recovery. There is extensive literature on the relationship between patient motivation, patient expectations, and the success of treatments that include psychotherapy, medications, and a combination of both. Therefore, if a person with panic disorder is displaying significant depressive symptoms, it is probably imperative to treat those depressive symptoms, even if the person does not meet the diagnostic criteria for clinical depression.

General Treatment Strategy

First, it is important that a licensed psychologist or psychiatrist administer some standardized tests as well as a complete interview to determine the level of depression in an individual (these tests can often be given for anxiety, worry, and personality variables). Such a test can only be interpreted by a licensed psychologist or psychiatrist trained in the administration and interpretation of such instruments. These instruments often give the clinician a good picture as to the severity of the symptoms and may provide some direction for treatment protocols.

Next, the treatment of comorbid depression and panic disorder will often require the use of a combination of psychotherapy and medication. The problem with attempting to treat depression solely with medications is that the medications do not actively begin to reduce depressive symptoms in individuals for several weeks after they have been started. Therefore, it is extremely important that the patient receives immediate treatment for severe depression, especially in the case of a suicidal patient, and that the patient's mood be continually monitored as he attempts to gain control over his panic disorder. Typically in patients with comorbid clinical depression and panic disorder, the recovery is somewhat slower and patients need more psychotherapy sessions in addition to any medications in order to benefit.

Finally, patients with a history of depression comorbid with their panic disorder need longer follow-up sessions in order to ensure that their symptoms do not return. A competent clinician will schedule follow-up sessions even after the treatment has been deemed effective and keep the door open for future consultations with these patients.

ESSENTIAL

The safest policy regarding diagnosis is that trained mental health workers, such as psychiatrists and psychologists, should be diagnosing psychiatric disorders. Primary care physicians are not fully qualified to diagnose psychological/psychiatric disorders in individuals and should refer people suspected of having these disorders to a qualified mental health care provider.

Other Considerations

The high instances of comorbid panic disorder and depression, anxiety disorders and depression, and anxiety symptoms and depressive symptoms may actually suggest something quite different from what is commonly acknowledged by the DSM diagnostic criteria. The comorbidity between panic disorder and depression has led some to believe that these may not be separate disorders. Comorbidity between panic disorder and depression appear to be the norm rather than the exception. Much literature indicates that depression is comorbid with many disorders; however, panic disorder seems to predate depression in individuals who have comorbidity for these disorders. This may signal a progression of symptoms. Some of the considerations regarding the comorbidity of depression and panic disorder are:

1. The comorbidity of depression and panic disorder is a result of overlapping diagnostic criteria in the DSM.
2. The comorbidity of depression and panic disorder represents true comorbidity: two separate and distinct disorders occurring at the same time in the same individual.
3. The mixed presentation of depression and anxiety is a separate psychiatric/psychological disorder that has not been fully recognized.

4. Panic disorder may predispose you to developing depression.
5. The observation of comorbid panic disorder and depression represents one specific disorder with one specific cause; however, this disorder is expressed in two different phenotypes (a phenotype is the physical expression of a genetic cause).

While any one of these possibilities could be true, many mental health researchers would probably accept the notion that panic disorder or having high levels of anxiety predisposes a person to develop depressive symptoms. Remember, at the beginning of the book, the disease model of panic disorder was rejected in favor of a model of panic disorder as a psychological disorder. Therefore, do not accept the idea that anxiety disorders and depression are separate "diseases" that one can "catch" or develop like a common cold and the flu. Instead, they represent disorders of behavior that are often related. If you accept this notion, then you cannot consider them to be mutually exclusive but, instead, must acknowledge that their symptoms can be interrelated.

Once the person with panic disorder begins to experience depressive symptoms, these symptoms can interfere with the treatment of their panic disorder (or can interfere or stop the person from even seeking treatment). Thus, the appearance of depressive symptoms as a reaction to panic attacks and panic disorder may represent a relatively common progression of panic disorder. The way psychological disorders are diagnosed at this time using the DSM is not conducive to understanding panic disorder in this manner, even though many clinicians would most likely agree that having panic disorder could produce depressive symptoms in a person. In fact, the experience of depression and anxiety, while common symptoms in all psychological disorders, is not considered to be a symptom of other disorders and is not listed in their diagnostic criteria. (For example, having depression or being sad as a reaction to panic attacks is not listed as a possible symptom of panic disorder in the DSM diagnostic criteria for panic disorder.) Moreover, while it may be theoretically valid to assume that if a person could learn to control their panic attacks, their depression would lift, this is not as easy as it sounds because the depression will often interfere with the treatment of panic disorder by reducing the person's motivation to get treatment or to continue treatment.

Because of issues like this, new research funded by the NIMH (National Institute of Mental Health) is designed to develop a new way to classify psychiatric/psychological diagnostic types, concentrating on both biological markers (such as the presence of certain genes or other physical signs) and behavioral markers (such as panic attacks or avoidance) for these disorders. Such a classification system may find common genetic markers for panic disorder (or anxiety disorders in general) and depression. Such a system could help integrate all of the feelings one experiences and help develop more effective treatment approaches. At this point this is pure speculation, but in a decade or so, many of these issues may be resolved by successful attempts to improve the DSM classification system.

ALERT

No matter if the comorbidity of depression and panic disorder represents separate disorders occurring together or some new unclassified disorder, it is important to remember that it is not unusual for someone with panic disorder to also experience significant depressive symptoms. Anyone undergoing the diagnostic process for panic disorder symptoms should be sure to report any depressive symptoms they experience.

CHAPTER 9

Understanding Research and Treatment for Panic Disorder

In order to continue learning about panic and its effects, it is important to understand exactly how research is gathered by medical professionals regarding this disorder. You will probably look at the headline of this chapter and want to skip it. Please do not skip this chapter unless you already have a college-level understanding of research methodology and statistics. This chapter will attempt to explain what research can do, when research can show cause and effect, and what clinical proof is. In addition, this chapter will help you arm yourself with as much information as possible about panic disorder, which is essential to recovery. Take your time and read on . . .

What Is Empirical Evidence/Research?

Consider these two "common-sense" proverbs:

- He who hesitates is lost.
- Haste makes waste.

Is there any discrepancy between these two sayings? Yes. In fact, they both express the exact opposite viewpoint. Oddly enough, both of these conditions can be true depending on the context in which they are considered. So when does "haste make waste"? When is "he who hesitates," "lost?" It depends.

Human beings are prone to a number of cognitive biases that allow them to think and make decisions quickly, but these biases can interfere with reasoning when the outcome of something is based on probability.

For example, suppose that you and a friend were betting on whether or not a coin toss would be heads or tails. Your bet is it will turn up heads; your friend's bet is it will turn up tails. You both start flipping the coin. Each bet can be increased or decreased depending on how confident you feel that the coin will either be heads or tails. The first four coin tosses in a row have all been heads and you have won a lot of money. You decide to bet on one final coin toss. Should you bet more money now since there have been four heads in a row and the result is more likely to be tails on the final toss?

Actually, the fact that there have been four heads of a role has no impact on the outcome of the fifth toss. The probability of getting either heads or tails on any single coin toss remains 0.5 despite what has happened on previous tosses. Nonetheless, many people would believe a tails result is imminent. Gambling casinos make billions off this type of thinking and this particular scenario is even termed the "Gambler's Fallacy."

Despite the claim by a best selling book that intuition is better than reasoning, when outcomes are determined by probabilities, intuition is a relatively poor way to make decisions. Common-sense reasoning led to the view that the world was flat, that the earth was the center of the universe, that bleeding a patient who was ill removed the bad blood and cured her, and a number of other faulty beliefs.

When it comes to trying to determine if a specific treatment is effective in treating a mental disorder such as panic disorder, intuition and common sense are often ineffective when compared to the use of the scientific method.

ESSENTIAL

There are times when using more automatic, fast, energy-efficient mental processes such as intuition is appropriate, and there are other times when using more controlled, slow, energy-intensive mental processes is important. Remember that this chapter is not downplaying the use of intuition; it is explaining when it is important to remove potential bias in decision making.

Empirical Research

Common-sense reasoning often occurs after some event has taken place. Most people evoke common sense to explain events after they have occurred. This is due to something called a hindsight bias, where an individual will reason that she should have been able to tell the outcome of an event after it has happened. However, after that person already knows the outcome, it is very easy to determine what it should have been or how it occurred.

Conversely, research is often done in an effort to predict an outcome. Empirical research is an attempt to gain knowledge by means of observation. The record of a researcher's observations is called empirical evidence, and this evidence can be analyzed in a systematic fashion to determine the probability that the observation/outcome was a chance observation or if it occurred as a result of some other influence. The particular research design used to evaluate empirical evidence depends on the type of question being asked and the point of view one wishes to adopt. Empirical evidence is often called data: recorded observations that can be analyzed in a systematic fashion to determine their meaning.

FACT

Qualitative research attempts to make a detailed description of the observations, whereas quantitative research attempts to classify data and use statistical techniques to explain observations. Quantitative research is more useful in determining the effectiveness of a particular type of treatment for a particular condition. Qualitative research is useful in describing the subjective experiences of people in treatment.

In order to determine if a particular form of treatment or intervention is effective for a particular disorder, one must apply a standardized procedure that is designed to eliminate bias in decision making. Empirical research is designed to follow such a standardized observation procedure and to prevent subjectivity and bias from determining what actually happened or prevent such biases from affecting outcomes.

Do Your Research

The scientific method is a standardized procedure that acts as a set of guidelines that scientists and researchers follow in order to determine the types of evidence that are meaningful and eliminate bias from their decision making. The scientific method works something like this:

1. Begin by observing some aspect of the world.
2. Develop a speculative description of this observation (called a hypothesis) that is consistent with what was observed.
3. Use the hypothesis to make predictions about future events.
4. Test those predictions through experiments or correlational observations.
5. Determine if the hypothesis is consistent with what has been observed.
6. If there are discrepancies, develop new hypotheses and repeat steps three, four, and five until there are no discrepancies between your hypothesis and your observations, or change the hypothesis/theory in light of your results.

When the method is followed and completed, the hypothesis can become a theory and can provide rational information that can explain an entire class of phenomena. Observations are explained, and predictions about behavior, or whatever the topic of research is, can be made. Personal knowledge can be used to construct hypotheses, such as "There seems to be an increase in intelligence when people listen to Mozart" (which, by the way, has not been supported by research), but hypotheses must be tested by an objective method designed to rule out bias and chance.

ALERT

There are times when intuition and common sense are applicable and times when the scientific method is applicable; neither method is applicable all the time. For example, one does not need an empirical study to decide to run if being chased by a rabid dog; however, one does need empirical evidence to determine the effectiveness of a particular treatment.

Some Terms

At this point, it is appropriate to clear up some terms. Something that is said to be theoretical or a theory is often deemed as being a type of guess. Thus, for many people, the term *theoretical* lacks credibility in that they believe it describes something that is untested. However, this is not the scientific notion of a theory; scientists would call that untested notion a hypothesis. A *hypothesis* describes a potential or calculated relationship between two or more variables (observations) that need to be objectively examined. In scientific circles, a theory is a much broader set of conditions that have been supported by empirical evidence (theories are supported by hypothesis testing). For instance, gravity is a theoretical concept, but it is doubtful that many readers would jump off an overpass into oncoming traffic because they believe that the theory of gravity is untested. Theories regarding human behavior are based on probabilistic data and change as new data is accumulated. This aspect of scientific reasoning is very hard for many people to understand.

ALERT

It is important to remember that a theory is not fact. Theories can sometimes predict some aspect of reality, but they are not laws. Scientific theories are based on hypothesis testing and can be altered many times based on objective research.

Types of Research (In Basic Terms)

Again, this explanation will remain very general. There are some references/referral sources at the end of this book that interested readers can use to find more in-depth explanations of these basic ideas. There has been a lot of interesting research on how people, including scientists, have difficulty interpreting events and estimating the probability of an outcome.

One of the major cognitive biases that all of us exhibit is something called a confirmation bias. The confirmation bias occurs when we selectively seek and pay attention to information that conforms with what we already believe and ignore information (often a much larger body of information) that is in contrast to our belief. A common manifestation of the confirmation bias occurs when one is thinking of a song and then turns on the radio to find that the song is playing. Many individuals mistakenly consider this to be evidence for extra sensory perception (ESP), when in fact such occurrences conform to the rules of probability (ESP is a proposed sort of mental ability where people are believed to be able to determine events before they occur or be able to read other people's minds). What most people fail to consider is the number of times they were thinking of a song and it did not play on the radio. Instead, we tend to concentrate on the very rare occurrence and use it to confirm such a belief.

Other biases include viewing two things and believing that they are related when in fact they are not, the hindsight bias that occurs when people view an event that has already taken place and reason that they knew the outcome all along, and the gambler's fallacy, where people misinterpret the probability of an upcoming event based on previous independent events. These are all quite common in everyday decision making.

Perhaps the most common bias that we engage in is inferring that one thing causes another thing to happen, when, in fact, the two things are associated, occur in unison, or one occurs slightly before the other. For instance, some very famous psychological research showed people a display with a square moving from right to left and stopping right before another square that began moving from right to left. The vast majority of people viewing this scene believed that the first square caused the second square to move, even though there was no evidence that this was even possible. In general, there are two basic categories of research (there is actually a type of research that combines features of these two basic categories, but for simplicity's sake this book will stick with the two basic categories of research).

Correlational Research

Correlational research is research that looks at relationships and associations between variables. Correlational research often consists of surveys and questionnaires, observational studies where people are observed in the laboratory or in the real world during some type of manipulation, case studies, and archival research where researchers go back and look at data previously collected by others and analyze it. Correlational research is very beneficial in determining how things are associated with each other. It allows investigators to test hypotheses and to confirm or disconfirm aspects of certain theories. For instance, the NCS-R cited in this book is an example of extremely useful correlational research on the various presentations, epidemiological factors, and other associations of the psychological/psychiatric disorders in the DSM. One finding from the research was that panic disorder was two-and-a-half times more common in females than in males.

The main issue with correlational research is that while the findings are often very useful and informative, this type of research does not allow the investigators to make cause and effect statements regarding the findings. For example, the NCS-R data cannot make the statement that, because panic disorder occurs two-and-a-half times more often in females than males, being female causes one to develop panic disorder. A proper inference from this data would be that panic disorder occurs two-and-a-half times more often in the females surveyed than in the males surveyed. In order to determine cause and effect between the variables in a particular research study, one must perform a true experiment.

Experimental Research

True experiments allow researchers to make cause-and-effect inferences. However, true experiments are often costly, difficult to design and implement, and have some methodological issues that can limit their ability to generalize outside the participants in the study. The difference between a true experiment and a correlational design is actually quite simple. The participants in a true experiment are randomly assigned to the different conditions in the experiment. What this means is that each and every participant in the experiment has an equal chance of being selected for any one of the different conditions. This random assignment is a way to control all the outside extraneous factors that can affect the outcome of the particular research. Random assignment statistically evens out all the potential confounding influences in the subjects. Here is a very simple example:

A researcher is interested in the efficacy of a new drug on individuals with panic disorder. The researcher recruits forty subjects, all diagnosed with panic disorder according to DSM criteria, and randomly assigns them to two different groups of twenty participants. The first group gets a new medication and the second group gets a placebo. At the end of the duration of the research, the experimenter compares the symptoms of distress between both groups to determine if the medication works better than a placebo.

This is a very simplified example, but would qualify as an experiment with a control group. Unfortunately, there are other factors to consider before this would actually be considered a good study, but it is an example of a true experiment, and the researcher would be able to determine if the new medication did indeed cause the symptoms of panic disorder to lessen compared to a placebo in the participants in the study.

Most true experiments in treatment research for psychological disorders have some sort of control condition or control group along with one or more treatment groups. A control group allows researchers to compare their intervention with a standard. In many cases, mental disorders such as panic disorder are not stable, and symptoms wax and wane over time, so it is important to have a control group in the experimental design (control groups can also be a part of correlational research as well).

FACT

The key component of a true experiment is the random assignment of the participants in the experiment to different conditions. Sometimes researchers will randomly assign participants based on some stratified criteria like age, gender, etc., in order to make the sample of the experiment resemble the population of those the study wishes to generalize.

Good experimental research allows the researcher to make cause-and-effect inferences, but small sample research in behavioral science does not prove anything. Correlational research describes relationships, helps make inferences about how things are associated, and helps develop hypotheses to explain things, but cannot make cause-and-effect inferences or prove anything. When reading research about panic disorder, be sure to keep these ideas in mind. Take everything with a grain of salt.

ESSENTIAL

Neither type of research is "better" than the other. The specific research design investigators choose depends on a number of things, including the questions being asked, the practicality of the design the researchers wish to use, and the theoretical constructs and hypotheses involved. Both types of research are very important in determining issues surrounding mental disorders.

Important Research Issues

The issue of cause and effect has been discussed previously. One issue with true experiments is that the more internal control these experiments exert (the more the experiment controls for all the outside influences other than the one under observation that can affect the outcome), often the less the experiment resembles real-world conditions. So while many very tightly controlled experiments can infer cause and effect regarding their outcomes, they may not resemble the way these variables act in the real world very well.

Making Generalizations Outside the Study

The ability of a research study to generalize outside the conditions of the research design is known as the external validity of the experiment. For example, many observational studies have very good external validity, but it is nearly impossible to determine cause-and-effect relationships from them due to the large number of intervening influences. Another way for a researcher to make his findings more in-line with real-world individuals is to use a technique called random sampling. Random sampling occurs when every person in the population being studied (e.g., all people with panic disorder) has an equal chance of being selected for the research study. Random sampling is a good theoretical construct; however, it is difficult to initiate in most circumstances because no one can identify every particular panic disordered person and it is next to impossible to offer everyone with panic disorder an equal opportunity to participate in the study. However, researchers develop certain types of sampling techniques so that the research participants can resemble the known demographic features of the population under study.

Specific Problems

Researchers often criticize their own findings while they discuss them. A number of issues can cloud the findings in research that is designed to determine the effectiveness of certain treatments for certain mental disorders. These include, but are not limited to, the affiliation of the authors (authors affiliated with drug companies rarely publish negative findings for their drugs), the characteristics of the sample participants, whether or not the researchers and the participants knew what condition they were in (the term *double-blind experiment* means that neither the researchers nor the participants knew what condition the participant was in), the dropout rates in studies that look at treatments for various disorders, the duration of the study, follow-up, etc. When attempting to determine side effects or long-term effects of the use of medications, many research studies fall short since the duration of these studies is typically only a few months or a few weeks.

FACT

Randomized controlled trials (RCT) are considered the gold standard that treatment studies should follow. The studies have randomized assignment and a control group, and when they are double-blind RCTs, they are considered even more effective. However, even these research designs are still susceptible to individuals who misrepresent the results or report results that were not found.

When studies have positive findings, it is very important for researchers to try to replicate them. Replication studies often are able to point out some inconsistencies in the original studies. Often it takes quite a bit of training in research design and statistics to be able to understand the issues in many types of studies.

The Notion of Clinical Proof

First, one thing needs to be made quite clear: the notion of "clinical proof" regarding results from small sample research is a misnomer. *Proof* is a strong word and works in legal contexts, but clinical research does not prove anything. The only real proof would come from the study of a population, not a small sample. For example, suppose that you wanted to prove that all crows are black. In order to prove this, you would have to collect all the crows in the world today, collect every crow that has ever existed, and somehow collect every crow that ever will exist. If all these crows were black, you could prove the statement "All crows are black." However, this is impossible. Likewise, the notion of "clinical proof" is a ridiculous statement used by advertisers to sell certain products like medications. Small sample research and the methods by which hypotheses are statistically tested do not provide proof that a hypothesis is true.

In essence, any research that uses samples as opposed to populations cannot *prove* anything. This is especially true in research that looks at different types of treatments for different types of behavioral disorders, such as panic disorder. Research can find support to infer that a treatment is effective for a particular disorder or to disprove that the treatment works on alleviating symptoms of a particular disorder, but research with samples of subjects can never *prove* that some treatment, such as a medication or a type of therapy, is effective for treating the disorder. You might think that the difference between *proof* and *support* is insignificant; however, consider if advertisers stated the truth and said that a medication has clinical support or clinical evidence for its efficacy. There is a big difference.

Due to the nature of small sample research, differing findings in research with the same parameters, and the subjective nature of most psychiatric/psychological disorders, no study or set of studies can offer "clinical proof" that some treatment is effective. Researchers understand this and use the terms *empirically validated* or *evidence-based* when referring to treatments that have a solid base of research findings to support them. Researchers and clinicians never speak of a "clinically proven medication" or a "clinically proven therapy."

Why Empirically Validated Treatment Methods Are Important

Now it should be clear exactly why this section of the book is so significant. It is very important to establish empirically validated treatments for any type of disorder or illness to eliminate the types of biases that individuals are prone to have. Using empirically validated methods offers the best opportunity to establish reliable and valid treatment options for mental disorders, physical diseases, and a host of other medical problems. The effects of treatments are studied under standardized, controlled conditions that significantly reduce bias, misinterpretation, and chance.

Empirical validation helps determine the pros and the cons of a specific treatment and also helps identify which individuals are at risk when using the treatment. Sticking to empirically validated treatment methods allows treatment providers to offer the most effective and safest treatments for individuals with particular disorders and diseases, and it allows for standards to be set in terms of what will be acceptable for treatment and what will not be. The use of peer review also helps ensure rigorous standards and honest reporting of results. However, no safeguard is perfect, and there is no way to be absolutely sure that the system will not be abused. The best thing that can happen is that the system self-corrects in cases of abuse and becomes more stringent and reliable.

ALERT

Certainly there are a number of faults in the system; one fault is the ability of large corporations to get around checks and balances of peer review and clinical validation. However, empirical validation and peer review are still the best ways to help ensure that only valid treatments are widely prescribed. Instances of fraud or manipulating the system should be dealt with vigorously when detected.

Treatments That Are Not Strongly Supported by Research

In some cases, research is ongoing for certain treatments that lack clinical validation to support their use. No reputable clinician would advise a client to use a potentially dangerous treatment option that is not clinically validated, due to the potential for harm to the person (and of course the potential for litigation). Likewise, any reputable clinician should be able to list the pros and cons of clinically validated treatments for her specific area of expertise, or should be able to find them if needed.

In keeping with the spirit of recommending empirically validated treatments, those that do not have solid clinical evidence for their use for panic disorder will not be recommended. This does not mean that they are not necessarily ineffective or unsafe (although in many cases this can be determined); there is just not enough evidence to support their use at this time. Until such evidence either for or against these types of treatments can be determined, it is the recommendation of this author to not engage in their use. Be sure to ask your doctor whether your proposed treatment is clinically validated.

The Placebo Effect

A puzzling disorder occurring with alarming frequency in the 1700s and 1800s was *hysteria*. Hysteria was a group of disorders that present as neurological (caused by CNS dysfunction), but have no apparent physical reason (this class of disorders is now called conversion disorders). In the late 1700s, Franz Mesmer, a healer in France, claimed that certain forces in the body based on "animal magnetism" could be manipulated to cure hysterical disorders. This individual developed an elaborate method of putting people in a pot with water and magnets and then moving around them while chanting and staring. Interestingly, this method was relatively successful in "curing" these patients (who were primarily females) and resulted in the first medical review panel to review this treatment (in fact, the panel included the then–American ambassador to France, Benjamin Franklin). Though the review panel found no reason to think the treatment was actually effective, Franz Mesmer remains in the annals of psychiatry as the prototypical example of the use of a placebo effect and hypnosis (in fact, the word *mesmerize* comes from this whole incident).

Placebo effects are quite common in conditions that have symptoms that are very subjective in nature. Such conditions include many types of chronic pain and many psychiatric/psychological disorders. While placebo effects are not as common in physical diseases, such as cancer, they are still present in many, just to a much smaller degree. Despite a wealth of research on placebo effects, no one really understands why they occur. There are some interesting explanations for them, though, including the power of belief, certain neurobiological contributions, and the inaccurate notion that many of these disorders are "just in the person's head." Placebo effects remain very important to ascertain in empirically validated research for most psychological/psychiatric disorders because they can be quite strong in these disorders. Validated treatments must be significantly more effective than a placebo in order to be recommended.

Placebos Are Not Treatments

It is wrong to think of a placebo effect as a treatment effect. When placebo effects occur, like in Mesmer's cure, there is no reason to suspect that the effect produced by the placebo should have any effect on the condition whatsoever. For example, the color of certain medications, such as antidepressants, can add significantly to their effectiveness, and it has been noted that medications administered by a physician are more effective than medications administered by a nurse (there are numerous similar placebo effects). If the medication is effective for some particular condition, it should not matter what color the pill is or who gives it to you. Likewise, antianxiety medications have been shown to be significantly more effective when the person is told that the medication he is getting is for his anxiety, as opposed to not being told what it is for. Again, effective medication should be effective to the same degree whether or not the person knows what the medication is for. Simply knowing that a medication is for anxiety is not a treatment effect.

This is another reason why empirically validated treatments are very important when we are discussing psychiatric/psychological disorders like panic disorder. It is important to determine what interventions provide real treatment effects beyond placebo effects for the very reason that it is unethical for clinicians to knowingly administer placebos to patients as bona fide treatments, as they are quite unreliable. If placebos were fully effective and ethical to administer, then there would be no reason to design treatments for these conditions. Clinicians could just charge to do what Mesmer did and use anything on individuals that apparently looks like it is working.

FACT

Research has questioned the effectiveness of nearly all types of anti-depressant medications based on the recent finding in the clinical trials submitted to the FDA for approval that antidepressant medications were no more effective than active placebos (an active placebo produces sensations that feel like side effects so one thinks he is getting the medication, but he is not).

There are instances where someone given a placebo may change certain lifestyle factors that contribute to the condition he thinks that he is being treated for and thus improve; however, this could also occur with an empirically validated treatment, so the use of placebo effects in actual treatment of patients remains unethical. Moreover, placebo effects are not reliable and often do not last.

Anecdotal Evidence versus Empirical Evidence

There is a large number of untested claims that many different types of things can "cure" many different disorders or diseases, including certain herbs, diets, "new" therapies, etc. The Internet is full of many such endorsements. Anecdotal evidence consists of nonscientific claims and endorsements from people who report that something has worked for them (a type of self-report or endorsement). These do not qualify as evidence-based arguments. These claims are subjective in nature and are identical to the type of claims Mesmer made. Often people who support these claims may not have had a true disorder, but just had some symptoms. In fact, many of the claims regarding untested treatments are not targeted at true disorders but at normal experiences of anxiety or sadness. Remember that having a disorder is not the same thing as normal variability in emotions and behavior. Placebo effects are not treatments, and therefore cannot be ethically used as clinical treatments for disorders.

Anecdotal evidence can certainly motivate research to investigate the objective nature of the claims, but cannot be recommended as evidence that a treatment is effective unless it is supported by objective evidence designed to control for bias and chance factors.

CHAPTER 10

Medications Commonly Used in Treating Panic Disorder

This chapter very briefly reviews the major medically based treatments for panic disorder. Several classes of medications can control some of the symptoms of panic attacks, but in order to treat the full disorder, you may need to try something beyond medication use. Some medications can work quickly; some take longer before they are effective. Medication is nothing to fear. Of course, medications for any condition should only be taken under the close supervision of a medical doctor.

A Brief History of Medication Use for Anxiety Disorders

The search for an effective way to control anxiety dates back many centuries and covers many different types of drugs. This brief history will simply outline some major developments of this process so you can get a better idea of the treatments for panic disorder.

The search to control nervousness or anxiety goes back many centuries. For example, alcohol use. Years ago, alcohol was used medicinally to treat nervousness or anxiety, for which it worked quite well; however, by the eighteenth century, the addictive properties of alcohol became recognized. The temperance movement and its offshoots in the United States, such as Prohibition in the early part of the 1900s, resulted in the medicinal use of alcohol being mostly limited to its antiseptic properties.

Opium use also has a history extending back thousands of years, but again, in the nineteenth century its addictive properties became recognized and its medicinal properties were primarily limited to use as analgesics, such as morphine. A class of drugs called bromides was used to treat epilepsy in the 1870s (these were also used as sedatives), but again these drugs were found to have a high potential for addiction.

Barbiturates were actually discovered accidentally, but were introduced as hypnotic or sedative drugs in the early 1900s. These drugs were quite popular for some time in treating anxiety. But they were highly addictive, and the potential for overdose using these drugs is quite high.

In the 1970s, the benzodiazepines, minor tranquilizers, became popular for the treatment of anxiety (especially the use of the drug Valium). Interestingly, benzodiazepines were initially considered not to have the addictive properties of barbiturates, but it eventually became quite clear that they were also highly addictive. Nonetheless, benzodiazepines remain popular today in the treatment of anxiety disorders, and there are many different types of benzodiazepines on the market.

Other medications, such as antidepressants and beta-blockers, were originally approved to treat different conditions. In the context of their clinical use, though, it was noted that they appeared to reduce anxiety in individuals who took them. Several of these drugs (antidepressants) underwent clinical trials to determine their efficacy for the treatment of anxiety disorders and have since been approved in the use of treating panic disorder.

Antidepressant Medications and Panic Disorder

There are three general classes of antidepressants that are commonly used for both depression and for panic disorder (other classes of antidepressants are being developed). These three classes are: selective serotonin reuptake inhibitors (SSRIs), tricyclic antidepressant medications, and MAO inhibitors (a newer class, serotonin and norepinephrine reuptake inhibitors [SNRIs], is also available, but not widely used for panic disorder at the time of this writing). Each of these classes has a number of different medications that have a slightly different molecular configuration, but these medications still operate by a general principle that is common to the particular class in which they belong. The most common class of antidepressant medication used in the treatment of panic disorder is the SSRIs.

FACT

Before jumping in, a few term descriptions may be useful. *Anxiolytic drugs* refer to drugs that are used to treat anxiety (most often benzodiazepines are referred to with this tag). *Psychotropic medications* are used primarily for the treatment of psychiatric disorders (some may have other uses as well).

Selective Serotonin Reuptake Inhibitors (SSRIs)

Some literature indicates that many psychiatrists believe that all SSRIs are effective for the treatment of panic disorder. SSRIs block the cellular reuptake of the neurotransmitter serotonin, which has done its job and has been released in the synapse. This way, it remains in the system. Serotonin is believed to be important in mood, and decreased levels could lead to depression or anxiety. Thus, these medications are used in disorders where decreased levels of serotonin are suspected. SSRIs were originally developed for the treatment of depression, and while these drugs were not noted to be more effective than the other antidepressant medications in treating depression, they did demonstrate fewer side effects. This made them more attractive than the previous two classes of antidepressant medications. Sertraline (Zoloft) and fluvoxamine (Luvox) have been noted to be the best tolerated SSRIs for panic disorder. Empirical research has suggested that paroxetine (Paxil) offers some sedative effects (helpful with anxiety) and may have the quickest mechanism of action of the SSRIs for panic disorder. SSRIs are considered to be effective not only in the treatment of panic attacks, but also in lessening the worry, behavioral issues, and depression often associated with panic disorder.

SSRIs do not exert their effects until between two to six weeks after they are started. Because of this, clinicians will often use a benzodiazepine with an SSRI to offer immediate relief. Most patients start with low to moderate doses of an SSRI, and then the dose is increased in small amounts as the person gets used to the medication.

Tricyclic Antidepressants

The tricyclic antidepressants include a large class of drugs that affect several different neurotransmitters as opposed to just affecting serotonin. Several members of this class of antidepressants have been demonstrated to have some effectiveness in the treatment of panic disorder; however, the full clinical benefit of these drugs may not be reached for eight to twelve weeks, as clinicians need to slowly increase the dosage to get the clinical effect. These drugs also tend to have a much more salient side effect profile than the SSRIs. Tricyclic antidepressants may be useful in the treatment of people who have panic disorder and chronic pain, but since the advent of the SSRIs, these drugs are less widely used.

MAO Inhibitors

MAO inhibitors work by reducing a substance that contributes to the breakdown of certain neurotransmitters in the brain (monoamine oxidase). The neurotransmitters remain in the system and are not broken down and this theoretically leads to improvements in mood. There is some data to suggest that phenelzine (Nardil) and tranylcypromine (Parnate), both types of MAO inhibitors, have some effectiveness in the treatment of panic disorder. However, like the tricyclic antidepressants, they may require quite some time before the person can acclimate to the full dosage. These particular antidepressants require dietary restrictions when they are being taken. Therefore, today these medications are rarely used in the treatment of panic disorder.

The Pros of Antidepressant Medications

Antidepressant medications, especially the SSRIs, have a fairly large body of evidence to support their use in the treatment of panic disorder. Antidepressants have been reported to reduce the symptoms of panic attack, anxiety, worry, and behavioral problems that are involved in the entire panic disorder spectrum, as opposed to simply reducing symptoms of panic attacks.

The potential for physical addiction is much lower in antidepressant medications than for some of the other medications used to treat panic disorder. In addition, these medications (especially SSRIs) are relatively well tolerated by many people. This has led to the use of SSRIs being the first line of treatment by psychiatrists for many cases of panic disorder.

The Cons of Antidepressant Medications

Even though SSRIs have fewer side effects than other antidepressants, the side effect profile for SSRI antidepressant medications remains one of the major complications of their use. The common side effects of SSRIs include nausea, nervousness, manic behavior, sexual dysfunction, headaches, dizziness, weight gain, withdrawal if stopped abruptly, cognitive issues, and increased suicide risk (especially in children and adolescents). There can be even more severe (but rarer) side effects as a result of using SSRIs. The other classes of antidepressants tend to have even more severe side effects that SSRIs do. The understanding regarding the long-term use of SSRIs is still in its infancy. If you have any concerns before going on these medications, speak with your doctor.

While SSRIs have been noted to affect the symptoms of panic disorder and not just panic attacks, they often are not full-scale treatments that stand on their own. This is because individuals with panic disorder still experience some anxiety, worry, and behavioral changes even if the medication is shown to be effective. The general thinking in psychiatry is that the use of antidepressant medications and other pharmacological treatments should generally continue for eight to twelve months before the person is slowly weaned from the medications. However, the potential for relapse in anxiety disorders and other disorders like depression is quite high if only medications are involved in their treatment. Research suggests that people who are treated with medication only are at risk for relapse once the medication is discontinued. Therefore, in order to achieve effective long-lasting treatment, SSRIs and other medications may not be enough.

FACT

At the time of this writing, the FDA has approved the use of five specific medications in the treatment of panic disorder. These medications include the SSRI antidepressants fluoxetine (Prozac), paroxetine (Paxil), and sertraline (Zoloft). The benzodiazepines clonazepam (Klonopin) and alprazolam (Xanax) are also approved. Other medications have empirical support for their use, but are not FDA-approved.

Antianxiety Medications and Panic Disorder

One advantage to the use of benzodiazepines in dealing with panic attacks is that they have the most rapid onset of action against panic attack symptoms. What this means is that benzodiazepines work very quickly at reducing the symptoms of an oncoming panic attack. Most benzodiazepines prescribed for panic disorder work on a neurotransmitter known as GABA (gamma-aminobutyric acid). GABA is the major inhibitory neurotransmitter in the CNS; an inhibitory neurotransmitter reduces the firing of other neurons when it is released into the system. Thus, benzodiazepines increase the amount or action of GABA in the brain, resulting in a decrease in neuronal firing, which, in turn, results in a decrease in the symptoms of anxiety.

The major differences between the different benzodiazepines are how quickly they begin working, how long they are retained in the body, and individual responses to them. Not everyone will have the exact same response to the same medication. Any benzodiazepine could potentially be used to treat panic disorder, but the most common benzodiazepines used in the treatment of panic disorder are listed as follows.

ALERT

The *half-life* of a medication refers to the time it takes the potency of the medication in the system to be reduced to half its original strength. This is important because people who take these medications frequently are at risk for overdose. A benzodiazepine overdose could result in a shutdown of the cardiac and respiratory systems and is potentially fatal.

Xanax

Probably the most widely prescribed benzodiazepine for panic disorder is alprazolam (commonly known as Xanax, but it also goes by several other names). If you take Xanax, the medication will work very quickly. For many people, 90 percent of the full effects of the medication occur within an hour or less. This has made Xanax very popular in the treatment of panic attacks. The person who begins to experience the symptoms of an oncoming panic attack can take the medication and experience very fast relief from the anxiety. Many people have claimed that Xanax has been extremely helpful in the reduction of their panic attacks, and there is a fairly substantial body of research that supports the use of Xanax in the treatment for panic attacks.

With the approval of antidepressant medications for the treatment of panic disorder, Xanax is often no longer considered the first-in-line treatment for panic disorder, but is still considered to be helpful in the initial stages of treatment. One problem with Xanax is its relatively long half-life, although it has the shortest half-life of most of the commonly prescribed benzodiazepines. Taking Xanax or any benzodiazepine too often can be dangerous because the amount of the medication in your blood may still be quite high, and taking more medication before a significant amount of the drug has been eliminated from your system can lead to overdose.

Ativan

Lorazepam, commonly known as Ativan (although there are other generic names as well), is another benzodiazepine that has a fair amount of empirical research to support the notion that it is effective in the treatment of panic attacks. Ativan has a quick onset of action, but also has a relatively long half-life.

Klonopin

Clonazepam, known as Klonopin, is another benzodiazepine that has some empirical research to support its use in the treatment of panic attacks. Some sources report that Klonopin is as effective as Xanax in the treatment of panic attacks, and others indicate that Klonopin does have some effects, but may not be as effective as Xanax or Ativan. The disadvantage to using Klonopin is that it has an extremely long half-life and a much longer onset of action compared to Xanax or Ativan.

Valium

Diazepam, commonly known as Valium, was at one time the most pre-scribed psychotropic medication in the United States. It has a short onset of action, but a much longer half-life than most of the other benzodiazepines used in the treatment of panic disorder. Valium has received much notoriety for its strong potential for addiction; however, this is a problem with most of the benzodiazepines.

The Pros of Benzodiazepines

Benzodiazepines have the most rapid onset of action against panic and anxiety. This makes them very popular with psychiatrists and other medical doctors who treat patients with anxiety disorders. However, with the use of certain antidepressant medications in the treatment of panic disorder, par-ticularly SSRIs, benzodiazepines are probably not considered to be the first-line treatment for panic disorder. They do offer almost immediate relief for anxiety and the symptoms of an oncoming panic attack. This quick relief from anxiety is a major advantage to their use. Many physicians use them as a first agent in the treatment of panic disorder, often prescribed with an SSRI that is slowly being taken in increasing doses to reach its therapeutic effect. Then, the patient is asked to slowly taper their use of the benzodiazepine as the SSRI begins to take effect. Benzodiazepines can be taken daily, two or three times a day, or just on an as-needed basis.

ESSENTIAL

Benzodiazepines, minor tranquilizers, are often referred to as antianxiety medications because these medications were specifically designed to treat the symptoms of anxiety. However, technically any drug used in the treatment of anxiety symptoms is an antianxiety medication. Most often when mental health professionals refer to antianxiety medications, they are referring to benzodiazepines.

The Cons of Benzodiazepines

As with most psychotropic drugs, the side effect profile of benzodiazepines is often cited as a major complication in prescribing these medications. The major reservation for prescribing benzodiazepines for panic disorder is that they have a strong potential for addiction (dependence), as benzodiazepines can be very physically addicting. Many people develop tolerance to benzodiazepines very quickly (they need to take more of the drug to get the same effect) and experience severe withdrawal symptoms if the drug is discontinued abruptly. The strong potential for addiction can be enhanced in people with anxiety disorders because the addiction to the drug gives them both a physical and psychological crutch to depend on. They develop a type of belief system in which they see the drug as being essential to their everyday functioning.

In addition, because of their mechanism of action, someone using benzodiazepines can be at risk for an accident when driving or using heavy machinery. It is important to note that these drugs can produce lethargy, drowsiness, and significantly decreased reaction times or problems with concentration. Other side effects from benzodiazepine use may include memory loss, dizziness, nausea, loss of coordination, disinhibition, and sexual problems, and there are some instances of paradoxical effects where benzodiazepine use has actually increased anxiety or was associated with mania and increased aggression in some patients. The action of benzodiazepines can be significantly enhanced with alcohol use or other drug use, so people taking these drugs are strongly encouraged not to drink alcohol.

Beta-Blockers and Panic Disorder

Beta-blockers are a class of drugs that target the beta receptors in the heart muscles, arteries, kidneys, and other organs associated with the sympathetic nervous system. Recall that the sympathetic nervous system generally "speeds things up," so the sympathetic nervous system is often implicated in panic disorder and stress responses. Beta-blockers interfere with the binding of the neurotransmitter epinephrine (adrenaline) and certain stress hormones, which results in a dampening of the activation of the sympathetic nervous system.

Research has indicated that beta-blockers are effective in inhibiting symptoms of anxiety such as feeling jittery, sweating, and feeling nervous. Propranolol (Inderal) is a beta-blocker that is often used in the treatment of high blood pressure, but also appears to be effective in treating symptoms of anxiety, such as those observed in panic disorder or social phobia. Typically beta-blockers are only used in the treatment of panic disorder for a short time while other forms of treatment are being initiated. These drugs do not have the potential for addiction as do benzodiazepines and can be used in place of drugs like Xanax.

Other Medications Used to Treat Panic Disorder

Buspirone (Buspar) is an anxiolytic medication primarily used to treat generalized anxiety disorder. It is sometimes used in the treatment of panic disorder. Buspirone enhances the effects of serotonin in the brain. It appears to be effective in decreasing general worry and anxiety, but is not as effective in treating panic attacks, although there is some literature that indicates that it might be effective for panic attacks in some cases. It appears to have a side effect profile similar to SSRIs.

Valproic acid is an acidic chemical compound that has been used in the treatment of epilepsy and bipolar disorder. There is some research to indicate that it may be helpful in treating some cases of schizophrenia as well. There has been some empirical research that has indicated that valproic acid can be a useful medicine in addition to the primary medications, such as an SSRI, for the treatment of panic disorder. However, if used in conjunction with a benzodiazepine, it may cause excessive sedation.

Verapamil (known as Isoptin, Verelan, and several other names) is a calcium channel blocker used to treat hypertension, angina, migraine headaches, and cardiac arrhythmias. It has been noted to be a vasodilator, and early research identified it as a potential treatment for panic disorder, but with the increasing use of SSRIs, this medication is not used for panic disorder often.

Other substances used by physicians will be discussed in upcoming chapters.

ALERT

There are a number of factors that must be considered before a person is prescribed psychotropic medications. Most of these medications should not be taken by pregnant women, people who drink alcohol excessively or use illicit drugs, or people who have certain medical conditions, among other things.

Nonresponders to Medications

Certain conditions may direct the clinician's use of a particular drug or type of drug. For example, when immediate relief for severe panic attacks is needed, the use of a benzodiazepine such as Xanax or Ativan is often combined with the use of an SSRI to give the patient some relief until the SSRI can become effective. In cases of panic disorder with comorbid generalized anxiety disorder, clinicians may opt to use Effexor, an antidepressant that works on the neurotransmitters serotonin and norepinephrine. When the patient suffers from panic attacks but is able to anticipate a situation in which a panic attack may occur, clinicians may use Klonopin instead of Xanax. When a patient is prescribed a medication that has a partial effect on the patient's symptoms, the physician will often add medications to work with the medications the patient is already taking. These particular combinations of medications can be quite variable and can be a combination of benzodiazepines, antidepressants, and other drugs.

The general approach in psychiatry is that if a person fails to respond to one class of drugs, another should be tried. Many psychiatrists will use a combination of an SSRI and a tricyclic antidepressant, or a benzodiazepine, an SSRI, and the drug lithium (which is typically used for bipolar patients), or the use of medications that are commonly used in other disorders, such as antiepileptic drugs, which are sometimes used as mood stabilizers for bipolar disorder.

Clinicians tend to approach patients from two perspectives:

1. A statistical perspective, where the patient is treated in conjunction with what is generally effective for most of the population
2. An individual perspective, where the patient's specific symptom constellation and sensitivities must be considered in order to design an effective treatment program

FACT

One drawback to a medication approach for treating panic disorder is that many of these psychotropic medications produce side effects. Physicians often prescribe more medications to treat the side effects of the medications that they themselves prescribed to the patient in the first place. When a patient's symptoms are created by a physician, they are referred to as "iatrogenic symptoms."

Psychiatrists who fail to consider the individual needs and the individual presentations of their patients, and who rely solely on a statistical approach to treatment, are more apt to get involved in symptom management as opposed to actually treating their patients. Unfortunately, it is not unusual to see a person on several different psychotropic medications with numerous iatrogenic symptoms that might be better regulated by reducing the number of medications the person is taking.

Are Psychotropic Medications Effective?

There has been a re-evaluation of the research used to gain approval of the use of antidepressant medications in the treatment of depression. The re-evaluation, spearheaded by psychologist Dr. Irving Kirsch, intended to look at placebo effects in these clinical trials, but unexpectedly found that in these clinical trials, antidepressant medications were not more effective in relieving depressive symptoms than active placebos (an active placebo has no treatment effect but produces side effects so the person receiving the placebo thinks that she may be on a medication). In addition, there have been several additional sources that have re-evaluated much of the research performed by pharmaceutical companies on their psychotropic medications and have come to the conclusion that many of these medications are not effective in treating the disorder in question.

There has also been some research that suggests that the effectiveness of antianxiety medications is significantly enhanced if the person receiving the medication is told that the medication is designed to specifically relieve her anxiety. In essence, this suggests that these medications have strong placebo effects because a true treatment effect should not be significantly enhanced or decreased by the simple knowledge that one is taking the medication (certainly there should be some placebo effect for any treatment, but clinically significant effects due to expectations or wanting to get better suggest that there is a strong placebo effect in these medications). Nonetheless, there are a number of people with panic disorder who strongly endorse the medications that they have been taking, and there is independent research to suggest that these medications have empirically validated evidence to support the fact that taking them helps people with panic disorder.

This competing research is important for several reasons. Recall that clinicians who knowingly administer placebos to patients are engaging in significant ethical violations of their profession. The question of whether or not psychotropic medications are actual treatments or are primarily placebos is one that will continue to be debated. Most people who suffer from panic disorder and see a psychiatrist will be placed on some type of medication regime, so instead of debating this question further, it will be more useful to discuss how you should approach using medications for panic disorder.

Some Guidelines to Medication Usage

The classes of medications discussed in this book will only work if they are taken according to the instructions on the label or given to the person by her psychiatrist or physician. It is also important to understand that medications often do not resolve all the symptoms of panic disorder and that medications, such as SSRIs, take some time before they actually produce an effect. It is important to remember to follow these basic guidelines when taking medications in order for them to be most effective:

1. It is not a crime to ask questions about a prescription medication. Too many people simply nod their heads without knowing what to expect. Ask questions such as: "How should I expect this medicine to help me?"; "Should I avoid certain foods or beverages?"; "What side effects might I expect?"; and "What type of interactions with other medications can I expect?" Be proactive.

2. Always disclose every prescription medication, dietary supplement (including herbs and vitamins), alcohol or other drug usage, and even nonprescription medicines that you take when getting a prescription to treat panic disorder.

3. Make sure to understand how to take the medication (when, how often, after meals or on an empty stomach, etc.) and find out how long you should expect to wait before noticing results.

4. It is always a good idea to make sure to have after-hours contact numbers for the prescribing physician in case one begins to experience side effects.

5. Make sure to schedule follow-up appointments.

ALERT

Contact your physician if you experience side effects, even if you are not sure that a symptom or feeling is caused by a medication. Do not stop taking a medication or cut down on a medication without consulting with a physician, as sudden discontinuation or cutting back may result in health risks.

CHAPTER 11

Psychotherapy and Panic Disorder

When considering the various treatments for panic disorder, one of the more popular approaches you may want to explore is psychotherapy. With psychotherapy, you work with a trained professional to gain control over your anxiety and panic. Psychotherapy is the most conventional treatment for panic disorder and, when done properly, can yield some very promising results. In fact, there is a large body of evidence to support the use of several types of psychotherapy for panic disorder. You shouldn't feel pressured to stick with one specific type of psychotherapy if it doesn't work for you. Just remember, everyone is different. What one patient finds inspiring, you may find anxiety-provoking. The best thing you can do is to learn what kind of therapy you feel more comfortable with. The following chapter will help you do just that.

Major Psychotherapy Schools

There are literally hundreds of different types of psychotherapy. Don't worry, though. For purposes of this book, *psychotherapy* will be used as an overall term that refers to a contracted treatment between a trained professional and a person or group of people with the goal of solving a specific set of problems, lifestyle conditions, or the effects of some type of mental disorder.

The problems or issues addressed in psychotherapy vary considerably, so don't ever feel as though your problems are not appropriate for this treatment. The method used in psychotherapy involves a number of different approaches that revolve around verbal communication, reflection, uncovering thoughts and feelings, learning to change behavior, etc.

A number of different trained professionals are qualified to perform psychotherapy. When searching for your own mental health professional, there are a few facts you'll want to keep in mind. First, despite the depiction in the media, psychiatrists typically do not engage in much psychotherapy; they are trained in the use and management of medications for specific types of issues (most psychiatrists receive minimal training in psychotherapy). Licensed psychologists (typically those with a PhD), licensed counselors, and social workers are the main groups of individuals that typically deliver psychotherapy services. Many states allow licensure with a master's degree in social work and counseling or a limited license (a limited-licensed individual must have a fully licensed supervisor overseeing his work).

It is important to make sure that the professional in question is licensed and certified to perform the specific type of psychotherapy that he practices. Often people seeking psychotherapeutic services do not inquire about the experience and training of the individual they consult. For the treatment of panic disorder, it is imperative to inquire about the therapist's experience in treating panic disorder. Not every licensed psychotherapist has been trained in treating panic disorder, which can make a difference in the outcome of the specific case. Just like it would be wrong for a person with suspected heart disease to consult with an oncologist, a person with panic disorder will fare much better in treatment with someone who has the specific training and experience to deal with his particular disorder.

If you're not sure where to begin, the types of questions to ask would include: What is the clinician's training and background as it relates to panic disorder?; Does the clinician have any special certification regarding treating panic disorder?; What is the major method or type of therapy that the clinician uses?; etc.

In general, all the different types of psychotherapy approach treatment from one of two major perspectives: an *insight-oriented perspective* or an *action-oriented perspective*. It is important to understand that these designations are not mutually exclusive, but represent the major focus of the therapeutic paradigm in question. Most therapists will have an initial free consultation in order to determine if they can help you. It is during the first consultation when you should also be asking questions. Don't be intimated. This is your health, after all.

FACT

The degree of the therapist (PhD, PsyD, MSW, etc.) is not as important as special training in the area of panic disorder (although an MA is the minimum degree). Other important issues include how well the client trusts the therapist, how much at ease the person is when disclosing issues with the particular therapist, and other factors that make the client comfortable.

Insight-Oriented versus Action-Oriented Therapies

Insight-oriented psychotherapies attempt to help a patient discover what causes his behaviors. The major mechanism in these psychotherapies is the insight, realization, or learning that comes from the self-awareness one develops regarding one's own motivations, desires, etc. If you are more comfortable just talking about your problems, this might be the best treatment plan for you.

Action-oriented psychotherapies focus on having the person actually do something to change a particular behavior. The major mechanism of action of these therapies is the learning of a new way to behave, look at things, or change patterns of thinking or behavior.

One way to view these two different psychotherapies is that one is more of an intellectual approach and the other is more hands-on. However, no particular type of theory or therapy is fully insight-oriented or action-oriented. You will most likely be involved in a combination of these therapies during your treatment. For instance, types of therapy that are considered primarily insight-oriented also include techniques for the direct changing of behaviors and thoughts, while types of therapy that are primarily considered to be action-oriented involve a great deal of learning and insight as to one's motivations. This designation is used to identify the *major* mechanism of change that the particular school of therapy concentrates on.

As mentioned previously, all types of therapy use both approaches, but most therapists will stress one approach as guiding the other. The actual type of therapy that works for an individual depends on a number of factors, especially the relationship between the therapist and the client, the client's background, and the therapist's background. To make things simple, the following section groups all types of therapy into four major schools.

Four Major Schools

Psychodynamic therapy consists of a number of different types of therapy that got their start in the Freudian tradition, including psychoanalysis. These types of therapies tend to lean more toward the insight-oriented approach and view the individual as a "dynamic" system that develops beginning in childhood and progresses from there on. Early experiences occurring in childhood and adolescence are considered very significant. For example, conflicts that occurred with your parents are considered to be important in the types of relationships and issues that you developed later on in life.

There is still quite a bit of focus on unconscious mental processes and how they affect overt behavior in this particular therapy paradigm (remember, the majority of actions people perform are performed automatically). Therapists from this paradigm often view all behavior as meaningful no matter how trivial it may seem. To them, almost all of your current actions represent many of the unconscious issues that were developed in childhood.

The *behavioral school of psychotherapy* is really not widely practiced without being combined with some other paradigm (most often behavioral therapy is combined with cognitive therapy). Behavioral therapy concentrates on unlearning patterns of learned dysfunctional behaviors. Behaviorism and behavioral therapy are traditionally action-oriented. Motivations, goals, and desires are considered to develop as a manner of contingencies. The important aspects of behavior are the antecedents (things that occur before the particular behavior), the behavior itself, and the consequences of the behavior (how the behavior is either reinforced or punished). These techniques attempt to change the antecedents and consequences of the behavior as a means to therapeutic change. For instance, a therapist may learn that a person begins to get anxious before going to work and the anxiety sometimes leads to a panic attack. The person stops going to work and the anxiety goes away (this is an example of negative reinforcement). The therapist may instruct the person to practice relaxation every morning before going to work in order to control the anxiety.

The *cognitive school of psychotherapy* concentrates on your thoughts and beliefs. According to this school, behavior results from how you view the world, interpret the events in the world, and what you expect to happen when you behave in a certain way. When there is an issue with behavior, cognitive therapists look at the person's beliefs and expectations regarding his behavior and attempt to make these beliefs and expectations more in line with reality. The cognitive school tends to be more action-oriented, but there is a great deal of insight involved in this process as well. The major offshoot of cognitive therapy is the cognitive behavioral psychotherapies (CBT) that combine both behavioral techniques and cognitive techniques. CBT is composed of a large group of different therapeutic methods that have received a great deal of empirical support and popularity with practicing psychotherapists. If you like the idea of combining behavioral therapy and insight-oriented therapy, CBT might be a perfect fit for you. CBT also has the largest body of evidence to support its use in the treatment of panic disorder.

ESSENTIAL

Eclectic psychotherapy combines different techniques from different therapies. Most of the hundreds of different types of psychotherapy recognized today have their roots in these four major paradigms or a combination of these paradigms. In general, it appears that most types of psychotherapy are effective for a wide range of different problems. However, there are questionable therapies that are not recommended.

The *humanistic school of psychotherapy* (also termed *existential psychotherapy*) considers someone's desire and drive to become self-actualized (think of this as becoming self-fulfilled or self-realized) the most important influence on his actions and behaviors. There is a hierarchy of needs that people seek to fulfill. Issues develop when you adopt standards and beliefs about how you should act from others as opposed to understanding your own inherent needs. This school tends to be more insight-oriented, but also uses a number of action-oriented methods.

Psychodynamic Therapy for Panic Disorder

Psychodynamic therapies include many different approaches ranging from object relations therapy to interpersonal therapy (which combines cognitive-behavioral principles with psychodynamic therapy). Before discussing the general effect of this approach on panic disorder, it is important to briefly discuss the current status of psychoanalysis, which is the prototype for this school of therapy.

Psychoanalysis, especially as practiced by Freud and his early followers, probably represents the common stereotype that many people have when thinking of psychotherapy. You might imagine psychotherapy as a client lying on a couch with the therapist sitting behind him, and the client talking on and on until the therapist asks a question like, "How does that make you feel?"

Traditional psychoanalysis is not widely practiced today for several reasons. First, traditional psychoanalysis is quite time-consuming (it can last for many years of several weekly sessions), and many insurance companies do not pay for such lengthy psychotherapeutic services. Second, the psychodynamic school of therapy has differentiated quite a bit since Freud initially developed the core principles of this paradigm, and many of the newer psychodynamic methods are time-limited and more direct in their approach.

As mentioned previously, traditional psychoanalysis is a long and drawn-out process that often takes years to complete. Many of the problems addressed in today's therapeutic environment require much quicker and more practical solutions. A specific type of dynamic therapy called panic-focused psychodynamic psychotherapy (PFPP) has been developed specifically to treat individuals with panic disorder.

Panic-Focused Psychodynamic Psychotherapy

Psychodynamic therapy for panic disorder (PFPP) has been tested in several relatively well-controlled studies that have demonstrated that this therapy does produce positive effects for people with panic disorder. Several of these studies have compared psychodynamic treatments with established treatments, such as cognitive-behavioral therapy and applied relaxation training, and have found that psychodynamic treatments are comparable with these established treatments for panic disorder.

Psychodynamic techniques attempt to get at the emotional and relational issues that produce panic attacks. The focus is on the root causes of the panic attacks. The psychodynamic viewpoint is that people who are prone to panic attacks have developed a fearful dependency on their significant caregivers (as a result of a diathesis-stress model). These people are insecure in their attachments and have an underlying feeling of inadequacy. This results in their needing to have attention from others to feel safe, and separation or perceived separation from important people in their lives leads to panic and fear. These people are burdened with both fear of separation and anger about being dependent on others. As a result, this develops into a very vicious cycle of fear and anger with themselves.

Panic disorder is often triggered by significant stressors that bring up these feelings from the unconscious part of the mind. The therapy is aimed at understanding these issues and making the patient aware of these specific issues as they occur based on his background and experiences. Understanding the causes of your insecurities and anxieties helps you take control over your panic and other issues.

ALERT

Make sure that the therapist targets the intervention directly at panic disorder before exploring other issues. PFPP to treat panic disorder does appear to be effective, but there is the potential for therapy to focus on issues not related to panic disorder if this is not agreed upon. Once the panic disorder is under control, other issues can be explored.

Behavioral Therapy for Panic Disorder

Most of the research looking at strictly behavioral techniques in treating panic disorder is rather dated. Many behavioral techniques have been combined with other forms of therapy, such as combining behavioral techniques with cognitive techniques into cognitive-behavioral therapy (CBT). CBT has become the primary type of psychotherapy that is used for treating depression and anxiety disorders.

Very few therapists use only behavioral techniques these days. Nonetheless, a brief word about behavioral techniques is important when discussing treatments for panic disorder because most of the psychotherapies for panic disorder use some type of behavioral intervention.

Recall from earlier that behaviorism concentrates on learning. Behavioral therapy is used to unlearn dysfunctional behaviors such as overeating, feeling depressed, smoking, etc.

FACT

Techniques from the behavioral school of psychology have been borrowed by a number of different psychotherapeutic paradigms. This is because these techniques are very effective in helping change a wide number of behaviors and problems that people experience, from breaking habits to changing entire long-standing patterns of unwanted behaviors. These techniques can be applied to anyone and any issue.

There are a number of different behavioral techniques that have been incorporated with other therapeutic schools to treat anxiety disorders such as panic disorder. One of the most used behavioral techniques for treating anxiety is relaxation training, which will be discussed in a separate section. Other behavioral techniques often used in the treatment of panic disorder include techniques such as exposure (recreating the panic conditions or symptoms at lower and increasing levels in order to learn to control them), breathing (which helps with relaxation), recording and documenting instances of panic and anxiety, and learning the antecedents and consequences of one's panic attacks, worry, or the behavioral changes associated with panic disorder. These techniques can be practiced in vivo (in real life) or in vitro (under simulated conditions), or both. By learning and reinforcing positive strategies of coping with panic attacks and their effects, the person can learn to control his anxiety and reduce the symptoms of panic disorder.

Cognitive-Behavioral Therapy for Panic Disorder

The school of psychotherapy that has received the strongest empirically validated support for treating panic disorder is cognitive-behavioral therapy (CBT). CBT has developed and expanded greatly into a number of different types of therapies, all with the goal of changing how one perceives her own actions, the actions of the world, and her ability to affect things. Cognitive theory views panic disorder as being maintained by biased thinking and beliefs about one's panic attacks and what they might do. Typically these fearful beliefs focus on the negative outcomes associated with panic attacks and the possibility that the panic attack may lead to some catastrophic event like hospitalization, ridicule, paralysis, or even death. There are several aspects of CBT that have well-established empirical evidence for the treatment of panic disorder.

Cognitive Restructuring

CBT therapists use examples from discussions during therapy and homework assignments given to the client to identify the types of thoughts, biases, and potential misinformation reflected in the person's beliefs. The therapist's goal is to identify and challenge these thoughts, beliefs, and assumptions in order to test them in the real world. Often these assumptions are converted into predictions of what would happen if the client should actually do something that she fears. Then these predictions are tested through behavioral experiments. These behavioral experiments involve having the client actually perform a feared task as an exercise to see what types of things will actually occur when the client is confronted with her fears and if what actually does happen matches the client's expectations.

Under such scrutiny, the validity of these catastrophic thoughts and beliefs is challenged and often disproven. Once the client is aware of the invalid thoughts and beliefs that fuel much of her concern, the therapist and the client work on developing new and realistic beliefs and expectations. Cognitive restructuring follows four basic tenets to help the client gain control over her panic attacks and her fears:

1. Panic disorder is perpetuated by a set of rigid and often unrealistic thoughts and beliefs about the consequences of a panic attack.
2. The first step is to identify and challenge these fearful and unrealistic thoughts and beliefs.
3. Dialogue and homework help identify and challenge these thoughts and beliefs.

4. Once these thoughts and beliefs are challenged, they can be changed and restructured. Decatastrophizing reduces the client's worry and need to avoid situations that may result in panic.

ESSENTIAL

Cognitive restructuring may help you to decatastrophize your expectations regarding your panic attacks. This is often accomplished through a series of questions aimed at determining what would happen if your worst fears about your panic attacks came true. Once you verbalize these consequences, you may come to the realization that your worst fears are really not that bad.

Breathing and Relaxation

Teaching the client to control her breathing helps her to develop a sense of control over her feelings of anxiety and panic. Studies have shown that producing hyperventilation in people with panic disorder often produces panic attacks. The breathing techniques that are taught as a part of the behavioral component of CBT are designed to induce relaxation and control. When you are stressed or anxious, you begin to breathe quickly and engage in short breaths characterized by the use of the upper chest. CBT combats this breathing by teaching you to breathe more slowly and to use your diaphragm to breathe, resulting in a decrease in anxiety. You will quickly learn to control your breathing when you begin to experience anxiety.

You will also learn progressive muscle relaxation to help you gain a greater sense of control over your body. This progressive relaxation is practiced daily, decreases tension, and helps you prepare for exposure to anxiety-provoking thoughts and situations. Breathing and relaxation are often used in conjunction with visualization. During therapy sessions, clients are often taught to breathe and relax and to visualize the situations that occur during a panic attack. By visualizing the panic attack in as much detail as possible while being relaxed, the client gains a sense of control.

Exposure

Exposure techniques are designed to extinguish panic by gradually approaching anxiety- and panic-provoking stimuli, whether they are bodily sensations or external events.

Interoceptive exposure exposes the client gradually to the sensations that are associated with her panic attacks, such as rapid heart rate, dizziness, etc., by having the client deliberately induce these sensations and learning to tolerate them during states of relaxation and breathing.

Exteroceptive exposure involves approaching feared activities or situations that are associated with panic attacks. This could be different depending on the client's experiences. The goal of this exposure is to reduce anxiety associated with these situations or stimuli, to increase control and predictability, and to eventually extinguish the fear associated with the situations.

Most likely the therapist will have you develop a hierarchy of your fears or situations that produce panic attacks, starting with the least anxiety-provoking to the most fearful or anxiety-provoking situation/stimulus. Then you and the therapist can work together, doing exposure exercises while you are relaxed and breathing. You will start with the least anxiety-provoking situations, working until these are mastered, and then move up the list. This type of *systematic desensitization* reduces the client's fear, reduces avoidance and worry, increases the client's control over her panic attacks, increases her confidence, and extinguishes fear and panic.

ALERT

Exposure is a very specific technique and should only be practiced by a licensed professional with experience in using it. You should never attempt to do any type of exposure on your own without supervision of a trained mental health professional. Doing so could potentially result in making your issues worse instead of better.

CBT has become the treatment of choice for panic disorder, and there have been many well-controlled research studies that have suggested that the effects of CBT continue long after the sessions have discontinued. This makes CBT more advantageous than using medications alone; however, there is also a great deal of research that suggests that the use of medications in conjunction with CBT is more effective than using either treatment alone. CBT treatments tend to be briefer in terms of the number of sessions needed than psychodynamic treatments, which is often also an advantage.

Relaxation Training

A behavioral component of CBT is relaxation training. In addition, *applied relaxation* has developed as a type of behaviorally oriented therapy to treat the symptoms of anxiety. This technique will teach you to relax in successively shorter time periods and to relax more quickly in everyday situations. This skill equips you with a strategy to control your reactions to stress and to panic attacks as they occur. Applied relaxation consists of six components taught in succession:

1. *Tense-release relaxation* is a method of relaxation where the individual learns to tense specific muscle groups and then release them, concentrating on the release portion of the relaxation technique as a means of experiencing muscle relaxation. This method works all muscle groups in the body and typically takes between fifteen to twenty minutes to complete. This technique is also typically taught as *progressive muscle relaxation* in CBT.

2. Next, individuals are taught the *release-only* relaxation technique, where the tension part of the above technique is removed and the client learns to simply relax major muscle groups without tensing them. This results in significantly less time to achieve a relaxed state.

3. *Cue-controlled relaxation* is the next step. This form of relaxation focuses on breathing. The client is first instructed to relax using the release-only method. Once the client is relaxed, he is instructed to simply recite the word *relax* as he exhales. Over many repetitions, the relaxation of the body is associated with the word *relax*, and this becomes a cue for whole-body relaxation (this is a type of conditioning).

4. *Differential relaxation* is taught next. This type of relaxation occurs while the person is engaged in some form of activity. The person learns to control his levels of muscular tension, first while sitting and then when standing and doing different activities. This technique teaches the individual to rid himself of excess muscle tension during activity.

5. *Rapid relaxation* is then taught to the client in order to further reduce the time it takes for him to relax. This is also practiced in everyday situations. Often the client's environment is arranged in such a manner to remind the client to relax, such as marking a telephone and other objects with a particular color that is relaxing to the client. Every time the client looks at these marked objects in his environment, it reminds him to release tension in his body. This is typically accomplished by having the client take a slow breath, think the word *relax*, and then exhale, removing tension from his body. This is practiced many times daily until it becomes habitual.

6. *Application training* occurs as the client practices learned relaxation skills in many different situations, especially in stressful or anxiety-provoking situations.

Relaxation techniques are important components of psychological treatments for panic disorder because relaxation and anxiety represent two different ends of the spectrum of bodily feelings. It is physically impossible for a person to feel anxious and relaxed at the same time. Once one can continue to feel relaxed during his panic attacks, the anxiety is extinguished.

Applied relaxation has been shown to be more effective than placebo or a simple no-treatment control group in empirical research for the treatment of panic disorder and has also been demonstrated to have enduring effects. However, the combination of exposure, breathing, and relaxation, as used in CBT, appears to have the most consistent empirically validated support for the treatment of panic disorder. Most of the therapists that use applied relaxation also include CBT components such as exposure.

Other Psychological Treatments for Panic Disorder

There are several other types of psychological treatments that have been used for panic disorder. One of these is *psychoeducation*, which involves learning about panic disorder, the rationale for various treatments, and the different models of the various treatments. Psychoeducation often prepares the individual for a specific treatment regime as opposed to being a stand-alone treatment itself.

Gestalt therapy is a type of experiential psychotherapy (insight-oriented) that grew out of the psychodynamic tradition. Here, the client is encouraged to become aware of his emotions as they exist in the present, not as a result of the past. Gestalt therapy is comprised of principles from a variety of therapeutic philosophies and can be quite intense. There is evidence that Gestalt therapy can be useful in the treatment of anxiety disorders such as panic disorder.

Interpersonal psychotherapy is a short-term psychotherapy that grew out of the psychodynamic philosophy. This school focuses on the connection between interactions between people and the development of symptoms such as panic attacks. There have been several good studies that have demonstrated its effectiveness in reducing the symptoms of panic disorder.

Rational emotive behavior therapy, developed by the American psychologist Albert Ellis, is a form of CBT that specifically targets faulty thinking and faulty beliefs that result in maladaptive behaviors. This therapy is based on the notion that the specific interpretations of events that occur in one's life lead to anxiety and unhappiness and not the events themselves. It is more confrontational in nature than traditional CBT but remains an action-oriented therapeutic intervention.

Dialectical behavioral therapy is a form of CBT that adds emotional regulation techniques and becoming mindful of oneself (trying to be more self-aware of momentary thoughts, feelings, and actions) from Buddhist meditation. There have been several studies that suggest that this therapy can help reduce panic disorder symptoms.

Other types of psychotherapy-based techniques used to treat panic disorder include eye movement desensitization and reprocessing, hypnotherapy, and biofeedback training. These will be discussed individually later on in this book.

ESSENTIAL

There are many different claims for psychotherapy "breakthroughs" on the Internet by people trying to sell books, promote self-help programs, or even solicit therapy clients. Most of these techniques consist of minor revisions to CBT, combinations of proven techniques, or alternative methods without evidence. These are marketing strategies that often apply anecdotal endorsements. Do not let them fool you!

CHAPTER 12

Group Psychotherapy for Panic Disorder

This is a social world where personal relationships are extremely important. Psychotherapy that occurs in a group environment provides the added comfort of a social arena where members of the group can learn about their strengths and weaknesses. This is done by working through their interactions with both the therapist and other group members. People with panic disorder can learn that they are not alone in their suffering and can learn from the experiences of others. This chapter briefly examines how group therapy can be useful in the treatment of panic disorder.

The History of Group Psychotherapy

Most historians date the beginning of group psychotherapy to the twentieth century when Boston physician, Dr. Joseph Pratt, brought tuberculosis patients into a group to show them how to combat their disease. It is said that Pratt noticed that the patients benefited greatly from group instruction as opposed to traditional individual instruction. Later in 1925, the psychiatrist, Trigant Burrow, begin experimenting with using psychoanalysis in groups as opposed to just seeing individual patients. By performing psychoanalysis in a group environment, Burrow found that he could lessen the authoritarian presence of the therapist and more effectively examine interpersonal reactions in the group. He also noticed that many of the traditional psychoanalytic processes occurred between the group members, between individuals and the therapist, and between the group and the therapist. The increase in the channels for psychoanalytic processes, which traditionally only occurred between the therapist and the client, resulted in even stronger overall therapeutic effects.

In the 1930s, Louis Wender and Paul Schilder began to perform group therapy sessions with groups of prison inmates and patients that had been discharged from mental hospitals. Psychiatrist Cody Marsh is said to have included group therapy in a hospital environment that also consisted of group dance classes. Freud began to recognize the dynamics of group therapy, and several of his followers began seeing patients in groups as well as individually. The development of Alcoholics Anonymous in the 1930s was one of the major contributions to the number of self-help groups in existence today.

During World War II, there was an increase in group psychology and the use of approaches using groups for selection and allocation of work responsibilities in the professional arena. Following the war, group therapy received quite a push, as large numbers of soldiers required psychological treatment following the war. Groups were also becoming popular when treating children. The psychologist Kurt Lewin was responsible for interest in group processes during this period. Lewin was responsible for the notion that groups are often more than the sum of their individual components and that groups of people exhibit emergent properties that cannot be found in individuals alone. Group therapy reached its zenith in the 1960s, beginning with T-groups and other personal growth groups, along with transactional analysis, Gestalt therapy, and other innovations in group psychology. Many of these different types of groups died out in the '70s, but the major psychological paradigms in psychotherapy retained group therapy as part of the paradigm's practice.

ESSENTIAL

There are as many forms of group psychotherapy as there are individual psychotherapies. There are some instances where empirical evidence has indicated that certain conditions are addressed better in a group environment, such as with low-income rape victims. However, for the most part groups and individual therapies are equivalent in their effectiveness.

What Is a Group?

A *group* is defined as "a collection of individuals whose association is based on their commonalities," like particular interests, goals, norms, or values. Groups can form by chance circumstances or by choice. Psychological treatment groups are often ongoing; even though certain members may reach their goals and "graduate" from the group, the group continues on. There are some groups that develop for a specific purpose and once the purpose is reached, the group disbands, but most psychological treatment groups are ongoing.

Group therapy is a type of psychological care in which more than one client meets with at least one therapist at the same time. The clients form a support group for one another in addition to receiving therapeutic advice from the therapist. A group model is particularly effective for psychological issues that require quite a bit of support from others, such as anxiety disorders, but may not be effective in other cases. Although different types of groups have different goals, psychotherapy groups exist as entities in and of themselves, and the group becomes central to all the individual members' goals. The nature of the group interaction allows the group to take on an identity that becomes a function of its members, and yet this identity is different than any single member. This group entity becomes an active participant in the treatment process and is fostered by the interactions between the group members themselves, the interaction of the therapist with the group, and the interaction of the therapist with each individual member.

Many types of issues are treated by the combination of individual and group psychotherapy, such as substance-abuse or addiction treatment, where people often see a therapist on an individual level and attend a twelve-step group or another addiction group. This way one learns from discussions in the group and can make personal strides toward improvement in individual sessions.

Types of Group Psychotherapy for Panic Disorder

Psychotherapy groups can literally be formed from any specific school of psychotherapy. Therefore, it is not unusual to find CBT groups for panic disorder, psychodynamic groups for panic disorder, behavioral groups for panic disorder, etc. Often psychotherapy groups tend to have one major orientation, such as CBT, but because of the nature of the different group processes will be a bit more eclectic in their approach than the individual therapist might be during individual sessions (in the group the therapist will be more apt will combine different ideas). Typically groups will combine more insight-oriented and action-oriented techniques that occur in individual therapy sessions (although almost all therapists these days combine these methods to some extent). The focus of the group is often an open forum where individual group members discuss their specific issues with one another and the therapist keeps the group on target and in check. Group members listen intently to each other and offer suggestions based on their own experience or knowledge as to how particular members of the group can improve their own experiences. It is also not unusual for the members of the group to see the group therapist for individual therapy as well.

Two different types of psychotherapy groups are opened and closed groups. Psychotherapy groups aimed at the treatment of panic disorder are rarely closed groups. A closed group is one that starts with a particular set of group members and does not allow new members into the group as the group progresses toward its goal. Once the goal is reached, the group disbands. Closed groups are typically formed for specific purposes, such as reaching specific goals at work, committees to address a specific problem, etc. Some psychotherapy closed groups may develop to help the members reach specific goals and then disband.

The majority of psychological treatment groups are open groups. These groups may start with a specific set of individuals, but will allow new individuals to enter the group. This results in the members of the group all being at different levels in their treatment. Some members may be beginning treatment; some members may be intermediate; and some members may be nearly at the end of their treatment, with most of their issues surrounding their panic disorder relatively under control. Open groups allow new members to learn from more experienced members, allow more experienced members to learn by teaching newer members their experiences, and allow for the interplay of many complex psychological group processes to occur.

Group psychotherapy for panic disorder is offered on a number of different levels. Specific psychotherapy groups for panic disorder may be offered by private licensed therapists in addition to their individual treatment programs. More general groups for anxiety disorders are often offered by hospitals and community services (and sometimes by private therapists). These groups will address issues regarding panic attacks, panic disorder, and other anxiety disorders. They often are not specifically focused on panic disorder, but individuals may still benefit from them by learning how to deal with negative thoughts, panic attacks, anxiety-provoking situations, etc. Certain hospitals and community services may also provide specific panic disorder groups. Local newspapers or community mental health services often list the types of groups in their area that address these disorders.

Couples and Family Therapy

Two special types of group therapy are couples or marital therapy (the husband and wife comprise the group) and family therapy (where the group in treatment is typically the immediate family). In these types of therapies, the group is treated as a cohesive unit and issues surrounding the relationships of the members, power struggles, and dysfunctional tendencies of the family/couple are addressed. The general opinion is that family or couples therapy alone is not recommended as a sole method of treatment for panic disorder; however, it may be useful in addressing relationship issues associated with the panic disorder of a member or members.

It can also be beneficial to include significant others in aspects of individual therapies such as CBT. There is a form of CBT that uses partner-assisted exposure therapy. In these cases, the family member helps the person with panic disorder during and between therapy sessions and homework practices. Psychoeducation for significant others about the nature of panic disorder and having family members help the individual improve his adherence to treatment are also useful practices.

ESSENTIAL

Group therapy offers acceptance and the strength of numbers during treatment. Groups can also provide accountability for members. Certain individuals are often more inclined to work on their goals when they are held accountable by others. Group therapy can help instill a sense of belonging, hope, and inspiration in someone who has been severely affected by his panic disorder.

Support Groups for Panic Disorder

A support group differs from a psychotherapy group in that these groups typically do not have a licensed therapist or professional running them. These groups are often formed by individuals with similar problems to support causes or to provide support for individuals with certain types of personal issues. Support groups actually appear to be a modern outgrowth of traditional fraternal organizations such as the Freemasons. Probably the most well-known type of support group is Alcoholics Anonymous, which is a support group of individuals who want to maintain abstinence from alcohol. These groups are administrated by volunteers and meet in community centers and churches. The groups consist primarily of individuals who get together and discuss their problems concerning their drinking of alcohol and their desire to remain sober. The entire membership of the group shares the same problem and meets at regular intervals so individuals can discuss how to cope with the problem, offer advice to other individuals who need help, develop a network of individuals to assist one another when the group is not meeting, and give incentive and support for new members. These groups are maintained by the members that attend them.

Some communities may have professionally operated support groups where the group is headed by someone, such as a therapist or medical professional, who does not have the problem addressed by the group. In these cases the professional heads and guides the group and takes care of all the administrative issues, but mostly lets the group run on its own.

There are two major issues with using support groups for the treatment of panic disorder. The first issue is that the research on the efficacy of support group use alone is lacking, and the available research suggests that the exclusive use of a support group is probably not an effective way for individuals to address their panic disorder. Instead, support group use should be used as an adjunctive type of treatment; an additional type of treatment that can enhance the effects of primary treatments. For this reason it is not suggested that an individual simply attend an anxiety disorder support group to treat his panic disorder.

The other issue with support groups for panic disorder is that it appears that they are not as available as other types of support groups. There are some resources at the end of this book that interested readers may wish to follow up on to determine if there are some support groups that might be helpful in their area. But, due to these two factors, the use of support groups alone is not recommended in the treatment of panic disorder.

ESSENTIAL

A number of online support groups and therapy groups are available for different issues, including anxiety disorders. The research on the effectiveness of these groups is variable, but there does seem to be some evidence that these groups can help people. However, types of online treatment should be supplemented with actual person-to-person contact, such as with a therapist or medical professional.

Is Psychotherapy Effective in Treating Panic Disorder?

There is a large body of empirical evidence that indicates that psychotherapy is quite effective in treating panic disorder. Even though there is some empirical evidence for several different types of psychotherapy regarding the treatment of panic disorder, CBT remains the psychotherapy of choice based on the available evidence and is most often indicated for clients with panic disorder. CBT generally lasts between ten to fifteen weeks and can be successfully undertaken in both individual and group therapy arrangements. Panic-focused psychodynamic psychotherapy (PFPP) also has empirically based evidence to support its use, but this evidence is not as strong as the evidence for CBT.

In any event, PFPP also has demonstrated efficacy for panic disorder, although its evidence base is more limited. PFPP therapy may serve as an initial form of treatment based on the preference of the patient. The research determining what types of clients respond better to CBT or PFPP therapy has not been able to reliably determine client differences that would allow the recommendation of one form of treatment over the other. Other types of psychotherapies have some empirical evidence regarding their effectiveness, but CBT is generally considered the first-line therapeutic intervention. In addition, group CBT is recommended over other forms of group therapy for treating panic disorder.

The Pros and Cons of Psychotherapy

Psychotherapy was not always considered to be effective. Some years ago, researchers questioned the effectiveness of psychotherapy. Using a statistical technique called meta-analysis, they evaluated many of the studies looking at the effectiveness of psychotherapy that were available during that time and came to the conclusion that psychotherapy was not effective in treating mental disorders. However, a large body of subsequent research, including many meta-analytic studies, has provided solid evidence that psychotherapy is indeed an effective treatment (the original study had some flaws in its methods).

It is generally considered that the vast majority (over 80 percent) of people who are involved in psychotherapy get better. However, one interesting finding regarding psychotherapy is that many of the different types of psychotherapy are often equivalent in their effects, despite offering radically different philosophies as to what to concentrate on, what techniques to use, etc. A number of different studies have indicated that what have been determined as the "common factors of therapy" appear to have significant effects on the people who engage in psychotherapy. These common factors include things like the relationship between the therapist and the client, the alliance between the client and therapist regarding solving the issues at hand, and certain therapist factors, such as the therapist's ability to remain caring and empathetic and to view the client as positive, regardless of the issues involved.

FACT

Make no mistake, psychotherapy for panic disorder is work! There is no magical revelation where one is suddenly cured, as seen in many films. Treatment for panic disorder requires facing anxiety in successive steps, performing homework assignments outside of the weekly or biweekly sessions, and actually getting involved in treatment. This means taking responsibility for wanting to get better.

It is generally considered that psychotherapy is effective and that the effectiveness of psychotherapy is more enduring than the effectiveness of medications (the effects last longer once the treatment has been stopped). Psychotherapy allows clients to develop a relationship with a trusted individual, learn about their motivations, apply their learning to new situations, and develop skills that can be used in the future. However, the effects of psychotherapy regarding a disorder like panic disorder are not immediate. These effects usually take weeks or even longer to be fully realized. In addition, psychotherapy is a proactive exercise in development. What this means is that the client actually has to *do something*. The therapist can only guide and direct the client, but in the end, the client has to actually do the work. Often this results in facing and experiencing one's fears, one's doubts, and one's insecurities. Not everyone will find this easy to do. Moreover, any form of psychotherapy can get quite expensive, and if one does not have the insurance to cover it, psychotherapy may not be practical. In addition, in instances where the client and the therapist do not make a good match, psychotherapy can become burdensome and lead to deleterious effects.

Pros and Cons of Individual Therapy

One advantage to individual therapy is that the sessions are all devoted to one client. There is more time to concentrate on individual issues. Often it is easier to reveal one's issues to a single trained professional than to a group of people. The therapy can be tailored to the person in question.

On the other hand, individual therapy is often more expensive. One must contribute for the entire session. The success of the therapy falls on only two people, who must agree to work together and remain vigilant to the issues at hand. This means that the client must trust and like the therapist.

Pros and Cons of Group Therapy

One advantage is that group therapy sessions are usually less expensive than individual sessions. In addition, in the group one gets to listen to and learn from others with the same issues. One learns to understand that she is not isolated. Group therapy can help one develop extensive bonds with others that often help her control her anxiety.

On the other hand, in individual therapy, only the therapist knows all the secrets and weaknesses one displays. In a group, others learn about all of the insecurities and foibles one has. In individual therapy, the therapist concentrates on one person; not so in a group. One will have to listen to others, and the time spent on any single person is often significantly less. Group meetings are inflexible; the person has to arrange her schedule to the meeting time of the group. If a person is shy or embarrassed, she may not disclose her issues as well in a group.

No treatment can claim 100 percent effectiveness. Certain private programs and other claims to this level of success are fabricated. (You can find many claims of success rates in the 90 and even 100 percentile on the internet. Be suspicious of them.)

ALERT

The choice of using psychotherapy in conjunction with medication is an individual one; however, the majority of experts on panic disorder strongly recommend that the person receive psychotherapy whether or not they take medications or try alternative interventions. The choice of group or individual therapy is a personal decision that depends on one's preferences and on the availability of therapists.

CHAPTER 13

Natural Remedies for Panic Disorder

The following chapters will cover what is called *complementary and alternative medicine* (CAM). Natural remedies are naturally occurring substances that are reputed to have some beneficial treatment effect on panic disorder. The notion of "natural remedies" is a little hazy because certain types of remedies, such as relaxation, breathing, etc., are also naturally performed. In this chapter, some of the most commonly touted "natural" remedies for anxiety and panic disorder are discussed.

Warning about Natural Remedies for Panic Disorder

You may object to a warning about natural remedies when there is no specific warning regarding medication use. However, as stated previously, prescription medications should only be taken and used under the direct supervision of a physician. The substances covered in this chapter can be purchased almost anywhere and taken in any amount without such supervision. This opens them up to some special considerations.

Many people who seek out alternative treatments or natural remedies for their problems typically have some kind of issue with Western medical approaches to treatment. There certainly is good reason to approach evidence from sources such as drug companies and pharmaceutical corporations with skepticism. Many say that there is a problem with the process used to approve medications by the FDA. This process is subject to a number of glitches and potential failures. These failures are often heavily publicized in the media, whereas the successes of the process rarely receive media attention because they are not news. So people are exposed to failures and not successes, which can create a type of bias toward the process.

Nonetheless, there is a great deal of potential for the research process to be taken advantage of by individuals and corporations that are interested in benefitting from the suffering of others. The gold standard for testing the effectiveness of any treatment remains randomized clinical trials (RCTs). This method is even more effective if the research employed is a double-blind or triple-blind RCT (where participants, researchers, and those analyzing the data are blind to the conditions). To say that RCTs are untrustworthy because the process is often taken advantage of by groups with ulterior motives is not as much a criticism of RCTs as it is of human nature. Would you say that all speed limits on roads and freeways should be abolished because many people do not pay attention to them?

When looking at research to determine if a specific treatment is effective, you need to consider the type of research (RCT or some other method), the affiliations of the researchers, and specific issues of the research, such as how the data was collected, the characteristics of the participants, the control groups, etc. The goal of this book is to discuss effective treatments for panic disorder. The gold standard in judging an effective treatment is the use of RCTs by independent researchers without secondary interests. One issue you may notice is that there are large numbers of RCTs for treatments like medications and psychotherapy, but few for CAMs. Thus, specific studies are discussed in these sections as opposed to generalities.

ESSENTIAL

Keep in mind that you can choose any treatment you want, but the recommendations in this book are based on the best available knowledge at the time of this writing. Any treatment that has good evidence to support that it works probably will not harm you.

Inositol

Inositol is a chemical compound that exists in several different forms. The most prominent form of inositol is called myo-inositol. Inositol is considered a member of the vitamin B group (B8), but since it is actually produced in the human body from glucose (sugar), inositol is not considered to be an essential nutrient. Certain vitamins and minerals are produced in the human body; however, many of them, such as niacin, are not produced in sufficient amounts to be beneficial without an additional dietary source. Inositol appears to be manufactured in sufficient amounts in the bodies of most people; therefore, it is not an essential nutrient. Nevertheless, dietary inositol is also considered a carbohydrate and is found in many foods, especially in fruits. As a dietary supplement, inositol is easily absorbed into the body. There is some empirical support for the use of inositol in the treatment of panic attacks. Some older studies have produced evidence that inositol is better than placebo and at least as good as one particular SSRI in reducing panic attacks.

A good study in 1995 used a double-blind RCT with a small number of panic disorder patients and found that over four weeks, panic attacks were significantly reduced in the sample compared to placebo. In 2001, a double-blind RCT with twenty patients compared inositol with the SSRI Luvox. Luvox is not one of the SSRIs formally recognized by the FDA as a treatment option for panic disorder; however, most psychiatrists and physicians are in agreement that SSRIs in general are effective in the treatment of panic disorder. In this study, inositol reduced the number of weekly panic attacks by an average of four, whereas Luvox reduced the weekly number of panic attacks by 2.4 in the sample. The difference between the two was not statistically significant, meaning that there was no statistical evidence that inositol was more effective than Luvox. When patients took the Luvox, they had significantly more side effects than when they took the inositol. As discussed previously, one of the main disadvantages to taking psychotropic medications is that they produce a number of side effects that can be irritating and even debilitating to the people who take them. The side effect profile of most psychotropic medications is the main reason that people discontinue using them.

Taking Inositol

Because it is water-soluble and excess levels are eliminated immediately, most sources suggest taking smaller doses of inositol throughout the day leading up to the maximum suggested dose. There are some mild side effects reported by most of the studies investigating the use of inositol that include stomach upset, flatulence, and mild insomnia at higher doses (twelve grams per day or higher). Inositol use at high doses may also block the absorption of other nutrients in the body. Due to the relatively small number of clinical trials, it is uncertain if inositol use over longer periods of time produces even more side effects. Nonetheless, the side effects are significantly less serious than many of the side effects that commonly occur with the use of antidepressants or benzodiazepines.

Both of the aforementioned studies were crossover studies, which means that both of the groups got received both treatments (e.g., one group took inositol and the other a placebo and then later the groups switched treatments) and the experimenters were not informed of which treatment the group was under. In addition, both studies recommend further research regarding the use of inositol for the treatment of panic disorder. However, remember that the studies found a reduction in panic attacks with inositol use over a short period of time, but the effects of the substance on panic disorder is still under question due to the need for more controlled studies and the fact that panic disorder consists of more than just panic attacks. There are a number of nonclinical reports that inositol is effective in the treatment of panic disorder and anxiety, but these are not empirically validated controlled studies and other than paving the way for further clinical research, these reports are not reliable or valid enough to be considered as empirically validated evidence. Nonetheless, there does appear to be evidence that inositol can reduce the intensity of panic attacks, and the side effects are minimal.

ESSENTIAL

Inositol has received both clinical and nonclinical support for its use in a number of conditions, including diabetes, some forms of cancer, and dementia. There are studies investigating inositol and its effect in treating other anxiety disorders and even depression that indicate that it may have beneficial treatment effects in a number of different psychiatric conditions. More research is needed.

Valerian Root

There are more than 200 plant species that belong to the genus *Valeriana*. The species most commonly used as an herb is *Valeriana officinalis*. Valerian is a perennial plant that grows from three to five feet tall and is found throughout the world. The root of the species has been used for medicinal purposes for many centuries due to its sedative effects. For instance, the ancient Roman physician Galen recommended the use of valerian for insomnia in the second century. Depending on the species of valerian, the chemical makeup of the plant can vary; however, it appears that most varieties of valerian contain the amino acid GABA (which you may recognize as the most prevalent inhibitory neurotransmitter in the brain) as well as the amino acids glutamine, arginine, and alanine. There have been several hypotheses regarding the mechanism of action of valerian root that include enhancement of GABA transmission in the brain as well as enhancement of serotonin transmission. A small number of clinical studies have investigated the effects of valerian root on anxiety and insomnia.

Insomnia

Because valerian root is popular as a sleep aid in the treatment of insomnia, a quick review might shed some light on its treatment effectiveness of anxiety. The clinical studies investigating valerian root as a sleep aid have not been consistent, and a recent review of eighteen RCTs did not find objective evidence that the use of valerian root reduced insomnia. Interestingly, there was some subjective evidence, based on self-reports, that those who took valerian root reported better sleep than those who did not. However, the lack of objective evidence calls this finding into question.

Some other evidence suggests that valerian root may be helpful for sleep, but only if taken over a long period of time. There have been some other RCTs that have found that taking valerian root in combination with other herbs may be effective in inducing sleep, and may act as a sedative when compared to placebo. These studies had some issues (for example, when taking combinations of untested substances, one cannot be sure if any effects are due to some or all of the substances in the combination). In addition, several follow-up studies failed to find that valerian root was more effective than placebo in inducing sleep in the participants. Thus, the sedative properties of valerian root are questionable at best.

Anxiety and Panic Disorder

A 2002 double-blind RCT using thirty-six participants investigated the efficacy of valerian, Valium, and a placebo in the treatment of generalized anxiety disorder. The study failed to find significant differences between the three groups or any significant reduction in a group's anxiety levels at the end of a four-week period; however, as there were only twelve participants in each group, there may have been some methodological issues due to the small samples.

Another study investigated whether valerian, propranolol (recall that this drug is a beta blocker sometimes used to treat panic disorder or anxiety), valerian and propranolol in combination, or placebo were able to reduce stress in a small number of healthy participants exposed to stressful social situations. The finding suggested that valerian and the combination of valerian and propranolol did significantly reduce stress-related anxiety. However, the induced stress in this study is significantly less intense than the stress and anxiety that occur in a panic attack.

One study compared a combination of valerian root and St. John's wort to Valium in the treatment of patients with anxiety. The combination of the herbs was significantly more effective in treating anxiety than the Valium in the sample of subjects. However, this finding would need to be replicated, and the effects of both herbs alone would need to be tested. None of these studies specifically looked at valerian and panic disorder. At this time, the evidence for the use of valerian root in the treatment of panic disorder is very scarce, and the lack of available evidence indicates that this substance should not be considered a primary treatment for panic disorder.

Use of Valerian Root

Valerian root is often taken in capsule form. It is on the FDA's list of generally safe substances, and even in high doses, it appears that only mild symptoms occur, such as stomach cramps, tightness in the chest, fatigue, lightheadedness, and in some cases mild tremors or feeling jittery. Using valerian root in combination with other herbs may produce more serious side effects. There are some animal studies with an extract of valerian root, which is more potent (valerenic acid), but clinical research with human participants needs to be done. Valerian should not be taken with prescription medications, especially benzodiazepines, sedatives, or antihistamines, as this may lead to oversedation. Likewise, valerian should not be taken with alcohol or by people with liver disease. Never take valerian before driving or operating heavy machinery. It is best to take valerian under the supervision of a physician.

ALERT

Because there are few studies looking at how different combinations of herbs and other natural remedies affect people, one should be careful when taking high doses of herbs or different combinations of herbs at the same time. Consult a physician before taking high doses of herbs, different combinations of herbs, or herbs and medication in combination.

Kava

Perhaps the most researched herbal treatment for anxiety is kava (*Piper methysticum*), a perennial plant that is native to various areas of the South Pacific Islands. The roots of the kava plant are usually prepared in some type of beverage for medicinal purposes. Kava is a member of the pepper family. Early research indicated that kava had an anxiolytic effect (reduces anxiety) similar to Valium in laboratory trials using animal models. Other research has also indicated that kava has anxiolytic effects.

A large review published in the prestigious *Cochrane Review* in 2003 evaluated kava's effectiveness as an anxiolytic. Twelve RCTs found kava to be significantly more effective than placebo in reducing levels of anxiety in patients with anxiety disorders. Most of the research looked at the effects of kava on generalized anxiety disorder, but several studies also had panic disorder patients included in the sample. A recent study in Australia found kava more effective than placebo in treating generalized anxiety disorder, with a few side effects noted in the sample.

The anxiolytic properties of kava have been studied, and the research suggests that these effects are due to a group of compounds known as kava-lactones. These compounds appear to facilitate GABA receptor activity, may result in more GABA receptors being formed, and inhibit the reuptake of another neurotransmitter known as norepinephrine. There has been a discrepancy between studies regarding the onset of action for kava, with some studies indicating a lengthy delay before the effects are realized, while others suggest the effects are realized within a week (perhaps these studies describing faster acting results are describing a placebo effect).

There has also been some research that compared the use of kava versus benzodiazepines in the treatment of anxiety disorders. The findings indicated that kava was at least as effective as benzodiazepines; however, there were some severe methodological issues in the studies. For instance, in one study the placebo group demonstrated equivalent effectiveness in the reduction of anxiety symptoms as did the benzodiazepine group. This suggests some issues with the participants defined as having anxiety disorders in the study.

Side effects from kava usage include impairment of coordination, light sensitivity, numbing of the lips, shortness of breath, dermopathy (changes in the skin that include scaly and yellowish patches), nausea, tremors, headache, and drowsiness. Due to potential drowsiness, it is best to take kava at bedtime. The FDA has set guidelines for kava usage. The FDA recommends a maximum dose of 250 milligrams a day, three times a week. In addition, the FDA recommends that after a person has used kava for a month, he discontinue usage for one week and not use kava for more than three months, unless under a physician's orders. There are potential untoward interactions with kava and alcohol, anticonvulsants, antianxiety medications (e.g., antidepressants and benzodiazepines), antipsychotic medications, and diuretics.

Kava Controversy

Probably the biggest concern regarding the use of kava is the reports of liver toxicity. An investigation of these reports indicates that cases of liver toxicity occurring with kava use may be extremely rare or occur in individuals with pre-existing liver problems, such as hepatitis C or alcohol abuse; however, liver damage is a serious concern. These reports of liver toxicity resulted in kava being banned in several European countries as a potential herbal remedy. Today the ban is lifted in all countries except for Poland, but the sale of kava remains regulated in several European countries. The manufacturing quality of the product, the method of extraction used, and differing doses are all potential concerns regarding kava, despite a qualitative study that found relatively few side effects with kava use.

Despite some pretty solid empirically validated research that kava may be an effective anxiolytic compound, there are several concerns regarding its use. In addition, as with all of these herbal remedies, there is the potential for untoward interactions with other herbs, foods, and medications, and these interactions are not well understood. Any reader wishing to use kava should do so under the supervision of a physician due to potentially serious complications.

FACT

A major problem with herbal remedies is that the manufacturing and content of these remedies is not well patrolled by the FDA. Several investigations have indicated that some manufacturers of these remedies list the ingredients and even potencies inaccurately on their labels. Therefore, it appears that buying herbal remedies is subject to a "buyer beware" warning. Buy from reputable companies.

GABA

Gamma-aminobutyric acid (GABA) is an amino acid that is also the central nervous system's most prominent inhibitory neurotransmitter. One can think of GABA operating in opposition to the excitatory neurotransmitters that increase brain activity and contribute to the anxiety in a panic attack. The presence of excitatory and inhibitory neurotransmitters in the brain helps to moderate brain activity and maintain equilibrium in the CNS. The logic behind the use of GABA supplementation is quite simple: Since many anxiolytic medications facilitate the transmission of GABA in the brain and reduce anxiety, taking an oral GABA supplement can increase GABA levels in the brain and reduce anxiety. There are numerous anecdotal reports of people taking oral GABA supplements and immediately relieving their anxiety; however, clinical research support for the use of taking oral GABA supplements to relieve anxiety is suspiciously lacking. Think about this for a second. There is no evidence that oral ingestion of GABA supplements allows it to cross the blood-brain barrier and reach the brain. Moreover, the process of taking amino acids or substances that are used in the CNS as neurotransmitters orally is not how the mechanism of action of antidepressants and other psychotropic medications are designed. These medications are not simply neurotransmitters in pill form.

Instead, most psychotropic medications are chemical compounds that increase or decrease the action of the existing neurotransmitters in the brain. Many of the alternative treatment supporters will point out that the big pharmaceutical corporations are only interested in profit and intentionally manipulate consumers and the system to market their products and make money. Thus, they defraud the public to market their expensive, but ineffective, treatments. If this philosophy of simply marketing neurotransmitters in pill form worked on anxiety, depression, and other psychological disorders, the pharmaceutical companies would develop and then patent special formulas for them and market them in an effort to capture the billion-dollar potential they offer. Likewise, taking GABA and then experiencing immediate reductions in anxiety levels suspiciously sounds like a placebo action. The degree to which orally ingested GABA can reach the brain is unknown at this time, and there is no solid empirically validated evidence to suggest that such a method is effective for treating panic attacks, let alone for treating panic disorder.

ALERT

Taking GABA may relieve mild anxiety in some individuals, and side effects from taking GABA supplements appear minimal. Taking GABA probably cannot hurt, but if you are being treated for panic disorder, you should consult with your physician before taking GABA. At the time of this writing, it appears that someone experiencing panic attacks should not use GABA supplements as her primary treatment.

Panic Disorder and pH Levels

Here's a quick overview of the science behind pH levels. The terms acidic and basic (alkaline) describe two chemical states that are extremes. Chemical pH scales measure the concentration of hydrogen ions in a medium. Mediums with high concentrations of hydrogen ions have low pH values and vice versa. From a more practical standpoint, the pH scale measures how acidic or basic (alkaline) a substance or medium is. The scale ranges from zero to fourteen, with values below seven representing more acidic states and values above seven representing more basic (alkaline) states. A pH of seven is a neutral state. Each pH value above or below seven is ten times more acidic or basic than the state at the next higher value. Lemon juice and vinegar are very acidic, whereas ammonia and laundry soap are very alkaline.

Recent studies have indicated that pH levels in the brain may be associated with fear. The pH levels of the brain represent metabolic factors. For the most part, the pH level in the brain is carefully regulated by the body. Drastic shifts in pH levels can lead to serious disruptions in brain functioning. Research has indicated that pH levels in synapses (the spaces between neurons that communicate with one another) can vary. The discovery of acid-sensing ion channels (ASICs) indicated that special proteins sense acidity levels in neurons. A very clever study using genetically modified mice that lack these ASICs indicated that the mice displayed disruptive capacities to express fear. Once researchers restored ASIC genes in the amygdala of these mice, they demonstrated normal fear behaviors. So the amygdala, a part of the brain often associated with fear behaviors, appears essential in displaying fear as well as recognizing it, at least in mice.

The Findings

What does all this have to do with panic disorder? Well, researchers also demonstrated that having normal mice inhale carbon dioxide (which has an acidic action) triggered strong fear behaviors, and these fear behaviors were at least partially dependent on the presence of ASICs in the amygdala. Recall that a consistent finding on panic disorder patients is that they are very sensitive to hyperventilation or carbon dioxide inhalation. People with panic disorder will often experience a panic attack when inhaling air with levels as low as 35 percent carbon dioxide, a level that typically does not affect people without panic disorder.

Moreover, first-degree relatives of people with panic disorder who do not have the disorder themselves also appear to be hypersensitive to carbon dioxide inhalation producing anxiety. There has been previous research that has suggested that people who have panic disorder may generate excess lactic acid in their brains. Lactic acid is a product of glucose metabolism (the brain's food) and is constantly being produced in the brains of everyone, but people with panic disorder may experience abnormal buildup of lactic acid in their brains. People with panic disorder may generate excess lactic acid in their amygdalae, and this may be at least in part responsible for their recurrent panic attacks. Such a finding suggests that there is a genetic vulnerability (something already generally accepted) to panic disorder that may involve this process of lower pH levels in the brains of people who develop panic disorder.

ESSENTIAL

The CO_2 levels in the body are regulated by respiration. There is some research that suggests there is a subtype of people with panic disorder who have some breathing irregularities. In addition, other types of panic disorder might be related to inherently higher levels of acid (lower pH) in the brain.

What Does It All Mean?

Let's take a step back. These findings are correlational in nature, that is, they are associations. There are a number of other possible reasons that could explain the relationship between pH levels in the brain and vulnerability to panic attacks. These findings are all speculative, and more research needs to be performed in order to understand what these findings actually mean. In addition, there has been research that has found that panic attack patients had higher pH levels in their urine (more alkaline) than normal controls, which could be contradictory to the notion that higher acidity levels in the brain are associated with panic disorder (it could also be that these higher pH levels were associated with more rapid breathing in those who had recent panic attacks). While this research is quite enlightening and will open the doors to exploring other treatment methods for panic disorder, at the time of this writing there are no medications, herbs, special diets, or any other methods that have been developed to specifically address this particular situation.

Jumping on the Bandwagon

Once the findings of potentially higher acidity levels in the brains of people with panic disorder were released, of course a whole slew of low-pH diets were recommended by observers to "cure" panic disorder and depression. As would be expected, many anecdotal claims that people have been cured by diets surfaced (of course this is exactly the same type of process that many accuse pharmaceutical companies of engaging in). As of this writing, there are no solid empirically validated clinical trials that indicate that low-pH diets effectively treat panic disorder; however, that does not mean that eating a balanced diet is not helpful. There is research that indicates that nutrition and anxiety levels are related in many different ways, and eating a healthy, balanced diet may have positive effects on a person's anxiety levels (for instance, a person who ingests caffeine or sugar may experience more intense levels of anxiety). So while, at the time of this writing, it does not appear that a diet that attempts to control acidity levels in the body is a stand-alone treatment for panic disorder, there is quite a bit of evidence that following good dietary habits, getting exercise (which helps one regulate lactic acid levels in the body), getting plenty of sleep, and not engaging in such activities as smoking or overdrinking are quite beneficial in reducing overall anxiety levels. Engaging in a more positive lifestyle will have all-around beneficial effects and can be combined with other forms of treatment to produce positive effects.

Other Herbs and Vitamins

There are many different herbal remedies and supplements that are reputed to have anxiolytic effects. Many of these claims are anecdotal in nature or are made by the manufacturers of the various products that contain these substances. A few of them are briefly discussed in this section.

St. John's Wort

St. John's wort (*Hypericum perforatum*) has been used for centuries in the treatment of anxiety and depression. Records indicate that the Greeks and Romans used this plant for medicinal purposes. Of all the plants and herbs used in treating psychiatric disorders, St. John's wort has probably received the lion's share of research, especially regarding treatment for depression. The available evidence suggests that St. John's wort has effects on the neurotransmitters dopamine, serotonin, and GABA due to two active main components, hypericin and hyperforin, making it an attractive candidate for treating anxiety and depression. There are several clinical studies that have suggested that St. John's wort is more effective than placebo in the treatment of mild depression. There are also some studies that indicate that St. John's wort may have some efficacy in the treatment of generalized anxiety disorder, but the results of studies looking at its effects in the treatment of social phobia and obsessive-compulsive disorder have been mixed.

St. John's wort has gotten quite a bit of popular support in the treatment of depression and anxiety, but studies that use clinical samples as opposed to the general literature are often mixed. It appears that St. John's wort can relieve mild depression and mild anxiety in individuals taking it, making it a possible adjunct treatment for normal sadness or everyday anxiety, but it is probably much less useful in the treatment of a panic attack or panic disorder, except to decrease mild anticipatory anxiety.

The most common side effects from the use of St. John's wort include fatigue, dizziness, sedation, and occasional confusion. St. John's wort should not be taken by women on contraceptive pills. People with psychotic disorders should not take St. John's wort, as it may aggravate psychosis. There have also been some findings that using St. John's wort may lead to light sensitivity and susceptibility to sunburns in some individuals.

FACT

Remember that there are major differences in the type of anxiety experienced in an anxiety disorder and the anxiety that occurs in the context of normal living. It is easy to misinterpret the notion that because something works on relieving sadness or mild anxiety, it also works for psychiatric disorders. This is often a mistake made by the general public.

Passionflower

Passionflower (Passiflora incarnata) is a plant found in the southern United States, Brazil, and Argentina. It has been consumed for centuries due to its antianxiety properties and is sold as a treatment for sleep disorders and nervous tension. It is thought that the anxiolytic properties of passionflower are related to activation of GABA receptors or the inhibition of monoamine oxidase, which breaks down certain neurotransmitters in the CNS. There is some research that suggests that passionflower may be useful in the treatment of generalized anxiety disorder compared to the benzodiazepine Serax (oxazepam, which may have the slowest onset of action of the benzodiazepines). In one study, Serax and passionflower were equivalent in reducing the anxiety levels of generalized anxiety disorder patients; however, passionflower had a much slower onset of action than Serax and also had fewer side effects. At the time of this writing, there is little evidence that passionflower use would prevent the onset of a panic attack, but it might be useful in treating anticipatory anxiety that occurs in panic disorder.

Ginkgo Biloba

Ginkgo biloba comes from the ginkgo tree, one of the oldest living tree species. Its leaves are among the most used and extensively studied herbs. Gingko supplements are among the best-selling herbal medications in the United States and Europe. There is a double-blind RCT comparing ginkgo to placebo in the treatment of generalized anxiety disorder that found that ginkgo was superior to placebo in the treatment of anxiety. However, the study would need to be replicated, and it is important for the reader to remember that the anxiety experienced during a panic attack is much more severe than the anxiety experienced in generalized anxiety disorder. Like several of the other herbs discussed in this section, ginkgo may reduce anticipatory anxiety in between panic attacks. Ginkgo appears relatively well tolerated by most people but may produce nausea, dizziness, or skin reactions, and may result in internal bleeding in some cases. Ginkgo probably should not be used by people who take medications that act as blood thinners.

Vitamin Supplementation

Eating a healthy diet and taking vitamin supplements may actually reduce panic attacks and help individuals who have seriously inadequate intake of vitamins and minerals. In some cases, B vitamin supplementation or omega-three fatty acids may reduce panic attacks in individuals who are deficient in their intake of B vitamins. In addition, leading a healthy lifestyle is associated with fewer psychological problems, including a lower prevalence of psychological disorders. Thus, it pays to be vigilant concerning one's health.

The Bottom Line

Here's the scoop: The objective evidence regarding the use of the aforementioned natural remedies in the treatment of panic disorder is generally lacking. There is evidence that inositol and kava are effective in treating anxiety and panic attacks, and perhaps a couple of others can reduce mild levels of anxiety in individuals, but most of these probably will not quell a full-blown panic attack. This means that using some of these remedies might be helpful in reducing anticipatory anxiety, other forms of worry, etc., that occur in panic disorder. However, it is extremely important that people choosing to use these methods make sure that they discuss this with their physician before using them. There are potential serious side effects with a couple of these (e.g., kava), and the potential interactions between these substances and other drugs, herbs, etc., are not well understood. As a comparison, few people would advocate taking antidepressant medications or benzodiazepines without being under a physician's supervision. If these "natural" substances can produce their own set of effects it only makes sense that they also should be taken under the supervision of a physician. In addition, the FDA does not regulate the contents of many of these remedies, and there have been instances where the listed ingredients of such remedies are not accurate with regard to what actually is in them when these products are examined. Therefore, it is recommended that anyone choosing to use any of these substances does so with caution and under the supervision of a physician.

CHAPTER 14

Alternative Treatments for Panic Disorder

Essentially any treatment that is not considered to be a mainstream treatment is a CAM, or alternative treatment. In this chapter, various alternative treatments to traditional types of psychotherapy that have been used for panic disorder are discussed. These alternative treatments can often be more expensive and more labor-intensive than traditional psychotherapy techniques, although the CAM label is attractive to some for the reason that these may offer some mysterious or miraculous alternative to traditional methods.

Warning Regarding These Alternative Treatments

The major issue with choosing one of these alternative treatments is making sure that you choose someone who is specifically trained in the use of these techniques for treating panic disorder. Like psychotherapy, there are many practitioners who claim to use these techniques, but may not be specifically trained in their use for panic disorder. Just because someone is trained in hypnotherapy for depression does not mean that they understand panic disorder, how to treat it, and the numerous complications and potential causes of panic attacks that can be treated by correcting a medical issue. Alternative treatments are often sought by people who have the same issues with the medical system as were discussed in the previous chapter. Individuals who seek out "alternative" methods often have a distrust of the more mainstream methods due to past experience or a philosophical stance, but again, if people expose the same amount of scrutiny to these alternative treatments as they do to mainstream treatments, they will often develop a different viewpoint of what treatments are effective and what treatments are not.

ALERT

It is extremely important that a professional employing any techniques for panic disorder actually has training and experience in treating panic disorder. See certifications from the provider. The good news is that, for the most part, there are no potential serious side effects associated with most of the following types of alternative treatments; however, you get what you pay for.

Hypnotherapy

Hypnosis is one of those techniques that has been severely misrepresented in popular culture, the media, and other venues. Hypnotherapy refers to the use of hypnosis as a form of treatment, whereas stage hypnosis refers to hypnosis used in entertainment. The word *hypnosis* comes from the Greek word *hypnos*, which means "to sleep." Recall from the discussion on research that Franz Mesmer used a form of hypnosis in his cure for hysteria. The use of hypnosis has a long history in psychotherapy, beginning with Freud and continuing to the present day.

Hypnosis is a type of psychological state that resembles sleep on the surface, but represents a state of extreme relaxation and openness to suggestibility. Because it is a psychological state, people will naturally vary in their ability to be hypnotized and will also vary in their ability to benefit from hypnosis. People under hypnosis are believed to have heightened senses of focus and concentration, which allows them to block out distractions and focus on suggestions.

There are different theories as to what exactly a hypnotic state is and why it works. While there are some who consider hypnosis to be a form of unconsciousness resembling sleep, people in hypnotic states are fully awake and aware. People under hypnosis typically feel calm and relaxed. There is no evidence that anyone under hypnosis can be persuaded to do things or perform actions that he normally would not want to do (e.g., such as occurs in many films when people are hypnotized to commit murder, etc.) or that people who are hypnotized lose control of their behavior. No one can be hypnotized if he does not wish to be.

There is an extensive body of research that indicates hypnosis is useful in changing many types of unwanted behaviors, such as overeating, smoking, etc., and there is good research regarding the use of hypnosis for the control of pain. There is also good empirical research that hypnosis can help people control their levels of stress and even control mild levels of anxiety.

Hypnosis for Panic Disorder

The empirical evidence demonstrating that hypnosis is successful in the treatment of people with panic disorder consists of few RCTs or specific reports of treatment for panic disorder. Much of the research that investigates the use of hypnosis in the treatment of anxiety disorders is concerned with generalized anxiety disorder, social phobias, and social anxiety, with some studies looking at hypnosis and PTSD or OCD. In many of these cases, individuals in the studies are described as having panic attacks, but the specific use of hypnosis in the treatment of panic disorder appears to be mainly documented in only several published case studies.

A case study is an intensive presentation of the treatment of a single subject using a specific therapeutic technique. It qualifies as empirically validated evidence; however, it is a weak type of empirical evidence in that its ability to generalize over multiple participants is limited. Nonetheless, there is good evidence that hypnosis does allow individuals with all types of psychological disorders to gain more control over their situations and to learn to relax.

Hypnosis may help individuals with panic disorder, and participating in hypnosis with a qualified hypnotherapist presents only a few risks. Some people have reported having headaches or increased anxiety following hypnosis, but these are very rare. There is a type of hypnosis that is practiced by certain people called "past lives regression," which has no empirically established reliability or validity to support its use. There is also the potential for a person to develop false memories under hypnosis, but this is rare when qualified, trained individuals use hypnosis. A person undergoing hypnotherapy will also most likely learn to induce hypnosis in himself and learn to make hypnotic suggestions away from the therapeutic environment.

ESSENTIAL

There are numerous self-hypnosis programs that vary in their quality and for the most part are not empirically validated. However, there is probably no danger in using them as an adjunct to formal treatment. Their ability to produce significant results remains questionable, but there are probably no risks aside from spending money on a product that you never use.

Acupuncture

Acupuncture is actually a collection of procedures involving the insertion of needles in the body and the electrical stimulation of certain points where the needles have been inserted. Acupuncture is an age-old component of traditional Chinese medicine and is among some of the oldest medical practices. According to traditional Chinese medicine, stimulating the acupuncture points corrects imbalances and the flow of life energy (*qi*) through channels in the body called *meridians*. Despite this age-old belief, there is no current scientific evidence for the existence of these meridians, and some acupuncturists who insert the needles do so without following traditional Chinese approaches and still report positive benefits.

It has been hypothesized that this procedure interacts with opioid pathways in the body or that perhaps it stimulates certain neurotransmitter releases, such as serotonin and norepinephrine. Specific research regarding the neurobiological effects of acupuncture in the treatment of anxiety has not been explored.

Acupuncture is a very popular alternative treatment method that, unlike many of the previous alternative and natural treatments, has a substantial body of empirical evidence regarding its safety and efficacy in the treatment of certain types of anxiety disorders and in the treatment of depression. However, the results of the literature indicate that there are some serious issues in being able to actually interpret the findings.

Acupuncture and Anxiety/Panic Disorder

A fair number of RCTs that investigated the use of acupuncture for the treatment of generalized anxiety disorder indicated that acupuncture was generally effective in treating generalized anxiety disorder, but the duration of the studies was generally limited (three to four weeks) and the sample sizes were quite small. Moreover, the studies differed by a lack of common procedures involved. The studies did not use similar treatment protocols for different individuals, relying on different sites of application for different individuals, and it appears that in some studies the same individual received different applications over different treatment sessions.

There is also evidence that indicates the placement of the needles in the treatment of chronic pain does not have a significant effect on the relief many individuals experience. For example, some studies have indicated that the needles can be placed nearly anywhere and individuals with chronic pain report relief from their pain. Other research has used sham needles, like the retractable fake knifes used in movies, and still got therapeutic effects from the "sham acupuncture." This type of research has led some people to suggest that acupuncture treatment consists of a strong placebo effect. There do not appear to be any RCTs investigating the use of acupuncture in the treatment of panic disorder specifically, although numerous sites on the Internet claim that acupuncture is an established treatment for panic attacks and panic disorder.

In reviewing the literature regarding acupuncture as a treatment for panic disorder, it can only be concluded that clear recommendations for its use are not warranted. It appears that acupuncture may be effective for short-term use in the treatment of mild anxiety, but its effectiveness for the treatment of panic disorder has not been well researched. It is unfortunate that more research with specific anxiety disorders, such as panic disorder, and acupuncture is not available, because acupuncture appears to be generally well tolerated and does not appear to interact with other forms of treatment, such as medication. Given the lack of research for the use of acupuncture with panic disorder specifically, any readers deciding to follow this approach should understand that there is no empirical evidence that this is a reliable and valid approach to treating panic disorder.

ALERT

Make sure the treatment is safe. Most acupuncturists use sterile, disposable needles, as poor sterilization methods can lead to infection or transmission of blood-borne pathogens, such as HIV. Make sure that the practitioner uses disposable needles or has a sterilization protocol and follow relevant directions from your physician before using this treatment.

Biofeedback Training

Biofeedback therapy works by helping to train you to control certain bodily functions that are typically controlled by the autonomic nervous system. These functions include breathing rate, heart rate, muscle tension, and skin temperature. Electrodes are placed on the skin to measure whatever physical processes are being trained, and these processes are displayed on a monitor. With the assistance of a therapist trained in the use of biofeedback, you can learn to control muscle tension, skin temperature, and even certain types of brain wave activity. Biofeedback became very popular in the 1970s and remains popular today to treat headaches, chronic pain, urinary incontinence, and in some cases high blood pressure. There have also been some studies that have looked at biofeedback training and reducing levels of anxiety, as biofeedback measurements allow for the immediate measure of a person's stress levels. There are several commonly used forms of bio-feedback therapy:

1. Electroencephalography (EEG) is sometimes referred to as neurofeed-back. This method is used to measure and control brain wave activity.
2. Electromyography (EMG) involves training to learn how to control muscle tension.
3. Thermal biofeedback is used in measuring and controlling skin temperature and is often useful in treating headaches.
4. Electrodermal activity (EDA) measures perspiration on the skin and can be used to treat chronic pain and anxiety.
5. Heart rate variability (HRV) measures heart rate and can be used to treat anxiety and other issues.

Biofeedback training for anxiety typically uses a progressive relaxation technique, visualization, diaphragmatic breathing, and the biofeedback instruments to allow a person to ascertain periods of stress and tension from periods of relaxation. It appears that using EEG training is the most beneficial for overall relaxation. The electrodes send signals to the monitor, which displays a light, a sound, or an image that allows the practitioner to get feedback as to one's level of stress and anxiety. By progressively relaxing and breathing, a person can fine-tune their relaxation response and reduce their levels of anxiety. Once the person associates his relaxed and anxiety-free body states with the biofeedback monitor, he can learn to reproduce this relaxed state without the biofeedback equipment. Biofeedback sessions last about thirty minutes. The number of sessions that a person will complete depends on a number of factors, but typically people will engage in anywhere from eight to twenty sessions.

Several reviews of EEG biofeedback and other types of biofeedback treatment for anxiety disorders noted that several research studies used very short durations of biofeedback training, much shorter than is typically used in clinical situations. Nonetheless, EEG biofeedback appeared to be effective for the treatment of generalized anxiety disorder in several studies. There have been several studies that have mixed samples of participants that had different types of anxiety disorders, and some of the studies included individuals who had panic attacks and even some participants who were diagnosed with panic disorder. There was a small study with four patients with panic disorder who underwent biofeedback training to lower their breathing rate. After four weeks of training, the sample demonstrated an ability to control their breathing during panic attacks; however, the small sample size is problematic to determine if the training can help panic disorder patients in general.

The overall findings for the use of biofeedback training in the treatment of panic attacks, panic disorder, and overall anxiety show that this method of treatment appears to have potential, especially when a sufficient amount of training sessions are used. This really should not be surprising, as biofeedback training appears to incorporate many of the techniques from cognitive behavioral therapies, such as exposure using visualization, progressive relaxation, and applying relaxation to deal with anxious states. Given this, you would expect that biofeedback therapy would be at least as effective as relaxation training and would approach the effectiveness of cognitive behavioral therapy depending on how much exposure is involved during biofeedback training.

Is the Equipment Necessary?

As stated previously, the reason why relaxation training is important in the treatment of anxiety disorders is that a relaxed state and an anxious state represent two opposite ends of the continuum. It is physically impossible to feel relaxed and anxious at the same time. Since biofeedback training is another way to train oneself to learn to relax, it can be a useful tool in the treatment of anxiety and panic disorder.

Under most circumstances, the biofeedback equipment is not necessary in order for one to learn progressive relaxation or to apply relaxation. There has been some research comparing progressive relaxation using muscle tension techniques and relaxation training without muscle tension techniques, such as biofeedback training. The findings are quite interesting. It appears that progressive relaxation training using muscle tension probably produces deeper relaxation; however, the participants in the studies often prefer to use relaxation training techniques that do not require muscle tension, such as biofeedback.

The bottom line is that biofeedback training is most likely useful in the treatment of panic disorder in terms of training panic disorder patients to learn to relax; however, it is not a critical or necessary component of the relaxation training associated with cognitive behavioral techniques, nor is there any reason to believe that biofeedback training is more effective than CBT. When CBT is compared to other types of treatment, most studies find in favor of CBT. Nonetheless, there is probably a subset of people with panic disorder that would prefer the type of feedback that this type of treatment offers. The research does not specify what groups of individuals biofeedback would be more suited for, and so this is probably best left up to the individual person and her treating clinician.

FACT

Most of the biofeedback research looks at generalized anxiety disorder but not specifically at panic disorder. However, it does appear that biofeedback training is a good adjunctive form of treatment for those in CBT or who are taking medication and experiencing difficulty relaxing, learning relaxation, or applying relaxation to their lives. It is probably less effective as a primary treatment.

Eye Movement Desensitization and Reprocessing (EMDR)

EMDR is a therapeutic technique where a therapist either waves a stick, a light, or his finger horizontally back and forth in front of the client, and the client is supposed to follow the moving object with his eyes and verbally discuss or visually imagine some past trauma or anxiety-provoking event. This combination of eye movement and visualization "reprocesses" the traumatic event and allows the individual to dissipate the anxiety associated with the trauma.

The therapy was allegedly invented by therapist Dr. Francine Shapiro, who actually received her doctorate at a now closed and never accredited professional school of psychology.

Nonetheless, it is claimed that EMDR is effective in the treatment of a number of anxiety disorders, traumatic disorders, phobias, learning disabilities, paranoid schizophrenia, pathological jealousy, and even more problems. This particular therapy has been marketed quite well despite a large body of evidence that indicates that the eye movement component of the therapy has no effect whatsoever and that most of the therapeutic effects either come from nonspecific effects or from the exposure component of the technique (visualization).

In the book *Science and Pseudoscience in Clinical Psychology*, the famous critic of ineffective practices in mental health Dr. Scott O. Lilienfeld and other authors claim that EMDR does not offer any "incremental clinical efficiency" (which essentially means that the technique adds nothing significant to conventional established psychotherapy techniques). Most of the independent research on this technique has found that the eye movement component of the technique adds nothing and that the visualization and exposure components, which are used with much greater efficiency in CBT, account for the therapeutic change in studies with positive effects.

ALERT

Pseudoscientific treatments come from nearly every branch of medicine and nonmedical fields and are much like the technique discussed by Mesmer earlier in this book. They often appear to be effective due to some new or alternative method; however, they are often unable to pass scientific scrutiny and yet remain popular due to anecdotal evidence and effective marketing.

One of the really big blows to EMDR was the finding that using finger tapping or tones as opposed to the eye movement component was just as effective for blind people as the normal technique was for people with sight. This finding is not consistent with the theoretical explanation of how this eye movement technique is supposed to work (which is based on sheer conjecture and pseudoscientific thinking). Despite such research, proponents of EMDR have still tried to explain away the findings and continue to use the technique. Even though there is a subset of therapists and patients that swear by this technique, this book cannot recommend its use in light of the substantial body of independent evidence that suggests that the eye movement component is nothing more than a sham treatment with nonspecific effects and the entire process includes elements of other psychotherapeutic techniques that account for its efficacy. In addition, EMDR can be much more expensive than traditional psychotherapy (another red flag). Why pay extra for EMDR when it is most likely CBT in disguise?

Diet/Lifestyle

There is little doubt that eating healthy and getting proper nutrition is a good thing. A balanced diet with proper nutrients and a lifestyle that balances exercise, rest, and is generally aimed at controlling the effects of normal stressors will in many cases prevent the onset of conditions such as arthritis, high blood pressure, and other such issues. As a result, there has been a rather large movement that endorses the use of megavitamin therapy—taking vitamins and minerals in doses many times higher than the recommended daily allowances provided by the FDA—as a potential cure-all or treatment for many diseases and disorders. *Orthomolecular medicine* has become a term for this type of treatment. There have been some cases where the use of high-dose vitamin therapy has been useful in treating some conditions, whereas in some cases the use of high-dose vitamin therapy has actually worsened the conditions it was supposed to treat. Nonetheless, there is a multimillion-dollar market for nutrition-based treatments, books endorsing nutritionally based treatments, and of course different nutritional supplements.

At the time of this writing, there is insufficient evidence to support the effects of vitamin supplementation or nutrient supplementation for the treatment of most of the anxiety disorders. There is a record of one double-blind RCT that reported a decrease in mild anxiety in generalized anxiety patients following three months of supplementation with magnesium compared to placebo. Another study indicated that following one month of nutritional supplementation, regular state anxiety (normal anxiety) was decreased in women with premenstrual symptoms, and another study indicated that amino acid treatment had some effects on stress-related anxiety in normal controls. A case study of mega-doses of niacinamide (vitamin B_3), a vitamin reputed to treat anxiety in high doses, indicated no effect on mild anxiety in the participants, although the dosage was deemed safe and there were no ill effects.

As discussed previously, inositol, another B vitamin, may have a potential role in treating panic disorder based on some older studies with small sample sizes. Anxiolytic nutrients might have an effect on the GABA system or on the major excitatory neurotransmitters in the brain, such as glutamate, but the formal research on inositol and other nutrients in the treatment of panic disorder is lacking. Therefore, outside of the obvious, well-established knowledge that good nutrition and a healthy lifestyle is important to overall health, it currently does not appear that megavitamin therapy can be recommended as a primary treatment for panic disorder. Further studies are needed to investigate these effects.

Other Lifestyle Changes

A good deal of research indicates that people with panic disorder smoke significantly more than people without a psychological disorder. The research on quitting smoking and increases in anxiety associated with panic disorder is mixed, with some studies finding no relationship between quitting and increases in anxiety and others finding the opposite. Some studies also find that people with anxiety disorders are less likely to seek help if they are smoking in excess, suggesting that perhaps they find a calming effect in the use of nicotine. In general, most researchers believe that quitting smoking does not lead to an increase in the intensity of panic attacks or anxiety in people with panic disorder, and reducing one's use of tobacco or quitting altogether is supported by mountains of research with regard to its positive health benefits.

Caffeine is the most commonly used psychoactive substance in the world. As a result of overuse, caffeine acts as a psychostimulant and may increase anxiety and the intensity of panic attacks and panic disorder. It appears that people with panic disorder are more sensitive to the effects of caffeine than other people. Most physicians and mental health professionals will suggest that people limit their use of caffeine if they're being treated for panic disorder; however, this can result in some mild withdrawal symptoms.

About one half of the people receiving treatment for alcohol abuse also suffer from an anxiety or depressive disorder. The abuse of alcohol may result in anxiety-related withdrawal symptoms once the alcohol is stopped, and alcohol is known to reduce levels of nutrients that are critical in healthy brain functioning. It appears that having a panic disorder can maintain or exacerbate a substance abuse disorder and vice versa. Of course the "self-medication" hypothesis suggests that people use alcohol or drugs to reduce their anxiety or stress. The use of alcohol or illicit drugs to deal with anxiety is not suggested, and individuals who have substance abuse issues comorbid with panic disorder need to be treated by mental health professionals and a physician concurrently.

FACT

The "self-medication" hypothesis that people use alcohol or drugs to medicate themselves in response to psychiatric disorders is popular with lay theorists; however, it is less supported in clinical research. One reason is that it cannot predict what type of substance a person with a particular disorder would use, when it should be able to do so beyond chance levels.

CHAPTER 15

Self-Help Treatments for Panic Disorder

Any treatment requires self-motivation in order for it to be effective. Even CBT or medication use requires quite a bit of self-motivation to be effective. If you are serious about coping with your panic, you can do anything. The following treatments are used by people without any professional advice and are given the designation "self-help treatments," but are also often considered CAMs. These treatments can be applied by simply reading an article, buying the necessary components, and going about applying the treatment/ technique by oneself. For some people this may be viewed as advantageous; however, it also leads to some special issues that need to be discussed.

Brief Warnings (Again)

On the positive side, most of these "self-help" treatments have no or very few detrimental side effects associated with them if used according to recommend guidelines. On the negative side, there are a lot of unsubstantiated claims that these types of treatments can cure almost anything or perform miracles, much like the claims for herbal remedies and nutritional supplements. Such claims often mislead people.

It is important to keep in mind as you read this section that just because one type of intervention may have evidence that it works for some specific issue, it doesn't mean it is true. Even treatments that have calming effects on "normal" people or that work with patients who have generalized anxiety disorder may be completely ineffective for panic attacks and panic disorder. By now you should understand that panic attacks and the anxiety associated with panic disorder is not "normal" by any means.

Aromatherapy for Panic Disorder

Aromatherapy is the practice of prescribing isolated volatile oils from plants for the treatment of various conditions. The oils are applied for treatment by a number of different methods, including inhalation, massage, and sometimes use internally. The oils can be extracted in a number of methods, such as steam inhalation or distilled into balms for massage. The supporters of this form of treatment suggest there are possibly two different ways through which aromatherapy works: The first method is the influence of the aroma (smell) on the brain. Smell is the only form of external stimulation that is sent directly to the brain without being further processed or broken down by several brain mechanisms, such as the thalamus (of course this occurs after the stimuli are processed through a sensory system, the olfactory system). Smells may have a direct effect on the limbic system, a part of the brain that deals with emotion and memory. The second possible hypothesis used by supporters of this type of therapy is that the essential oils have direct pharmacological effects, although there seems to be confusion as to what effects these are. Most of the supporters of this type of therapy believe that aromatherapy does not necessarily directly cure conditions, but instead helps the body to naturally cure itself or improve its response to stressors.

Supporters of this type of treatment make a number of different claims. There is quite a bit of literature about aromatherapy, as it is one of the most commonly used CAM treatments in the world. Nonetheless, there is really little direct clinical evidence for many of the claims made by its supporters.

Positive Effects of Aromatherapy

A recent systematic review of aromatherapy for the treatment of anxiety and anxiety disorders covered a twenty-year period and considered over fifty published reports. Only sixteen reports were methodologically sound enough to be included in the review (many were not RCTs and many did not focus on anxiety specifically). The review, which was published in a journal dedicated to contemporary and alternative medicines (*The Journal of Alternative and Complementary Medicine*), concluded that there were insufficient clinical trials that examined the effects of aromatherapy on people with anxiety disorders as their primary condition. Every one of the sixteen studies that had at least minimal methodological soundness investigated the effects of aromatherapy on secondary anxiety (symptoms of anxiety that occur with other disorders). This anxiety occurred in people with dementia, cancer, postpartum depression, and in healthy volunteers.

The levels of anxiety in the participants of all sixteen studies differed significantly from mild to moderate anxiety before the treatment was administered. As discussed previously, it is difficult if not impossible to compare the effectiveness of a treatment among participants with different disorders or vastly different levels of anxiety. Nonetheless, there were some positive findings. First, people who had mild levels of anxiety did not experience significant changes in their anxiety due to aromatherapy, whereas those with more severe levels of anxiety reported some remission of anxiety with aromatherapy. This suggests that aromatherapy may have some utility in the treatment of severe anxiety disorders such as panic disorder, but does not guarantee that this treatment is effective. The other major positive finding in this review was that over all sixteen trials, there were no significant adverse effects reported from aromatherapy.

Even though the review found no significant adverse effects, there are concerns. Essential oils should never be taken internally unless under a physician's supervision, as there can be severe reactions. All oils should be diluted with a carrier oil before being applied to the skin and may cause irritation after repeated use. Before engaging in aromatherapy, consult with your physician.

Music Therapy for Panic Disorder

There are a number of studies that have indicated that music has been effective in managing the anxiety experienced by patients getting ready to go undergo surgery, during surgical procedures, and following a surgical procedure. A number of studies suggest that playing music can significantly reduce anxiety in patients undergoing other types of medical procedures or medical examinations, and in patients on ventilators. Music therapy is an evidence-based type of therapy where music therapists apply music for individuals with a number of specific conditions and goals. Depending on the condition being treated, this could include listening to music, singing, songwriting, improvisation of music, etc. A growing body of evidence has indicated that music therapy can address a number of physical, emotional, and spiritual issues in a number of different disorders, including in people with terminal illnesses.

In many of these studies, music therapy has been found to significantly reduce anxiety levels in the patient groups being studied; however, there are no specific RCTs investigating the effects of music therapy on panic disorder. Instead, most of the Internet sites and other information regarding the use of music therapy on panic attacks cite the effect of music therapy on secondary anxiety due to other medical conditions. Because of this, it is difficult to ascertain the effect of music therapy on panic disorder specifically.

Due to a lack of research, music therapy cannot be considered a first-line treatment for panic attacks or for panic disorder. There is evidence to suggest that music therapy can be a very helpful adjunctive treatment for panic attacks or panic disorder. In addition, music therapy as applied by a trained and credentialed professional music therapist most likely has one of the lowest potentials for adverse side effects compared to most other forms of treatment. Therefore, music therapy is a safe adjunctive treatment option for patients with panic disorder, but is not recommended as a first-line or standalone treatment.

FACT

Music therapy can be used in many different contexts. One interesting use of music therapy is its ability to foster communication in individuals with brain damage. For instance, people with expressive aphasia, difficulty producing speech due to brain damage, can learn to communicate by singing.

Massage Therapy for Panic Disorder

Massages require a person to manipulate the skin, superficial and deep layers of muscle tissue, and connective tissue via some method that typically involves touching and kneading another person's muscles. By working and acting on the body with pressure, the result can be relaxing and even therapeutic. Professional massage therapists receive training in the type of massage techniques that can be used for therapeutic purposes, and if one is seeking massage therapy, it is important to make sure that one checks the credentials of the masseur or masseuse providing the treatment. The targets of such therapy may include muscles, skin, joints, gastrointestinal system, or any number of other bodily systems. The technique may involve the use of oil, may require the client to be clothed or unclothed, and can be done either standing, sitting, or lying down, depending on the reason for the massage therapy.

Therapeutic massage is one of the most popular contemporary and alternative medical treatments in the United States; however, there are very few rigorously clinical trials that investigate its use for people diagnosed with anxiety disorders. One recent study investigated the effectiveness of therapeutic massage for generalized anxiety disorder compared to thermotherapy (heat application), or relaxation therapy. A total of sixty-eight patients with generalized anxiety disorder underwent twelve weeks of treatment with one of the treatments. All three groups showed significant improvement in their anxiety symptoms following twelve weeks. No one therapy was superior to the other. The conclusions of the researchers were that the reduction of anxiety was due to a general relaxation effect and not to any specific treatment effects and that of the three treatments, the relaxation training and a relaxation room were the least expensive and therefore the most cost-effective methods for the treatment of generalized anxiety disorder.

Another study looked at chair massage for anxiety in patients withdrawing from cocaine, opiates, or alcohol. The participants were randomly assigned to either the massage or a relaxation control condition. Both groups experienced a significant reduction in their anxiety, with the massage group experiencing a greater reduction than the relaxation group. A different study looked at aromatherapy massage and CBT over a three-month period in reducing anxiety in cancer patients. There were some issues with the methodology; for example, the CBT patients only got eight sessions over three months, which is quite low. Nonetheless, both resulted in significant reductions in depression and anxiety, with CBT being superior for depression but both equivalent for anxiety reduction. However, the anxiety treated in this study was very low-level anxiety.

Potential Cons

There are some potential detrimental effects from massage therapy. The most common side effects from professional massage therapy are an increase in soreness following the treatment. Sometimes people can experience headaches, bruising, or fatigue. People who have significant chances to experience bone fractures, such as those with osteoporosis or cancer patients, should be wary of undergoing massage therapy. Other medical conditions that make people susceptible to getting blood clots or internal bleeding make the use of massage therapy questionable. Massage therapy may not be appropriate for women in the first trimester of their pregnancy or those with high-risk pregnancies.

In summary, the results for massage therapy suggests that there is some benefit for anxiety reduction in some different patient populations and in some different contexts; however, there is no direct evidence that massage therapy is effective in treating panic disorder. Thus, massage therapy can probably be used as an adjunctive treatment for people suffering from panic disorder but cannot be recommended as a first-line or stand-alone treatment for panic disorder, despite many claims from massage therapists and claims on the Internet. In addition, there are so many different types of massage therapy that it is unclear which particular type of massage therapy might be most efficient in relieving general anxiety or the more severe anxiety experience of panic disorder.

ALERT

There are many different types of massage, such as sports massage, deep tissue massage, Swedish massage, etc. Anyone seeking massage therapy as treatment for panic disorder should explain the reasons for the treatment and discuss all of his symptoms with the therapist. It is suggested that anyone seeking massage therapy consult with a physician first.

Yoga for Panic Disorder

Yoga is a mind-body practice that has a long-standing history of use and is generally defined as a practice that consists of three components: postures or stretching exercises, methods of breath control, and methods of meditation. There are a number of different types of yoga, and traditional East Indian yoga practices have become westernized. There are many claims that support the use of yoga techniques in different psychiatric disorders; however, most of these are not RCTs, and several of the studies that approach methodological adequacy often include quite a bit of diversity in the types of anxiety in the participants, making it difficult to determine exactly what type of anxiety yoga may be helpful for. There is also a "yoga psychology" movement that attempts to tie in yoga philosophies with certain psychological paradigms (most often the humanistic paradigm and Jungian thought are used).

One recent review of the effectiveness of yoga for anxiety was based on an extensive search of the literature over several different databases, and the results provided only eight studies that met minimum standards. The review commented that the methodology in the studies that were even chosen was generally poor. Only one study demonstrated adequate randomization, although six of the eight studies claim to be RCTs. Two studies claim to be double-blind; however, only one had participants who were blind to their condition. Most of the studies had a high dropout rate and short follow-up time with no explanation for either. In addition, there was a large diversity of the types of anxiety that the participants in the studies complained about. The most rigorous study was performed on twenty-two adult patients diagnosed with obsessive-compulsive disorder. Yoga treatment was found to be significantly more effective than the control condition in this study.

A 2013 review targeted twenty-seven studies but used less stringent criteria for the studies. Yoga practice was found to reduce general anxiety, but its effect on anxiety disorders is still questionable. Due to the poor methodologies in most of the studies and most studies not being RCTs, the conclusions from this review are questionable at best, especially when trying to ascertain if yoga is an effective treatment for anxiety disorders such as panic disorder. Moreover, the results of many of the studies are mixed, in that some studies show no reduction in anxiety between yoga and control groups, whereas others show significant reductions in anxiety.

The Bottom Line Is . . .

In summary, there is evidence to suggest that yoga has potential as an adjunctive treatment for panic disorder; however, actual solid clinical evidence is lacking. Yoga is quite popular and there are many anecdotal claims as to its effect on anxiety and its ability to promote good health, but without solid clinical evidence, these claims simply represent pseudoscientific reports and do not qualify yoga as an effective treatment for any anxiety disorder. Yoga is generally considered a pretty safe form of exercise. Detrimental effects from yoga practice could include overstretching and orthopedic injuries due to trying to do too much too fast. Some exercises, such as the shoulder stand, can put strain on the neck. People with orthopedic injuries or arthritis are cautioned to consult their physician before attempting to practice yoga exercises (anyone should consult their physician first).

ESSENTIAL

There are many different schools of yoga and literally thousands of books and DVDs that allow people to practice yoga on their own. Yoga is most likely a safe adjunctive therapeutic technique to assist in the treatment of panic disorder. It is best to practice yoga under supervision until a person is at least at an intermediate level.

Tai Chi and Martial Arts for Panic Disorder

Tai chi is a martial art and form of exercise from China that involves moving through a series of postures, much like a choreographed dance form. A recent review investigating the effects of tai chi and overall psychological health documented two RCTs and six nonrandomized studies that reported tai chi practice to be associated with significant reductions in anxiety when practiced four to six times a week. There were diverse issues for the anxiety, and none of the individuals was formally diagnosed with an anxiety disorder. Therefore, the specific effects of tai chi are difficult to interpret, and whether tai chi adds anything to normal physical activity or relaxation is questionable at this time.

There is some pretty decent research that has investigated the effect of other types of marital arts training on increased self-concept, increased grades in children, and more efficient self-control in several typically hard-to-work-with patient groups (e.g., ADHD children). Martial arts training has been associated with decreased normal levels of anxiety and there are some anecdotal reports of successes in treating panic disorder, but no real formal research that could be termed clinical evidence. Traditionally focused martial arts training as opposed to training aimed at competition has a lot to offer people with psychiatric disorders such as increasing self-esteem, concentration, etc, but most likely this training will not be successful as a first-line or stand-alone treatment. Martial arts training could be used as an adjunctive form of treatment for panic disorder for individuals who have a genuine interest in this type of activity. Of course some marital arts are very strenuous and some types involve falling and throwing techniques that may not be appropriate for everyone. Always discuss beginning this type of training with your physician before you start.

Meditation for Panic Disorder

The concept of meditation is not a unified one. There are many different types of meditation, and even the progressive relaxation techniques taught in CBT could be considered a form of meditation. Several types of psychotherapy borrow from Eastern meditation and have evolved into "mindfulness" therapeutic techniques. The development of mindfulness can probably be best explained as paying attention in a particular way such that attention is directed on purpose to the present moment and in a nonjudgmental manner. It should also be noted that both yoga, martial arts, and tai chi are techniques that also incorporate meditation into their practice. Due to the many different types of meditation and a lack of RCTs specifically looking at specific schools of meditation and panic disorder, there is no evidence that one form of meditation alone is better than another.

One recent study investigated the effects of an eight-week program of mindfulness meditation for stress reduction in twenty-two patients who were diagnosed with generalized anxiety disorder or panic disorder and in fifty-eight nondisordered participants who had high levels of anxiety. At the end of the study, and at the three-month follow-up eighteen of the patients and thirty-nine of the nonpatients experienced significant reductions in panic symptoms. The researchers also followed up with the participants after three years and found that eighteen original patients and a good number of the nondisordered patients retained their improvements regarding the reduction of their panic symptoms.

Another study looked at the efficiency of mindfulness meditation with forty-one patients who were diagnosed with either generalized anxiety disorder or panic disorder. In this RCT, the meditation group displayed significant decreases in anxiety and panic symptoms compared to the control group, which received only psychoeducation. A more recent study investigated mindfulness meditation compared to a waitlist control group. A significant difference was found in the meditation group compared to the control group in regard to generalized anxiety symptoms and panic disorder symptoms. These improvements were still present at a six-month follow-up. In a study that compared CBT and mindfulness meditation, both groups received significant reductions in generalized anxiety disorder symptoms, panic disorder symptoms, and social phobia symptoms, with CBT having a slight advantage over mindfulness meditation.

The Benefits of Meditation

There are a number of different claims as to why meditation and mindfulness meditation may be effective in reducing anxiety symptoms. First, through meditation training it is believed that negative thoughts may become viewed as simply transient thoughts, and their ability to trigger anxiety is thus reduced. Meditation is also believed to be a form of gradual exposure therapy, where during meditation, the prolonged exposure to anxiety-provoking thoughts in a relaxed state helps to dissipate them.

Neuroimaging studies indicate that meditation practice may be associated with a number of different changes in the brain, including an increased thickness of the cortex and changes in the frontal areas of the brain. Given the evidence, it appears that mindfulness meditation qualifies as a potential treatment for panic disorder; however, it is probably most effective if used in conjunction with a first-line treatment, such as CBT, medications, or other.

FACT

There appear to be minimal risks from meditation practice; however, there are cases of fragile individuals developing psychotic reactions to meditation. It is suggested that anyone who has a psychological disorder and engages in meditation be supervised by a trained mental health professional. As always, anyone engaging in meditation for a mental illness should also consult her physician.

Exercise for Panic Disorder

A lack of physical activity is an established risk factor for the development of many health problems including many psychiatric disorders. Regular physical activity appears to reduce all the risk of causes of mortality and premature death and is associated with improved emotional well-being in nearly all patient groups. There is also well-established evidence that regular physical activity is associated with a reduction in depression and anxiety symptoms, including those that occur in panic disorder. This type of correlational research does not effectively address any causal relationship. For example, it could very well be that people with panic disorder engage in less physical activity or that people who engage in more physical activity are less likely to get panic disorder.

There is some research that has indicated that prescribed physical exercise can relieve depressive symptoms, but there is less clinical evidence that prescribed physical exercise can relieve anxiety disorder symptoms. One review found that aerobic exercise was not superior to a combination of relaxation and SSRI treatment or relaxation and placebo in the treatment of patients with panic disorder. There is research to suggest that regular physical activity in conjunction with CBT and medication treatments can help reduce the intensity of panic attacks compared to CBT or medication treatment alone.

Other recent studies have associated greater levels of physical inactivity in people suffering from panic disorder and agoraphobia than control groups. Some recent findings indicate that in rodents, those that received regular exercise had a response in the hippocampus of their brains that allowed them to tolerate stressors better than sedentary mice.

There is good evidence that regular physical activity, such as walking or running, is effective in the treatment of depression and anxiety, but the relationship between mental and physical activity appears to be very complex, and there are always contraindications to more intense forms of exercises, such as running compared to walking.

The Bottom Line . . .

The overall evidence supports the use of graded exercise to reduce anxiety, and increasing physical activity is suggested in most cases of panic disorder after the individual has an appropriate health assessment. The evidence does not support using physical exercise in isolation to treat any psychiatric disorder; however, physical exercise alone can improve normal sadness and normal anxiety levels that are not associated with mental disorders. Thus, a complete assessment of the individual is appropriate before prescribing any type of physical activity to treat any type of psychological disorder.

FACT

Anyone attempting to start an exercise program of any kind, including walking or tai chi, is strongly urged to have a physical examination by a physician before beginning an exercise program. Not doing so can potentially result in consequences that are worse than the original problem one wishes to address through exercising.

CHAPTER 16

Panic Disorder in Children and Adolescents

From the time they are born, children in the United States are assessed, evaluated, and labeled in a number of different categories, including behavior, educational achievement, mood, personality, etc. Although there is agreement regarding the need to assess and understand children, there continues to be significant disagreement regarding how mental disorders in childhood should be defined. This chapter looks at some of the special issues and challenges for people under the age of eighteen when considering a diagnosis of panic disorder.

What Does Panic Disorder Look Like in Children and Adolescents?

Research on panic disorder indicates that it was initially thought to be an exclusively adult disorder; however, some studies indicate that up to 40 percent of adults with panic disorder reported having their first panic attacks before the age of twenty years old. Epidemiological studies indicate that the prevalence rates of pediatric panic disorder are estimated to be between 0.5 percent and 5 percent in community samples and much higher in clinical samples. Epidemiological studies also suggest that the rate of anxiety disorders in children is generally less than the rate of anxiety disorders in adults, but nonetheless, a pediatric panic disorder does exist.

According to the National Institute of Mental Health, the lifetime prevalence of panic disorder in thirteen- to eighteen-year-olds is 2.3 percent. According to this data, the prevalence rate for panic disorder increases with age, from 1.8 percent for youngsters thirteen to fourteen years old, to 2.3 percent in the age range of fourteen to fifteen years old, to 3.2 percent for those who are seventeen to eighteen years old. Most studies indicate that panic disorder is more common in female children and adolescents than in male children and adolescents, which is similar to the gender differences found in adults.

Normal Developmental Anxiety

The diagnostic criteria for panic disorder remain the same whether it is pediatric panic disorder or adult panic disorder. However, there are some specific issues regarding a diagnosis of panic disorder in children that should be considered. There are several periods of normal developmental anxiety that most children go through that could be mistaken for panic attacks. Normal separation anxiety can occur as children develop rudimentary notions of object permanence between four to seven months of age. When separated from a familiar caregiver, children at this age may throw tantrums, cry, and appear very anxious. Most of the time this behavior is normal and will dissipate as the child matures.

Stranger anxiety is a relatively normal occurrence that children between the ages of six to twelve months will display in the presence of unfamiliar adults. The onset of an episode of stranger anxiety can appear very much like a panic attack, but if this anxiety occurs in the context of being left with a stranger, it is probably not significant.

Other normal developmental episodes of anxiety can occur in a number of different contexts, including social contexts, unfamiliar situations, childhood fears of objects, childhood fears of animals, childhood fears of strange situations, etc. Young children have a diminished capacity to anticipate and predict future outcomes, and it is not unusual for young children to become anxious easily over things that would normally seem trivial. These "normal" developmental instances of anxiety will typically resolve if the parents show restraint, understanding, and empathy toward the child, but at the same time, parents should not indulge the child too much. Likewise, children learn from watching their parents, and children will easily model their behavior after their parents. If a parent is extremely afraid of spiders, a young child watching this may develop an irrational fear of insects. These rather normal types of anxiety that occur during development can often be mistaken for an anxiety disorder.

The key to handling normal anxiety is to be consistent with how problems and discipline are handled and administered. Children exhibiting anxiety are not exhibiting willful misbehavior, but are having difficulty understanding and controlling their feelings. Parents need to be patient and prepared to listen to them as opposed to being critical. Keep goals obtainable for children and maintain a consistent, but flexible routine for schoolwork and chores. Make sure to accept the child's mistakes as a part of growing up and listen to her expectations. When children appear overly worried about an upcoming event, such as giving a talk in class, help them practice it to reduce anxiety and show them how to deal with anxiety by preparing for it in a positive manner. Other concerns occur as children get older and become more focused on how their peers view them, the pressures of performing, and their developing sense of self.

There have been studies that looked at the incidence of fear and anxiety in children and adolescents not diagnosed with a psychiatric disorder. Typically these studies find that a good proportion of parents report that children between the ages of four and seventeen years often display a significant number of fears and anxiety-related issues, averaging between three and nine intensive fears.

Panic Disorder in Children

It is a mistake to think that children and adolescents are miniature versions of adults. Children and adolescents do not often understand their feelings (not that adults always do either, but children may lack the developmental capacity to understand their emotions). Young children will often not be able to explain what is bothering them, whereas older children will often not want to look weak or want to be labeled as being sick or different. There are several questions to consider when trying to determine whether a child or adolescent has panic disorder. These following questions are designed to help parents determine whether to seek professional help; they are not designed as diagnostic indicators, and parents should always refer children suspected of having psychiatric issues to a qualified mental health professional.

1. Who is doing the complaining? Sometimes the perceptions of adults complaining about a child's behavior may be more important in determining whether or not the child needs actual treatment than the child's behavior itself. Given that children typically experience more intense fears and anxieties than adults and that it is not uncommon for children to have issues with worry and anxiety, it must be determined whether or not the observations of adults are appropriate enough to consider treatment for the child. If the child's reactions are deemed appropriate and the child is being subjected to unrealistic demands or expectations, it may be the complaining adults that need treatment and not the child.

2. In consideration of the first question, an important question to ask is: How is the child's behavior problematic? If the child's behavior interferes with his ability to adjust to the environment, disrupts his goals or

normal obligations, or results in extreme discomfort and dissatisfaction, then the behavior should be examined by a mental health professional to determine if it represents some type of a psychiatric issue.

3. How are the fears in question related to other areas of the child's behavior? Often the fearful or anxious behavior reported by adults is not the problem that needs to be resolved. For instance, children who are extremely anxious about going to school may have learning difficulties or social problems, such as being bullied. It is important to understand how the child's behavior or fear relates to other areas of his life in order to determine if it represents a potential diagnosis of panic disorder. Often the fears are anxious behaviors that are related to some specific area and not to unexpected panic attacks.

4. How would things be different for the child without the problem? Here, one would need to ask the question "Would changing the fear be positive for everyone?" The classic example here is the childhood fear of dentists. The child's fear of the dentist or other medical procedures may be short-lived; however, if it is allowed to interfere with normal checkups, it may lead to permanent physical damage or poor health later on. On the other hand, an irrational fear of spiders in a child may or may not have such implications. Thus, looking at the potential implications of changing the fear is an important consideration before moving on to a formal assessment.

5. What are the implications of treatment for the child and others involved? Children are often embarrassed and resentful about getting treatment, and putting a child in treatment requires a great deal of expenditure of money, time, and effort by parents and the family. It is important to consider these variables before seeking treatment.

ESSENTIAL

Pediatric panic disorder has the same set of symptoms and diagnostic criteria as adult panic disorder. However, diagnosing children is much more complicated and should be left to experienced pediatric psychologists or psychiatrists. There are many clinical tools that have been developed to diagnose such issues in children, but these can only be administered by licensed, trained professionals.

Special Issues in School

It is not unusual for children who have panic disorder to have panic attacks while at school, although they may attempt to hide their symptoms at school more than if they were to have an attack at home. It is also not unusual for children to be reluctant to describe their behavior at school when it is related to panic attacks, which may lead to some confusion with teachers and others in school as to what is actually going on. Some things to look out for that may signal the child is having panic attacks are:

- The child has repeated and sudden interruptions during activities without clear explanations as to why she stopped. At these times, children may need adult intervention to help them understand what is going on.
- The child or adolescent displays difficulties with concentration that are caused by persistent worry (the key here is "caused by persistent worry"; concentration difficulties can signal other issues as well, such as ADHD). This difficulty concentrating may affect a wide variety of activities, including completing assignments and following directions.
- The child is reluctant to go to school, leave parents, or spend time with other children.
- The child has low self-confidence, specifically directed at academic activities and social situations.

These are just general guidelines that may require the parent or teacher to investigate further. There are also certain things that be done in school to help a child with panic disorder.

There are many ways that schools can help a child with panic disorder succeed in the classroom. Meetings between parents and school staff, such as teachers, guidance counselors, or nurses, will allow for collaboration to develop helpful school structure for the child. The child may need particular changes (accommodations/modifications) within a classroom. Examples of some accommodations, modifications, and school strategies include the following:

- Allow the child to be able to let the teacher know if a panic attack is occurring so that the teacher can get the child to a less stressful environment. In order to control false alarms or misuse of leaving the classroom, set up a reward system for the student when she remains in class during less anxiety-provoking situations and during panic attacks.

- Develop specific relaxation techniques to reduce anxiety for the classroom.
- Encourage the child to develop helpful interventions that will keep the child on task and lead to more successful strategies in dealing with her anxiety and school.
- Adjust homework loads and stressors to prevent the child from being overwhelmed. Use assistance for homework and classwork wherever possible.
- Anticipate issues and provide assistance with them. Transitions may be particularly difficult for a child with panic disorder.

Being flexible and supportive in the classroom is extremely helpful for a child with panic disorder, as for any child with special needs. Other issues to consider are side effects from medications, peer interactions and how they can be helpful and harmful, and forming a team environment to make the child feel as if she is not alone.

Special Issues at Home

Home should be a safe place for any child. The assistance of caring parents is extremely important in helping a child or adolescent deal with any psychological issue. It is important for parents to understand panic disorder and how it is experienced by the child. This will help parents empathize with the child's situation and the difficulties the child encounters. In order to help the child, there are several steps that a concerned parent can follow:

- Listen to your child or adolescent. Children who feel isolated are at risk for developing depression and low levels of self-worth. Parents often feel they have to correct things or offer advice; however, just having someone listen with a sympathetic ear, without giving any advice, has been shown to have a powerful and therapeutic effect.

- It is extremely important to keep calm and remain comforting when the child is experiencing a panic attack. This helps the child model relaxation and not overreact. Panic attacks typically do not last very long, so the best approach is to maintain composure, offer calming and soothing advice, be empathetic, and understand they may not be able to stop the panic attack. But it will go away.
- It is always helpful to gently remind the child that he has survived subsequent panic attacks, and this may help reduce his anxiety.
- Work with the child on relaxation, deep breathing, and developing a mastery over his feelings. This may empower him and improve his sense of control. Do not present relaxation and the homework from CBT or other therapies as a chore; present it as an activity to get better.
- Always praise and reinforce the child's efforts to control his symptoms and deal with his panic disorder. Even if improvements seem to be small, they are improvements. Develop a reinforcement system for practice.

Again, treating panic disorder in children is a team effort—it helps the child feel that he is not alone, gives him confidence, and also gives him a model to look up to. Children are often unwilling to admit that they are different or have some type of perceived flaw. Do not approach panic attacks and panic disorder as a flaw in the person. Instead, approach the situation as a problem that can be resolved.

It is more productive to treat a child's panic disorder as a solvable problem as opposed to a mental disorder. Parents can model appropriate behaviors and remain calm when the child feels that his world is crashing in. This gives the child a model to follow and also gives him confidence that the parents can help him overcome his issue.

The Use of Medications in Children

At the time of this writing, the only medication formally approved by the FDA in the treatment of pediatric panic disorder (in children ages six to seventeen years old) is the SSRI Zoloft. Recall that SSRIs have a broad spectrum of effects and were specifically developed as antidepressant medications, but were also found to have strong anxiolytic (anti-anxiety) effects. The other groups of antidepressant medications used in the treatment of anxiety disorders and panic disorder are tricyclic antidepressants, which are not generally recommended for children because they have potential cardiotoxicity effects, and MAO inhibitors, which require special dietary restrictions and are not considered appropriate first-line treatments any longer.

Even though Zoloft is the only antidepressant formally approved for the treatment of pediatric panic disorder, your physician still may prescribe other antidepressants. It is extremely important that before putting a child on an antidepressant, the child and the parents know the potential risks involved. Both the child and parents need to agree to try medication. Once a child is taking an antidepressant medication for panic disorder, it is extremely important to monitor the child's symptoms and behaviors to make sure that potentially harmful side effects do not occur.

Important Information Regarding SSRI Use

Recall the SSRIs are antidepressant medications that are proposed to work by increasing the levels of serotonin in the body by not allowing it to be taken back into the releasing neuron in order to be reprocessed. In December of 2003, the United Kingdom Medicines and Healthcare Products Regulatory Agency issued an advisory stating that most SSRIs were not suitable to treat depression in children under the age of eighteen years old. In October of 2004, the FDA required pharmaceutical companies to put a warning on all antidepressant medications that there is a small, but statistically significant, risk of an increase in suicidal thinking in children taking these medications. There has been quite a lot of controversy surrounding this issue, and what the researchers found is that as children continue to take the medication, these suicidal thoughts may begin to subside in the small percentage of children that get them. The risk for an increase in suicidal thoughts is not thought to occur in children who are being treated for anxiety disorders with these drugs; however, physicians and parents must closely weigh these risks and monitor any child taking these drugs for any signs of increased agitation, irritability, behavior changes, and of course any sign of suicidal tendencies.

ALERT

The other issue to be concerned about with antidepressant use for pediatric panic disorder is that children are typically more sensitive to the effects of drugs and can have more varied and more prevalent side effects, and that these medications may not be eliminated or tolerated in the child's system in the same way as they are in an adult's system.

Benzodiazepines

Benzodiazepines have a quick onset of action regarding panic attacks, but are not very good first-line treatment choices for children or adolescents with pediatric panic disorder. There are several reasons for this. First, benzodiazepines often cause a person to become disinhibited, and this effect may be more pronounced in children and adolescents. Secondly, tolerance to these medications develops rapidly, and more and more of the medication is needed to achieve the same effect. Third, once these medications are discontinued, withdrawal symptoms are almost inevitable. Fourth, these drugs all have high potential street value as drugs of abuse and can be misused by children and adolescents. There are several benzodiazepines that have been used in children to reduce panic attacks or anticipatory anxiety; however, benzodiazepines should only be used in conjunction with psychotherapy, such as CBT, and should be tapered off once a child begins to gain control of her panic disorder.

Other Drugs

Several drugs were discussed that have been used to treat panic attacks and panic disorder. Most of these are not recommended for children for several reasons, including potential side effect profiles.

There are pros to limited medication use for panic disorder in children. In children who have severe panic attacks, it may be necessary to immediately address the situation until the child can learn to gain a sense of control over her attacks. However, given the potential risks involved, it is the opinion of this book that any psychotropic medication use in children for anxiety should be time-limited and should only be used in conjunction with psychotherapy until the child begins to exert control over the situation. Once this happens, the child should be tapered off the medication.

Psychotherapy and Children

CBT is probably the preferred method of treating panic disorder in children and adolescents. CBT is time-limited, allows the child to develop a sense of control, and has relatively few risks involved. Other types of psychotherapy, such as psychodynamic treatment for panic disorder, do not appear to have a solid empirical basis for use with children. Probably the biggest issue regarding the use of psychotherapy for the treatment of pediatric panic disorder is making sure that the therapist is right for the child. This involves a couple of considerations.

First, it is important to understand that there is a difference between a psychologist or therapist that specializes in treating adults and one that specializes in treating children. The types of training experiences that each receives are quite different. It is very rare that a therapist or psychologist can adequately treat both children and adults, except in the context of family therapy (although there are therapists that are trained to treat either both adults or children). The first consideration that the parents should have when choosing a therapist for a child with panic disorder is that the therapist specializes in treating children or has specialized training in treating children.

The next consideration should be obvious. The therapist should have specialized training and experience in treating pediatric panic disorder. If the therapist does not have this specialized training, it is probably a good idea to find another therapist. Finally, it is important that the therapist and the child work together, and therefore there must be a good fit between therapist and child so they can form a healthy alliance. With children, it may be best to have the therapist and child be of the same gender (although this is not always necessary) and to have the child express the notion that he/she actually likes the therapist. There are also special adjustments that the therapist will need to make for children, so it is good to have a therapist with a flexible approach.

Cons of Psychotherapy for Children

If there is one fact of treating psychological problems, it is that not everyone will receive the same benefit from the same technique. While CBT is the preferred method of treatment for pediatric panic disorder, it will not work for every child. Sometimes this can be due to a lack of chemistry between the therapist and child; sometimes it can be due to a child's unwillingness to participate; and sometimes it can be due to issues with the therapist. When this occurs, it may result in a trial-and-error approach, with parents trying different therapists and different psychotherapies. This can be quite frustrating for both the parent and child.

Psychotherapy is not magic; it requires work and commitment from the therapist, the child, the parents, the child's siblings, teachers, etc. Parents and children often have the misconception that the therapist will make the child well. This is a sort of "magical thinking" that has probably been propagated by the media. Nothing could be further from the truth. Therapists are guides and human beings. Change coming as a result of psychotherapy requires work, commitment, and more work.

ESSENTIAL

Confidentiality is a major factor that establishes trust between the therapist and the client. If confidentiality is breached, clients will typically not trust the therapeutic environment and will often not benefit from treatment. The relationship between the therapist and the client has been empirically demonstrated to be one of the most important factors that contribute to positive outcomes in treatment.

A major consideration if you are planning on placing your child in psychotherapy is that the parents often do not have the right to know everything that is said in session due to confidentiality. Therapists are bound to protect the client's confidentiality, and in this case the client would be the child. There is a reason for this. If the child cannot totally trust the therapist, the child will not be totally honest in therapy. A lack of honesty is a major issue in therapy and often one of the biggest obstacles to realizing positive effects. The therapist will discuss all this with you before accepting the child into treatment; however, it is important for parents to understand that they have limited access to what occurs in the psychotherapy sessions. Some parents may find this to be an intolerable situation, but it is one that is undertaken with the best interest of the child in mind.

Alternative Treatments for Children

Most of the contemporary and alternative treatments discussed in earlier sections of this book were noted to have a lack of empirically validated evidence for their use in the treatment of panic disorder in adults. Therefore, most of these treatments would not be appropriate as first-line treatments for pediatric panic disorder. Some of them might be good adjunctive treatments, such as meditation, hypnotherapy, yoga, tai chi, exercise, and nutritional supplementation, but none of these can be recommended as a stand-alone treatment for pediatric panic disorder. One of the advantages to using some of these alternative treatments may be that the child does not feel like she is a patient or that she is "sick" when engaging in these actions. In addition, some of these activities can be incorporated by a good therapist in order to get the child to open up and talk in therapy. Certainly activities that can increase the child's confidence, give her a sense of control, and help her forget about her anxiety have potential uses as adjunctive treatments for pediatric panic disorder.

CHAPTER 17

Panic Disorder and the Elderly

People over the age of sixty-five years old represent a specialized group with its own specific needs and issues. In recent years, special fields of geriatric medicine and geriatric psychology have become increasingly important specialties because of the rising number of individuals in this subset of the population. This chapter briefly covers the manifestation of panic disorder in this population and the special needs of these individuals.

Defining Elderly People

The chronological age of sixty-five years old appears to be commonly accepted in most developed countries as the cutoff point for "elderly" individuals. However, this particular cutoff point does not transfer well to all countries, such as those in Africa where life expectancy is somewhat lower than it is in other countries. The United Nations agreed to set the age as sixty-plus years to refer to the "older" population, but there is no scientific or general agreement as to when a person actually becomes "elderly." Moreover, it is generally accepted that someone who is sixty years old or older in the United States today is a qualitatively different person than a sixty-year-old person was back in the early part of the twentieth century. The reason for this has to do with attitudes, better health care, and a better understanding of how to take care of oneself as one gets older. Because there is no actual scientific definition of what constitutes an "elderly" person, this book will define elderly as being over sixty or sixty-five years of age.

To complicate things even further, many researchers studying the elderly divide this category into even more designations that include:

1. The young old (sixty to sixty-nine years old)
2. The middle old (seventy to seventy-nine years old)
3. The very old (eighty years old and above)

FACT

Research has indicated that the three categories of the elderly represent socially and clinically significant designations. This is due to the vastly different historical events experienced by these groups and the effects these events produce. Moreover, the risk for many medical conditions, such as arthritis, Alzheimer's disease, etc., is significantly increased in the very old compared to the young old.

The reason for further defining this group of individuals is that there are significant differences in both the life experiences of these three groups and in the incidence and prevalence of different disorders and medical conditions. Researchers studying the elderly find it useful to divide the latest population into the separate categories. Whenever possible, this book will try to distinguish between the effects of panic disorder in the younger old compared to the older old; however, due to the limitations of the current research, this may not always be possible.

The important thing to keep in mind as you cover this section is that there can be some pretty significant difference in the way people react to having panic disorder, expressing panic disorder, and being treated for panic disorder depending on their generation. For example, someone who is 60 years old who has panic disorder will most likely have an entirely different outlook, an entirely different physique, and an entirely different set of expectations than does a person with a person with panic disorder who is 80 years old. The type of physical differences and dispositional differences observed between different generations of elderly people is often more pronounced than between the same age differences in younger groups.

What Does Panic Disorder Look Like in an Elderly Person?

Anxiety disorders remain the most common psychiatric disorder in the elderly, as they are in other age groups; however, the research is a bit mixed regarding the prevalence rates of anxiety disorders and panic disorder in people over sixty to sixty-five years of age. Nonetheless, the NCS-R study mentioned previously found that the prevalence rates for anxiety disorders and nearly all psychological disorders were lowest for individuals sixty-five years of age and older. Some studies have found higher rates of panic attacks for elderly people, whereas other studies have not replicated this finding. The available evidence suggests that anxiety disorders are as common in the elderly as they are in other age groups. Panic disorder, however, may be less common in elderly people than in younger age groups.

The diagnostic criteria for panic disorder and panic attacks in the DSM remain the same regardless of age, but there are several considerations for elderly individuals. Panic attacks in the elderly can present with a variety of symptoms, including the feeling that death is imminent, trembling, sweating, chest tightness, etc. Elderly individuals with panic disorder often report more physical symptoms and less psychological symptoms, perhaps due to a desire not to appear mentally vulnerable. Nonetheless, behavioral issues and concern about experiencing future panic attacks can be devastating for an elderly person, who may often hide these concerns. An elderly person experiencing a panic attack for the first time in his life should be evaluated in the same way that anyone who begins experiencing panic attacks is evaluated. This should begin with a full physical examination.

Because there is a higher prevalence of medical issues in elderly people and elderly people tend to be on significantly more medications than younger people, the sudden occurrence of panic attacks in an elderly person without a history of panic attacks is often a sign that there is a medical problem or medication problem. For instance, new combinations of medications or increasing doses of certain medications can lead to side effects that can bring on panic attack symptoms in the elderly. As people get older, disruptions in cardiac functioning or pulmonary functioning can create anxiety, which can also lead to the person experiencing panic attacks. An elderly person experiencing panic attacks for the first time should be evaluated by his physician as soon as possible.

ESSENTIAL

Elderly people often do not understand the meaning of their symptoms, especially symptoms that are new to them. Some research has suggested that the elderly may have fewer and less severe symptoms and exhibit less avoidant behaviors regarding their panic attacks than younger individuals experiencing panic attacks.

Medication effects are always a big concern in elderly individuals. It is extremely important that physicians know what medications elderly persons already taking before prescribing new medications (this means full disclosure of medications, supplements, herbs, etc.). Some elderly individuals are on so many medications that it is impossible to calculate the potential side effects from different combinations of medications. Moreover, elderly individuals often have different reactions to medications than do younger people. Before considering a potential panic disorder diagnosis in an elderly person who suddenly begins experiencing panic attacks is extremely important that the person undergo a medical evaluation with a full set of laboratory tests (e.g. blood work, thyroid evaluation, urine analysis, etc.) and an evaluation of the medications they are taking. Once medication issues or a medical condition that can result in panic attacks has been ruled out, there are some other considerations that should be explored.

Special Considerations with the Elderly

As mentioned above the occurrence of panic attacks in an elderly person warrants a full physical evaluation, as it would in anyone, but there are other special considerations for elderly individuals who experience panic attacks for the first time in their lives.

Depression

Panic attacks can be associated with depression at any age, and there is research to support the notion that panic attacks occurring for the first time in elderly individuals are often associated with depression. Often individuals who are severely depressed go through alternating feelings of anxiety, depression, and more even mood states. Depression is always a consideration in elderly people for a number of reasons and an elderly person experiencing panic attacks for the first time with no obvious medical causes should be evaluated for depression. There are a number of possibilities that could explain the association of panic attacks and depression in an elderly individual, including bereavement, feeling alone, and a loss of function or feeling useless due to declining health. If the panic attacks are related to depression and do not qualify for a diagnosis of panic disorder, the treatment would require addressing the reasons for the depression in the particular person and perhaps the use of medications.

Loss of a Spouse and Feelings of Isolation

Many elderly individuals will find themselves alone for the first time in many years. These people often have children who are grown and busy with their own families. They may have been separated from friends by either death or having to move to a new environment. Feeling isolated and alone often leads to depression. When an elderly person loses his or her spouse, the combination of bereavement and loneliness can lead to a number of different psychiatric symptoms, including panic attacks. Overwhelming fears of being isolated and alone can cause fear and panic to take over. Often the approach is to use medication for such individuals, but it may be more appropriate to use empathy, understanding, and companionship for such individuals. There is some older research that indicates that late-life panic disorder most often occurs in widowed elderly patients and is often mistaken for cardiac issues. Placement of an isolated individual in a senior's community with plenty of activities and peer support can often help.

Failing Health

The elderly often deal with declines in their physical well-being that can lead to anxiety and ultimately to panic attacks. Failing health of the elderly has been associated with depression, anxiety, and other psychiatric symptoms. For individuals who were formally very active and independent, the need to rely on others can be quite an adjustment. It can lead to feelings of despair, hopelessness, and panic. For elderly people not needing around-the-clock medical care, placement in a retirement community with same-age peers may be a solution as opposed to mere medication use.

Support

Certainly one of the best preventive measures against panic attacks in elderly individuals is social support. If at all possible, family members should try to include their elderly relatives in as many family activities as they can and should let these individuals know that they are not alone. Keeping an elderly person as active as possible can assist in the prevention of a number of problems. There is older research that elderly individuals who were given a plant or small pet to care for on a daily basis experienced fewer health issues than elderly individuals without such a task. Social support and feeling needed provides meaning and focus for a person's life, no matter what age he is.

ALERT

Social support is an important factor that influences physical and mental well-being throughout a person's life. Studies indicate that a person's perception of his social support system is even more important than the actual level of social support a person receives. Making an elderly person feel that he is not alone can be a potential remedy or preventative measure.

Dementia and Anxiety

Dementia is an umbrella term for a number of conditions that can be transient or permanent and lead to cognitive decline in elderly people. These conditions include Alzheimer's disease (the most common type of dementia), Lewy body dementia, dementia related to stroke, and many other conditions (including severe depression or medication effects). Studies have indicated that rates of anxiety are much higher in elderly individuals who have dementia than in elderly individuals without dementia. Elderly individuals with dementia are also prone to panic attacks. The treatment of choice for anxiety and panic attacks in elderly individuals with dementia is often medication as the dementia limits the effectiveness of other therapies. However, music therapy, light exercise, group activities, and other alternatives can also help.

Medication Use in the Elderly (Pros and Cons)

A person over the age of sixty-five should consider several issues before beginning medications for the treatment of anxiety or panic disorder. First, it is important to understand that medications do not cure panic disorder. Elderly people may believe that taking a medication "cures" the issue; however, this is not the case for panic disorder. Secondly, if the person is taking an SSRI or other antidepressant medication, she needs to be reminded that the effects of the medication typically do not begin to work until four to six weeks after the person starts taking it. Third, as many elderly people use a number of different medications, herbs, vitamins, etc., it is very important that they disclose what medications and supplements they are taking to the physician that is going prescribe an antidepressant or benzodiazepine for them. There are a number of side effects and interactions that can occur; some of them can be potentially dangerous. Finally, it is very important to instruct elderly people on how to take the medication they are prescribed. Antidepressants only work if taken on a regular basis; they are ineffective when only taken periodically. On the other hand, benzodiazepines can cause serious issues if they are taken regularly; their effectiveness is limited to the temporary relief of specific periods of anxiety.

It appears that benzodiazepines are the most commonly prescribed medication for elderly people with panic disorder, despite research indicating that SSRIs are also effective treatments. The research generally supports equivalent successful outcomes for medication treatment in elderly patients compared to younger patients with panic disorder; however, the research on the use of medications for elderly people with panic disorder is not nearly as extensive. Specific issues with the use of benzodiazepines in the elderly population include their potential for addiction and withdrawal symptoms when they are discontinued. The side effects of psychotropic medications continue to be a major reason for people discontinuing them over all age groups. The prescribing physician should be one with a specialty in geriatric psychiatry.

ESSENTIAL

The side effect profile of medications is a major concern for use with the elderly, and several studies report high attrition rates in this group of patients being treated with medications. It is suggested to use lower doses of medications for elderly people due to the extended half-life of many medications in the elderly. Lower doses may also limit the side effects.

Psychotherapy for the Elderly

The research on the use of CBT in the treatment of panic disorder for elderly patients is not as extensive as the research for the use of CBT with other patient groups; however, research indicates that CBT is an effective treatment for panic disorder in the elderly. Other types of psychotherapeutic interventions specifically aimed at elderly individuals with panic disorder appear to lack empirical validation due to a lack of research.

One of the cons regarding psychotherapy use in the elderly is that, as seen in the research on medication use in the elderly, there appears to be higher attrition rates (people dropping out) in older individuals than in younger age groups. There are several potential reasons for this: One reason is that psychotherapy benefits are typically not realized for several weeks, and people in the older age groups may lack patience in their anticipation of getting better. Another reason for high attrition rates is that teaching an individual who is in her upper seventies or in their eighties is somewhat different than teaching an individual who is in her thirties or forties. The approach to teaching and using progressive or guided relaxation and visualization techniques with elderly people should be different than it is with younger people as elderly people often need to understand the reason for doing something and need complete and practical explanations. It is probably more appropriate to have a trained geriatric psychologist work with individuals in their seventies and beyond, as these psychologists are trained to deal with this particular patient population.

Finally, psychotherapy is work; it is not simply a process of the therapist magically taking away someone's symptoms. Instead, it requires the collaboration between the therapist and client to address the problem in question, come up with an agreeable working solution to alleviate the problem, and then make adjustments as the solution is implemented. Sometimes people in psychotherapy do not understand this facet of therapy and become frustrated or disenchanted with therapy when they realize that they are responsible for working toward a solution to their issues. It may be that certain factions of people in their seventies and eighties are more prone to expecting quick results with little actual work on their own, due to older notions of how psychotherapy is supposed to work. While elderly people often have very good work ethics, they also needed to be committed to a particular activity before they devote time and energy to it. This requires that the therapist do a little "selling" regarding the techniques being taught, the need for the person to practice on their own, and how these relate to the person's specific situation. Complete explanations of the treatment and making sure the person understands and agrees with the treatment is often important. Elderly individuals may also require more time to learn new techniques and need to progress at a more even pace than younger individuals in therapy.

FACT

Geriatric psychologists and psychiatrists are specially trained to deal with individuals over the age of sixty. Geriatric issues are often best handled by someone who is trained specifically to work with this particular population. The "one size fits all" notion of a mental health professional has little empirical evidence to support it.

Alternative Treatments for the Elderly

Due to a lack of empirical evidence, many of the CAM treatments discussed in this book cannot be recommended as stand-alone treatments for panic disorder. Some of these treatments have potentially fewer risks associated with them, whereas others appear to have significant risks associated with them. There is a lack of empirical evidence associated with the vast majority of complementary and alternative medical treatments for panic disorder in the elderly, and little is known about their potential side effects in this population. It is the position of this book that any complementary and alternative treatment for someone over the age of sixty or sixty-five should only be considered under the supervision of a physician. Certainly light exercise, biofeedback, and meditation have potential uses with elderly populations, but the use of some of the herbs and other CAM techniques might bring about more complications.

CHAPTER 18

Agoraphobia

In the DSM-5, for the very first time, agoraphobia is treated as a separate disorder from panic disorder. Readers who may have been diagnosed with panic disorder before the DSM-5 was released may have gotten the diagnosis of panic disorder with agoraphobia or panic disorder without agoraphobia. Research has indicated that agoraphobia can occur in individuals who do not have panic disorder; however, agoraphobia is often associated with panic disorder and therefore warrants special discussion in this book.

Diagnosis of Agoraphobia

The diagnosis of agoraphobia now represents a separate psychological disorder. The main feature of agoraphobia is an intense fear or anxiety that is experienced in relation to the real or anticipated exposure to at least two of five specific situations. The DSM-5 defines these situations as:

1. Using any type of public transportation, such as a car, bus, plane, boat, etc.
2. Being in an open space.
3. Being in an enclosed place.
4. Being in a crowd or standing in line.
5. Being away from home alone.

These five specific situations are guidelines. For example, public transportation can be anything from a car to an airplane. An enclosed place can be a theater or restaurant, for example, whereas an open space can be nearly anywhere. There are several other diagnostic criteria that need to be met to be diagnosed with agoraphobia, including fear or avoidance that lasts for six months or more, significant distress or impairment in functioning, not being able to attribute the symptoms to another medical condition or psychiatric disorder, and fear that is out of proportion to the actual danger normally experienced in these situations. The fear one experiences in these situations may or may not lead to a full-blown panic attack. The agoraphobic situations are typically avoided by the individual (in fact, this is one of the diagnostic criteria). For example, someone who is afraid of using a car will walk for miles or not leave the house at all.

Active avoidance occurs when the person intentionally tries to minimize coming into contact with the feared situations. This avoidance can take any number of forms. The most severe forms of agoraphobia leave individuals homebound for lengthy periods, and in some cases these periods can last many years. The majority of people with agoraphobia also have some other mental disorder. Most frequently these comorbid disorders are other anxiety disorders, followed by depressive disorders, PTSD, and then alcohol abuse. The remission of agoraphobia without treatment of some type is very rare.

FACT

Females are twice as likely to have agoraphobia than males. The yearly prevalence rate of agoraphobia is recorded as 1.7 percent for those under sixty-five years old and 0.4 percent for those older than sixty-five. In two thirds of all cases of agoraphobia, the initial onset occurs before the person is thirty-five years old, but childhood onset of agoraphobia is rare.

Risk Factors and Complications

The comorbid diagnosis of panic disorder and agoraphobia presents some special challenges as compared to the diagnosis of panic disorder alone. According to the DSM-5, there are several associated risk factors with the development of agoraphobia in individuals.

Risk Factors Associated with Agoraphobia

There are several risk factors associated with the development of agoraphobia. One risk factor that turns up frequently is having a disposition toward the personality trait of *neuroticism*. Neuroticism has been identified as a risk factor for most of the other anxiety disorders as well. Neuroticism is a primary personality trait that has been identified by several different psychological personality theories. Neuroticism is often characterized by moodiness, anxiety, worry, guilt, depressed mood, and envy. Neuroticism is one of many personality traits, which are enduring attitudes and behaviors that a person displays over many different situations, often since adolescence or earlier. People who score high on the neuroticism trait on personality tests tend to have higher rates of anxiety disorders and depression. People predisposed toward neuroticism are often very self-conscious, have difficulty controlling urges, and have difficulty delaying their wants or needs.

Associated with neuroticism is a temperamental factor known as *anxiety sensitivity*, which is the belief that the symptoms of anxiety are harmful to the person who experiences them. Anxiety sensitivity is also commonly found in people who suffer from agoraphobia.

Negative events in childhood, such as the loss of a parent due to physical separation or death, being physically attacked, sexual abuse, etc., are often associated with an onset of agoraphobia. There is also some research that suggests that the families of people diagnosed with agoraphobia may be overprotective, but at the same time display reduced warmth in their interactions. Agoraphobia also appears to have the strongest genetic association of all the anxiety disorders.

Complications of Comorbid Panic Disorder and Agoraphobia

Probably the biggest issue in the treatment of comorbid panic disorder and agoraphobia is the tendency for people with agoraphobia to isolate themselves. The active avoidance behaviors associated with agoraphobia can become so severe that these individuals will limit their exposure to only a few areas that they have designated as being safe. Clinically these are sometimes referred to as the agoraphobic's "safe zones." These safe zones can create such restrictive boundaries for the person that they can interfere with all aspects of the person's life. It may be extremely hard to get the person with agoraphobia to leave her safe zone and come to therapy or to a doctor's office. Of course this can highly complicate attempts to try to provide treatment to an individual with panic disorder and to expose her to feared situations as a course of treatment.

ALERT

In many instances, people with agoraphobia will venture out of their safe zones with a trusted relative or companion. When this occurs, it is important for the treating clinician to take advantage and use the trusted individual in the treatment of the person with agoraphobia and/or panic disorder.

Comorbid panic disorder and agoraphobia may occur when the individual makes a connection between the onset of panic attacks and specific situations that may trigger the panic attacks. Typically these associations are made rapidly. Interestingly, this connection is often made in public places, such as being in a car, being at the movies, standing in line, etc. Few people make a connection between being at home and the onset of panic attack, because being at home is typically not viewed as a threatening place, even if one experiences a panic attack at home. In this case, the individual is more prone to making a connection between her thoughts or some other extraneous variable and the oncoming panic attack as opposed to thinking that being in her home is what triggers the panic attack.

Medication Use for Agoraphobia

SSRIs are often used in the treatment of panic disorder with agoraphobia. The SSRIs Paxil and Prozac are most often used for panic disorder with agoraphobia. These days it is less likely to be prescribed tricyclic antidepressants or an MAO inhibitor because even though they may be successful in the treatment of agoraphobia, there are more potential side effects, or in the case of MAO inhibitors, special diets are required.

Benzodiazepines are also commonly used in the treatment of panic disorder with agoraphobia. Most often these are Xanax or Klonopin. Treatment of comorbid agoraphobia and panic disorder with medications is typically performed under the same conditions as using medications for the treatment of panic disorder without agoraphobia. The same stipulations and pros and cons, discussed earlier in the section about the treatment of panic disorder using these medications, apply to the treatment of agoraphobia with these medications.

ESSENTIAL

The best long-term treatment program is probably using medications initially, then having the individual learn to control his panic disorder or agoraphobia via psychotherapy or some other treatment, and then tapering down on the medications as a person gets more control of himself.

Psychotherapy and Agoraphobia

CBT is the form of therapy most often used for treating the agoraphobic component of panic disorder if it occurs in an individual. There is some evidence that other types of therapy that are effective in treating panic disorder with agoraphobia are effective in treating agoraphobia alone as well. Psychotherapy for agoraphobia can be done on an individual basis or in a group environment. The pros and cons of treating panic disorder with particular psychotherapies, as discussed earlier, apply also to the treatment of panic disorder with agoraphobia and agoraphobia alone. One issue that often comes up in the treatment of agoraphobia is that the potential client does not want to leave his safe zone. Some therapists will begin treatment at the client's home or at one of his safe zones and then gradually try to improve the client to the point where he can come to the therapist's office. Some therapists may also offer phone sessions or sessions via e-mail; however, most therapists will not agree to providing the entire treatment in this manner, as resolving the agoraphobia is the goal of the treatment. The client will eventually have to come to the therapist as the client improves.

Alternative Treatments for Agoraphobia

There are some CAMs for panic disorder that, while they do not have the best empirically validated evidence as first-line treatments, appear to offer promise as adjunctive treatments. Typically these alternative treatments include things like some herbs and vitamins, meditation, yoga, etc., and their potential side effect profile does not qualify them as being potentially dangerous. On the other hand, there are some complementary and alternative treatments that may have some empirical evidence, but also have some potentially serious side effects (e.g., kava).

FACT

People with agoraphobia may find that support groups or self-help groups are especially useful adjunctive treatments. Going to one of these groups is often therapeutic in and of itself, as the person must leave his safe zone. Once a person gets to one of these groups, he can learn from other individuals that have the same problems/issues as he does.

At the time of this writing, it does not appear that any of the complementary and alternative treatments discussed earlier in this book can be recommended as stand-alone treatment for agoraphobia or panic disorder with agoraphobia. Some of the complementary and alternative methods discussed earlier may be helpful adjunctive treatments, such as exercise, meditation, etc. However, it is important that anyone attempting to use a complementary and alternative treatment notify his physician before doing so.

QUESTION

How do the three components of anxiety relate to agoraphobia?
The cognitive aspect of agoraphobia relates to thoughts and beliefs regarding perceived unsafe situations. The physiological component relates to the actual feelings of anxiety one experiences when he is exposed to one of these feared situations. The behavioral aspect manifests in a number of ways, including avoidance, needing a trusted friend to visit a feared place, and the need for safe places.

Addressing Agoraphobia

There are several considerations that can help an individual overcome some of the limitations of their agoraphobia. These are things to think about as one considers treatment.

Often agoraphobia occurs when a person begins to believe that they have a "safe zone" where they are protected from feeling anxious, experiencing panic attacks, or are protected from some other danger. The person begins to believe that by staying in the safe zone and limiting their activities they are able to prevent feeling anxious and avoid panic attacks. The safe zone can be one's home or can involve being within a certain distance from one's home; however, there are usually other factors involving the safe zones. Often people with agoraphobia will avoid any place where they believe they cannot escape if they are going to have a panic attack (clinicians often describe these situations as "traps"). A number of situations can be described as traps including traffic jams, standing in line, being in the store, being on the highway, etc. Therefore, it is important to understand that the safe zone it may not be just one's home but may also define boundaries and situations that the individual finds threatening. When considering what comprises one's safe zone make sure to include all of these factors. Having agoraphobia does not mean simply being homebound.

The next thing to consider is that when one that limits one's activities or travel these actions rarely result in positive outcomes. People who limit their activities may avoid some panic attacks; however, their anxiety does not disappear because they constantly worry about the next panic attack. Avoidance is actually a sort of "Catch-22" situation where the person avoids travel, but the more they avoid leaving their safe zone the more anxious they become regarding the next panic attack which results in more anxiety as they try to avoid future trips out of safe zones etc. This all leads to more and more anxiety in addition to complications that are associated with remaining in one's safe zone such as not visiting family, perhaps missing work, missing other social obligations, etc. In the final analysis limiting oneself to a "safe zone" only perpetuates the anxiety, it does not alleviate it.

The incentive behind agoraphobia is panic or anxiety. Having panic attacks actually deceives the person into treating these panic attacks as dangerous entities that one needs to protect oneself from. If panic attacks were actually dangerous and life-threatening it would be highly advantageous to create a strategy to protect one from them. However, panic attacks are not fatal and while they certainly imitate the type of feelings one may experience in real highly dangerous situations the panic attacks themselves are not really dangerous. The person gets tricked into thinking that the panic attacks are dangerous; however, no one has died from a panic attack and panic attacks *always* eventually go away and resolve over time. No one has perpetual panic attacks. When people trick themselves into thinking that their panic attacks are dangerous or life-threatening they simply increase their anxiety in the long run. As stated earlier, when people create elaborate strategies to avoid anxiety or panic attacks (such as in agoraphobic behavior) they are actually creating more anxiety than they controlling.

The problem will persist as long as the person allows themselves to be tricked into treating panic attacks as potentially fatal or dangerous situations and relying on avoidance behaviors to cope with them. The road to recovery from agoraphobia begins with understanding that while panic attacks are very distressing they are not potentially fatal. Moreover, panic attacks are highly treatable conditions. Once a person begins to gain control over their panic attacks there is no longer the need to employ safe zones to hide from them. The understanding that safe zones only exacerbate the situation and that panic attacks are not potentially dangerous experiences can help a person begin to address their situation, outline a strategy for change, and make positive changes.

In order to learn to deal with anxiety and agoraphobia the individual will at some point have to challenge their beliefs and learn that their safe zones are simply an illusion. There can be no resolution to agoraphobia if the person never ventures beyond their safe zones. Therefore, if one is truly committed to dealing with their agoraphobia one should understand that eventually they will have to be prepared to leave their safe zones and experience how to handle potential panic attacks away from these illusionary safe havens. There is no other way to confront agoraphobia except to actually face the situations one fears.

These considerations are extremely important for anyone who suffers from agoraphobia and wants to change their situation. Often, it helps to take an inventory of what situations a person believes to be safe situations and what situations are believed to be situations to be avoided. In addition, noting any special considerations such as a buddy a relative who makes one feel safe and allows one to venture outside their safe zones is also important. Defining the boundaries of one's safe zones and understanding that the safe zones are actually an illusion that are perpetuated by unrealistic beliefs and irrational thinking can help the person suffering from agoraphobia develop a strategy to begin to seek treatment.

The other thing to consider here is that agoraphobia rarely resolves on its own. Individuals who suffer from this type of thinking often feel that these feelings and their self-imposed restrictions "will just go away" over time; however, the research on agoraphobia indicates that this is most often not the case. Unless the person makes a decision to directly confront their beliefs and behaviors the situation will tend to be chronic and will perpetuate itself. One must confront one's fears in order to change.

CHAPTER 19

Stress and Panic Disorder

The relationship between stress and anxiety is well established. Likewise, there is an established relationship between stress and panic attacks. Research has repeatedly found an association between panic attacks (or having panic disorder) and stress. Many readers may believe that stress causes panic disorder or other psychological disorders; however, the relationship is not that simple. In this chapter, we will briefly look at some models of stress, see how stress is related to psychological/psychiatric disorders, and discuss the relationship between stress and panic disorder.

What Is Stress?

Stress consists of experiences or perceptions that result in *stress responses*. Stress responses are the series of physiological, bodily changes that occur as a result of some perceived or actual event. The term *stress* has been associated with negative or harmful effects; however, it is impossible to go through life without experiencing some type of stress. Not all stress is negative, and there are many instances where stress is actually a good thing (*eustress* is considered positive stress and *distress* is considered negative stress).

One of the oldest psychological theories is known as the *Yerkes-Dodson law*. This principle, developed in the early 1900s, describes the relationship between physical arousal, which can also be interpreted as anxiety or as perceived stress, and performance on various tasks. Although the theory has undergone some minor revisions, the basic principle of the Yerkes-Dodson law states that at low levels of stress (arousal) and at high levels of stress (arousal), performance on most tasks suffer, whereas at medium levels of stress (arousal), performance on most tasks is improved or optimal. The implication of the Yerkes-Dodson law is that certain levels of stress or physical arousal are motivating and optimal for performance on most tasks. This law is mediated somewhat by the complexity or familiarity of the task involved and personal perceptions; however, the general principle indicates that stress is not always a bad thing.

FACT

Response to stress varies. It is the person's notion of *perceived stress* that drives her physiological response to a particular event. For instance, a professional boxer will experience physical combat as less stressful than someone who has never had a fight, whereas the boxer may exhibit an extreme stress reaction when seeing a snake and someone else may not.

One Person's Stress Is Another Person's Motivation

Stress is considered to be potentially harmful when it is perceived as uncontrollable, chronic, and negative. There is a well-established empirical body of research that has looked at the various effects of chronic negative stressors in both animal models and in humans. This type of chronic psychological stress has been linked to negative changes in both physical health and mental health. Because it is the person's perception of stress that determines whether or not it is positive or negative, potentially harmful or not, or controllable or uncontrollable, all stressors that people experience are not equal.

When a stressor is perceived as controllable, it appears to have fewer deleterious effects on the organism than when it is perceived as uncontrollable. For example, most people consider getting married a positive event; however, you can probably also think of examples where couples getting married went through some very negative reactions to the wedding planning, issues with the wedding ceremony, etc. There can be a positive response to stressors that are perceived as healthy, and these often leave a person feeling fulfilled, whereas the negative responses to stressors perceived as threatening or uncontrollable can leave a person feeling drained and can affect a person's health.

ESSENTIAL

A famous rating scale for stressors came from researchers Homes and Rahe in the 1960s. The scale remains popular despite criticisms. The top-rated stressor for adults was death of a spouse, followed by divorce and marital separation. Marriage was the seventh top stressor. Death of a parent was the top stressor for children and adolescents, with marriage of a parent being rated third highest.

Models of Stress

One of the most often referenced theories concerning the effects of chronic negative stress on the body is the *general adaptation syndrome* proposed by endocrinologist Hans Selye. Selye's model was concerned with the effects of long-term stress and the breakdown of normal coping mechanisms that people utilize to deal with their short-term stressors. Seyle's theory incorporated the fight-or-fight response as it activates the hypothalamic-pituitary-adrenal (HPA; see below) axis. According to Selye, initially when people are exposed to a perceived stressful situation, the body goes into an *alarm mode*.

The fight-or-flight mechanism is activated, and hormones are released into the bloodstream to mobilize the body's resources to cope with stress (hormones are chemicals released into the bloodstream by glands that produce various effects in the body). This immediate reaction is productive in the short run but negative in the long run. A person's heart rate, blood pressure, and breathing levels increase; blood levels of certain hormones and glucose are subsequently elevated. These are signs of the second stage, *resistance*.

The body can only maintain functional active resistance for a short period of time. If the stress continues, the person's physical resources become exhausted (*exhaustion* is the final stage) and the person becomes susceptible to disease, mental health issues, and even death. Seyle's model has received empirical support, but has also been expanded by subsequent research.

Two Stress Response Systems

According to Selye, the activation of the HPA axis was responsible for the stress response. However, more recent theories have incorporated the sympathetic nervous system into the model, producing a two-system model of a response to chronic stress. Selye believed that stress activated the HPA axis, whether it was primarily physical or cognitive (mental). The modern view is that stressors can activate either the HPA axis or the sympathetic nervous system (or both). This leads to the release of epinephrine and norepinephrine (adrenaline and its counterpart, noradrenaline) from the adrenal medulla in the adrenal gland located above the kidneys. The effect of these hormones and other hormones that are released during perceived stress helps one adjust and meet the stressor in the short term, but if the stressor is chronic, these hormones can damage the system.

ALERT

There are cases of individuals with certain types of brain damage who suddenly no longer feel the anxiety associated with stress. These individuals have often been observed to make poor, impulsive decisions that they never made before the brain damage, such as gambling away their money, impulsively quitting their jobs, or ruining important relationships.

The Biology of the Stress Response

When you experience stress, a brain structure known as the hypothalamus sends signals to the pituitary gland in the brain and to the adrenal medulla above the kidneys (hence the hypothalamic, pituitary, adrenal, or HPA axis). The short-term response is the fight-or-flight response that is regulated by a pathway known as the sympathomedullary pathway (often abbreviated as SAM), where the brain affects the peripheral nervous system. The long-term response is regulated by the HPA axis. A very brief and simplified explanation of how these two systems work follows.

Stress and SAM

During stress, the hypothalamus in the brain activates the adrenal medulla, which is part of the autonomic nervous system and part of the adrenal glands located above the kidneys (recall that the autonomic nervous system consists of the sympathetic and parasympathetic nervous systems). Activation of the adrenal medulla results in secretions of epinephrine (adrenaline). The release of epinephrine leads to the arousal of the sympathetic nervous system (speeds up things) and the inhibition of the parasympathetic nervous system (slows down things). The epinephrine release results in increased heart rate, increased blood pressure, etc. The epinephrine release also leads to the release of glucose that is stored in the muscles. Glucose is the most important energy source in the body. The release of epinephrine directs blood flow to the muscles and prepares one for action in a stressful situation. This allows one to meet stressful challenges head-on by either resisting or running away. Once the stressor has been resolved, the parasympathetic nervous system acts to slow things down by bringing the body back to a balanced state (e.g., by releasing hormones such as norepinephrine).

The HPA

In the case of chronic stress, the hypothalamus stimulates the pituitary gland. The pituitary gland secretes a hormone called adrenocorticotropic hormone (abbreviated as ACTH). The release of ACTH stimulates the adrenal glands to produce cortisol. Cortisol maintains a steady supply of glucose that helps the person cope with the prolonged stressor. But cortisol release over the long run breaks down bodily tissues, including the liver. Cortisol also inhibits immune system functioning. The prolonged secretion of cortisol has been demonstrated to result in tissue damage, high blood pressure, slower rates of healing, and poor responses of the immune system to infection because these steroids continue to destroy healthy tissue over the long run.

Stressors also result in the release of peptide hormones in cells called cytokines. Cytokine release has been associated with inflammation of body tissues, and long-term stress can result in these inflammatory responses being chronic.

The immune system consists of certain organs and white blood cells that act as the body's defense mechanism against infections. The immune system responds to an invasion from unwanted infectious agents by either releasing specific types of cells to fight the infection (called cell-mediated responses) or producing specific chemicals to fight it (chemical-mediated responses). In the short term, the release of hormones prepares the body for action and is not damaging. In instances of chronic stress, cortisol can suppress the function of the immune system, leading to increased susceptibility to becoming sick.

The experience of anxiety, fear, and even panic attacks has been linked to the fight-or-flight response. Typically there is some trigger to set off anxiety or fear, but in cases like generalized anxiety disorder (where lower levels of anxiety are experienced every day) or an unexpected panic attack, the actual triggers may not be easy to define or may consist of stimuli not normally considered fear- or anxiety-provoking.

Chronic Stress and the Brain

Chronic stress has also been implicated in affecting certain areas of the brain. For instance, a brain area known as the hippocampus, which is crucial to the formation of new memories, appears to be very susceptible to the effects of chronic stress. The hippocampus has a very dense number of glucocorticoid receptors (cortisol is a glucocorticoid) that are designed to terminate the effects of stress. In cases of chronic stress, the high glucocorticoid levels in the hippocampus lead to a reduction in the ability of the cells to develop a response to, and learn from, new experiences.

FACT

The fight-or-flight response appears to occur in all mammals experiencing stress. However, in humans there appears to be a great deal of variation in both the level and type of hormones released in different individuals and in response to different types of stressors. Therefore, the above explanation as to how the stress response occurs in the body is a general one and is probably not complete.

Can Stress Cause Psychiatric/Psychological Disorders?

A cause is an action or event that produces a specific action or event itself. The key term in this definition is the idea that a cause produces a *specific* action or event itself. A cause can also produce a number of specific actions or events instead of just one; however, causes produce predictable consequences. You might be under the impression that a child who experiences physical or sexual abuse will develop some type of psychiatric disorder when he gets older. Many of the disorders discussed in the DSM-5 list psychological trauma or physical trauma as a child as a significant risk factor for the development of the disorder. Certainly experiencing traumatic events during childhood is a very powerful risk factor for the development of problems later on; however, most people experiencing some type of trauma, as young children or adults, do not develop a mental illness. Likewise, the research does not support the notion that stress causes any specific psychiatric disorder, but severe stress can be a risk factor for many different psychological issues.

Risk Factors versus Causes

The answer to the question "Does stress cause psychiatric/psychological disorders?" lies in the definition of cause and effect. If we adhere to the strict definition of cause and effect versus the definition of a risk factor, the answer to that question is "No." If we define risk factors as types of causes, then it is much easier to answer "yes" to that question.

Risk factors are events or actions that increase the probability of developing a particular disease or disorder. Having a single risk factor alone is typically not enough to produce the disorder. Risk factors tend to interact with each other in ways that are not understood very well by most researchers and clinicians. For instance, most genetic associations for most of the psychological/psychiatric disorders are risk factors and not direct causes. This is because not everyone with the genetic markers develops the associated psychological disorder (there are some genetic mutations that can be directly linked to some disorders, but these are rare).

Likewise, stress alone is not enough to produce a mental disorder in an individual. Therefore, the strict answer to the question posed by this section is that stress does not *cause* psychiatric disorders in people; however, stress is often a very powerful risk factor that contributes to the development of mental illness, and anyone who experiences a traumatic event or is under chronic stress is at significant risk for the development of physical health issues and/or mental health issues. Recall the diathesis-stress model discussed earlier.

FACT

Posttraumatic stress disorder (PTSD) occurs as the result of some life-threatening traumatic experience or witnessing someone undergo such an experience. However, most people who experience life-threatening events, like war, rape, etc., do not develop PTSD. The life-threatening event associated with PTSD interacts with a number of other risk factors that increase the probability that someone will develop this disorder.

Stress and Panic Disorder: Special Issues

A very consistent research finding is that there is an association between experiencing a high number of negative life events and experiencing the first panic attack in people who later are diagnosed with panic disorder. One of the observations about the association is that some of these patients are able to identify the negative life events as a precipitating event that they believe caused their first panic attack (however, this is their impression and does not represent an actual cause-and-effect relationship). The research also indicates that often when samples of individuals with panic disorder are compared to individuals without panic disorder (normal controls), the panic-disordered individuals as a group report significantly more negative life events within some specified time (usually a year or so) prior to being diagnosed with panic disorder than do normal controls for the same time period.

Trying to Make Sense of the Findings

There are a couple of caveats that must be discussed:

First, the studies are correlational and can only report associations; they are not able to determine cause-and-effect relationships or report that having more negative life events causes the first panic attack.

Secondly, it may be that people who develop panic attacks or panic disorder often remember normal life events or even negative life events as being more negative than they were and associate them with the panic attack compared to normal controls. There is some research that indicates that people with panic disorder report more overall significant life events that are both positive and negative than do normal controls. The inherent need for people to search for causes often leads to making associations that really do not exist or are not significantly related.

Third, the relationship might be in reverse; an undiagnosed panic disorder may predispose someone to place himself in more negative situations. For example, significant negative life events commonly remembered by those with panic disorder prior to the first panic attack include marital separation or marital conflict, domestic quarreling, or separation from a significant person in one's life. Disconfirming evidence for this notion might be that there are a number of individuals who report the death or illness of a significant other or events like miscarriages as the precipitating events of their panic attacks.

Finally, recall that stressful events are risk factors and not direct causes. Perhaps the most plausible explanation of the data is that stressful negative life events interact with other factors, including genetic predispositions, to make a person more vulnerable to experiencing anxiety and a panic attack. It is clear that anxiety is experienced differently in people and that the effects of negative life experiences and even traumatic experiences are not the same for everyone.

Therefore, the association of negative life events with a first panic attack is best defined as a risk factor that combines with other risk factors in order to produce a later panic attack or a diagnosis of panic disorder.

Social Support

One additional significant finding is that people diagnosed with panic disorder rate their perceived social support network lower than normal controls. This finding is consistent and indicates that people vulnerable to panic disorder rate their social support networks as less supportive. In terms of the applicability of such findings, it may very well be that people who are diagnosed with panic disorder may benefit from adjunctive family therapy or some type of group therapy that bolsters or increases their sense of perceived social support. A lack of social support or a perceived lack of social support may be another predisposing risk factor for the development of panic disorder.

The most common explanation for the interaction of the inherent and environmental factors in producing mental disorders is the *diathesis-stress model*. The diathesis is some type of inherent factor, such as a genetic vulnerability to a specific event or behavior that by itself will not trigger that behavior. Environmental events, such as stress, can interact with the diathesis to produce mental health issues.

When Are Stress and Panic Disorder Related?

There is no easy answer to this question. The reason for this is simple: Stress, negative life events, and lower levels of perceived social support are significant risk factors for the development of a number of different physical and psychiatric disorders. Relationships between high levels of stress, negative life events, and low levels of perceived social support have been found for cardiovascular disease, diabetes, chronic pain, multiple sclerosis, birth complications, tuberculosis, nearly all psychological problems, and many other issues. Therefore, stress and the related issues of negative life events and perceived social support appear to be general risk factors that can predispose certain people to certain types of diseases or disorders. There is no consistent method of predicting what type of stressor will lead to what type of particular disorder.

On the other hand, it is quite clear that someone who is already diagnosed with panic disorder has a better prognosis if these issues are addressed. The severity and outcome of treatment can be affected by such events. The experience of anxiety and of panic attacks, worry associated with future attacks, and other symptoms of panic disorder are exacerbated by perceived stress, a lack of social support, and experiencing life events that are perceived in a negative manner. Reducing stress or learning how to cope with stressors, bolstering perceived social support, and attempting to minimize the number of negative life events that a person is subject to can be useful as adjunctive approaches in the treatment of any mental disorder or physical problem. Therefore, any intervention program aimed at panic disorder should also target stress reduction techniques and social support building.

FACT

Stress reduction techniques are a big component of most psychotherapy interventions for panic disorder. This is one of the reasons that relapse rates are lower for individuals completing psychotherapy than for other interventions, such as medication. Stress reduction is also a component of meditation, yoga training, and several other CAMs. Stress reduction techniques teach coping strategies for the future.

CHAPTER 20

Other Issues

There are several other important issues to consider if you are dealing with panic disorder. These issues can complicate the treatment of panic disorder and also can sometimes be so severe that they themselves are comorbid mental disorders, whereas in at least one case the issue is highly overstated and may be more a product of lore than of actual fact. This chapter will look at five major issues commonly associated with having a diagnosis of panic disorder.

Suicide and Panic Disorder

Being diagnosed with panic disorder is associated with a number of negative factors, including high levels of occupational, social, and physical disabilities. People with panic disorder have the largest number of medical visits among the anxiety disorders, and panic disorder results in considerable economic costs due to lost productivity, increased medical expenses, and other factors. Often people with a comorbid diagnosis of panic disorder and agoraphobia have the strongest associations with these variables. Another significant risk factor for people experiencing anxiety disorders is having thoughts of hurting themselves or committing suicide.

There has been quite a bit of research over the past fifteen to twenty years that has indicated that people who have suicidal thoughts and people who attempt suicide are significantly more likely to have some type of psychiatric disorder. Recent research has indicated that people diagnosed with an anxiety disorder are at a high risk to have suicidal ideations (thoughts). This finding should not come as a surprise. However, having thoughts about suicide is not the same thing as attempting suicide. Since the majority of actual suicide attempts are preceded by significant periods of having suicidal ideations, we could easily conclude that having suicidal ideations is a significant risk factor for attempting suicide. The research confirms this conclusion.

ESSENTIAL

Having suicidal ideations is always serious. Someone claiming to be suicidal should be evaluated by a qualified mental health professional as soon as possible. In nearly every case, *such claims should not be assumed to be idle threats.*

Some research has indicated that individuals who attempt suicide are often diagnosed with at least one anxiety disorder. The research has also indicated that being diagnosed with panic disorder, agoraphobia, or some other type of phobia is a significant risk factor for having suicidal ideations and for attempting suicide, even after adjusting for other comorbid disorders. In addition, the risk of suicide attempts for other psychological disorders increases if the person has a comorbid panic disorder or experiences panic attacks. It is clear from the research that someone diagnosed with panic disorder is in a high risk group to experience suicidal ideations and to therefore in a higher risk group to attempt suicide.

Handling Suicidal Ideations

This section is designed as a guideline for readers. Anyone who suspects someone of being suicidal or anyone who is having suicidal ideations should be immediately evaluated by a licensed mental health professional.

Questioning someone about her feelings will not increase the potential for her to hurt herself. Clarifying if the person actually has a plan or is just feeling suicidal is important. Asking simple questions like "Are you thinking about hurting yourself?" or "Do you know how (or when) you would do this?" is appropriate.

Warning signs associated with suicide, aside from someone actually stating that they are suicidal, include the person having mood swings; being preoccupied with violence, death, or dying; wanting to withdraw and be left alone; increased use of alcohol or drugs; giving away belongings for no apparent reason; and saying goodbye or writing farewell notes to close friends and relatives. When someone is claiming to be suicidal, it is important that she not be left alone. It is also important to understand that getting emergency help may save the person's life. People having serious suicidal ideations often do not think about seeking help for themselves. Calling other family members or friends, calling the authorities, or taking the person to the emergency room are all viable options if a person is suspected of being actively suicidal. The person may need to be hospitalized. Do not try and treat such a person without professional help.

If you have suicidal thoughts, it is extremely important to discuss these with a very close friend or relative immediately. Do not keep them to yourself. If you have no one to speak to you can easily access several hotlines via the internet (see Appendix B for some direct access sites) or you can go to a clinic or ER and discuss these with the medical staff there. Do not wait; take action if you start to have these thoughts and you feel that your situation is hopeless. Do not fool yourself into thinking that no one cares or life is not worth living. Talk with someone immediately.

Substance Abuse and Panic Disorder

There are studies that have actually found that people with panic disorder are less likely to use alcohol compared to people with another psychiatric diagnosis. However, there have also been findings that indicated that people who have panic attacks might be more likely to self-medicate with alcohol and sedatives than people who do not experience panic attacks. These findings indicate that it is highly likely that someone who is experiencing panic attacks or has been diagnosed with panic disorder is likely to attempt to use substances, such as alcohol or sedatives, to self-medicate or control his anxiety *if he believes* that the substances will work in that manner. When individuals believe that the use of a particular substance will help with their anxiety, they are more prone to use it often, rationalize their use even if they experience negative consequences as a result of their use, and therefore are at increased risk to develop some type of substance abuse problem.

There are also smaller groups who are diagnosed with panic disorder that initially are brought into treatment for some type of substance abuse disorder. After an evaluation is performed, it is discovered that these people are suffering from panic disorder and their substance abuse is an independent comorbid diagnosis. When the figures are examined closely, it appears that about 20 percent of the people with an anxiety disorder also have some type of substance abuse disorder, and that about 20 percent of the people diagnosed with substance abuse disorder also have an anxiety or depressive disorder. For those with panic disorder and a comorbid substance abuse disorder, it is not often clear which came first.

In general, the research indicates that individuals who have agoraphobia or social phobia tend to begin using alcohol after they experience the symptoms of these disorders. For instance, someone with agoraphobia who is afraid of leaving his home, but must do so daily to go to work, may begin using alcohol to curb his anxiety. This makes it easier for him to leave home, but tolerance to these effects develops rapidly and he may begin using increasing doses. The substance abuse becomes a method of dealing with the anxiety disorder. However, the research on panic disorder and substance abuse indicates that people who have a comorbid diagnosis of panic disorder and substance abuse tend to start using substances about the same time they start having panic attacks. This finding suggests that the use of alcohol or other substances may precipitate panic attacks in these individuals and that the initial use may be in response to experiencing lower levels of anxiety that they then attempt to control on their own.

The comorbid diagnosis of substance abuse or dependence and anxiety disorders such as panic disorder often necessitates specialized treatment for both disorders. The research indicates that treating the substance abuse disorder typically does not make the anxiety disorder go away. This indicates that these two are separate disorders, but interrelated. The presence of both substance abuse disorder and panic disorder can complicate treatment. For example, benzodiazepines are highly addictive, so their use in a patient with panic disorder and a comorbid substance abuse disorder should be tightly controlled. Other medications with lower abuse and dependence potential, such as antidepressants, are often used, but their effects are not immediate. CBT is also often the treatment of choice for both the substance abuse problem and the panic disorder, but again the effects of CBT take some time before they are realized. If a person has a severe physical dependence on alcohol or another drug, the withdrawal from the drug will create anxiety and could result in the experience of a panic attack. Such individuals should be closely monitored by a medical team and mental health team as they go through their detoxification period.

FACT

Withdrawal from substances can induce panic attacks. You may visualize the withdrawal from drugs as a rather dramatic series of events, as depicted in the media; however, having a hangover is a sign of withdrawal. It is not unusual for people suffering hangovers to experience anxiety, elevated blood pressure, and increased heart rates. These symptoms can lead to panic attacks.

Panic Disorder and Vulnerability to Other Psychological Disorders

A common observation regarding the diagnosis of panic disorder in clinical settings is that panic disorder alone occurs rather infrequently. Panic disorder prevalence is much higher in individuals who are diagnosed with other psychiatric disorders, especially anxiety disorders like agoraphobia, mood disorders such as major depression and bipolar disorder, PTSD, and alcohol abuse disorders. Typically panic disorder is reported to have an earlier age of onset than other comorbid disorders. This suggests that having a diagnosis of panic disorder may be a risk factor for the development of other psychiatric disorders; however, sometimes people are diagnosed with panic disorder following the diagnosis of another psychological disorder.

According to the DSM-5, in individuals who have panic disorder and comorbid depression, about one-third will develop depression first and in the other two-thirds the depression occurs at the same time or following the onset of panic disorder. Most studies that investigate the comorbidity of other psychological disorders with panic disorder find that comorbid panic disorder and depression are quite common. With the designation of agoraphobia as a separate disorder, one can expect high rates of comorbid depression, panic disorder, and agoraphobia as well. Most studies indicate that the panic disorder precedes the agoraphobia in the majority of these cases. Thus, for depression and agoraphobia, it appears that having a diagnosis of panic disorder increases the vulnerability to developing these disorders.

Recall that panic disorder is not diagnosed in cases of people who experience panic attacks due to a medical condition or another anxiety disorder; however, higher rates of panic attacks are reported in certain psychiatric disorders. These include posttraumatic stress disorder and substance abuse disorders. The high rate of comorbidity with other psychiatric disorders and the potential for nonpsychiatric causes for panic attacks highlight the need for a complete physical and psychiatric evaluation by qualified individuals before one is diagnosed with panic disorder.

ESSENTIAL

Panic attacks have been observed in people diagnosed with a number of mental disorders, including bipolar disorder, impulse-control disorders, and substance abuse disorders. The presence of panic attacks is associated with an increased risk for later development of an anxiety disorder, mood disorder, and possibly other disorders, such as personality disorders.

Comorbidity and Vulnerability

Some researchers have suggested that the high rates of comorbidity in psychiatric disorders (and hence the theory that having one psychiatric disorder is a risk factor making one vulnerable to develop other psychiatric disorders) has more to do with the way the DSM series has approached diagnostic issues. The late Lee Robins, distinguished professor of psychiatric epidemiology, acknowledged that in the DSM series since the creation of the DSM-III, the same symptom could not appear in more than one disorder. For example, the specific symptom of anxiety, common in the diagnosis of clinical depression, could not appear in the diagnostic criteria for major depression. The way depression is presented in the DSM does not allow for the presence of anxiety in a patient with depression to be recorded as a symptom or as a specifier for the diagnosis. The concurrent diagnosis of major depression and panic disorder is encouraged by this policy, which is not explicitly stated by the APA but has been noted by distinguished psychiatrists such as Lee Robins.

A second reason for the large number of comorbidities in DSM diagnostics is the huge increase in the number of diagnostic categories in recent DSM volumes. For example, it is rare to see a patient with a diagnosis of an anxiety disorder that does not fulfill the requirement for another anxiety disorder. Such psychiatric categories as anxiety disorders, personality disorders, and so forth do not have clear boundaries among them and lead to the vulnerability to multiple diagnoses. Within the DSM diagnostic classification of mental disorders, there is a lack of a rule system that establishes a hierarchy in the disorders. For example, a person diagnosed with schizophrenia (a serious psychotic disorder) can also be diagnosed with panic disorder if she experiences panic attacks. In reality it may well be that the panic attacks experienced in schizophrenia (or depression or some other disorder) are different than the panic attacks a person with panic disorder experiences, or are a consequence of schizophrenia itself and therefore are best conceptualized as a symptom of this disorder. The worry and behavioral changes the person experiences may be related to her schizophrenia. Some researchers suggest that the more severe disorder, such as schizophrenia or a personality disorder, should be placed in a higher level of the hierarchy of symptoms and that other symptoms, such as anxiety, depression, etc., should be considered manifestations of these disorders.

ALERT

People who are diagnosed with panic disorder will most likely be diagnosed with at least one other psychological disorder. The positive result of this is that all of the issues get treated; the negative result is that people may get the impression that they are "sicker" than they really are. In some cases, this may interfere with positive treatment effects.

Cognitive Decline and Panic Disorder

There are a number of research findings that associate having a diagnosis of a psychiatric disorder with decreased cognitive capabilities. Qualitatively, many individuals diagnosed and treated for psychiatric disorders often complain of memory problems and cognitive decline. In many instances, these symptoms may be associated with the medications that are prescribed to these individuals, and in others they may be related to the psychiatric disorder itself. Individuals who suffer from anxiety disorders such as panic disorder do not appear to suffer significant cognitive problems as a result of their psychiatric disorder; however, when one is experiencing extreme anxiety, it is difficult to think clearly. Once the anxiety is reduced, people tend to be able to function at their normal cognitive capacity.

The cognitive dysfunction associated with panic disorder is most often confined to attention deficits and paying excessive attention to or experiencing hyperarousal by stimuli that are perceived as threatening. However, attention or attentional capacity appears to be affected to some extent in diagnoses with almost any psychiatric disorder. Fewer studies have found deficits in memory to be associated with the diagnosis of panic disorder, and it may be that individuals who have comorbid substance abuse disorders or who are taking benzodiazepines for the panic disorder experience memory issues. There is little evidence that having a diagnosis of panic disorder is consistently associated with decreased memory capabilities. There is also little evidence that having a diagnosis of panic disorder leads to an intellectual decline. The findings also suggest that mental processing speed may be accelerated in panic disorder and other anxiety disorders, especially mental processing speed for potentially anxiety-provoking stimuli. This would be consistent with learning theory via classical and operant conditioning.

FACT

The research suggests that having a diagnosis of panic disorder does not significantly increase the risk for developing cognitive issues. Other conditions, such as substance abuse or taking medications such as benzodiazepines, have certainly been shown to affect cognition; however, it appears that people with panic disorder do not normally suffer a cognitive decline due to their anxiety disorder.

Psychotropic Medication Use and Long-Term Effects

The medical profession, the pharmaceutical industry, and aspects of the media have put forth the impression that psychotropic medications are effective and safe in the long run. However, some of the research seems to paint a different picture. For example, a re-evaluation of the data used by the FDA to approve the release and marketing of several major antidepressant medications indicated that these medications were not more effective than an active placebo in relieving depression in those initial studies. A study by the World Health Organization indicated that recovery from schizophrenia in Third World countries, where medication use was not the norm, was much higher than in industrialized countries, where medication use was common. There has been evidence that the long-term use of antidepressant medications is associated with a rise in the diagnosis of bipolar disorder. Several studies looking at the longevity of individuals taking psychotropic medications have suggested that there is an association between long-term psychotropic medication use and decreased longevity. The issues are confounded by other clinical evidence that seems to suggest that these medications work and that they are generally safe.

Do Psychotropic Medications Work?

Because people's belief systems heavily affect their response to treatments and the type of subjective symptoms like those occurring in most psychiatric disorders, there are strong placebo effects associated with any treatment for nearly any psychiatric disorder. These placebo effects are much less pronounced for real physical diseases like cancer or tuberculosis, but smaller placebo effects have been observed in these disorders as well. Even if antidepressant medications are no more effective than active placebos, it would be incorrect to state that they do not work; however, it would also be incorrect to state that they are effective medications, as a medication should be more effective than a placebo. Moreover, it is unethical for a physician to prescribe a placebo in the treatment of any disease or disorder. Therefore, the findings suggesting that antidepressant medications may be no more effective than active placebos in treating depression should create ethical dilemmas in psychiatrists and physicians, but apparently this has not happened, as these medications are still commonly prescribed. There is a large body of evidence that suggests that these medications do relieve depression and anxiety in some people, but the mechanism by which this works is questionable at best.

Benzodiazepines are effective short-term solutions for the severe anxiety people experience during a panic attack. However, tolerance to these medications develops rapidly. What this means is that a person will need more and more of the drug to achieve the same effect over time. The development of tolerance and subsequent withdrawal symptoms when these medications are discontinued make these medications highly addictive. There are a number of other side effects associated with their use. Most physicians would agree that using alcohol to curb anxiety is a potentially counterproductive solution in the long term, but many of the same physicians continue to prescribe benzodiazepines for anxiety and panic attacks over the long term.

Psychotropic medications are tools that can be used appropriately or can be abused. Concerning the treatment of panic disorder, the empirical evidence is strongly in favor of interventions such as CBT, other forms of psychotherapy, and adjunctive treatments that are usually considered CAM treatments, such as meditation, yoga, mild exercise, inositol, and perhaps some other vitamins and herbs. Psychotherapy should only be performed by licensed, qualified individuals, and complementary and alternative treatments should only be used under the supervision or acknowledgment of a physician. Psychotropic medications can enhance the effects of these treatments; however, the goal should be to help a person get control over his panic disorder and then discontinue the medications. When the medications are discontinued and no other form of treatment, such as CBT, is used, the symptoms the person was experiencing typically return.

QUESTION

With all of these treatments, what do I choose?
Stick with treatments that offer empirical validation. Try to fit the treatment with your needs and preferences. Appendix C of this book offers a quick survey to help guide people toward the treatment approach that may be suitable for them.

The Long-Term Effects of Psychotropic Medication Use

Earlier in this book, the use of kava for the treatment of anxiety and panic disorder was discussed. There has been evidence that kava use may present some potential health risks; however, there is also evidence that the long-term use of psychotropic medications presents health risks as well. Again, to many it appears that the FDA is biased in its recommendations. The bottom line here is that there is evidence on both sides of the fence for treatments like kava and psychotropic medications. There is evidence that psychotropic medication use in the long term leads to more deleterious health effects and decreased longevity, and there is other evidence that the use of these medications over the long term is beneficial and does not lead to serious issues.

The fact of the matter is, no one really knows how any particular individual will react over the long term to exposure to these medications, and the research on the long-term effects of most of these medications is lacking or contains significant methodological flaws. There is sufficient evidence to question the efficacy of antidepressant medications, such as SSRIs. There are also quite a number of documented potential side effects and interactions that can occur with the use of these drugs, as anyone watching a commercial on television can attest to. If methods that have relatively few side effects and low risks can effectively treat panic disorder in individuals, it makes more sense to concentrate on these and attempt to discontinue medication use in the long run. Unfortunately, most medical doctors (this includes most psychiatrists) do not appear to view the use of psychotropic medications as temporary measures. This leads to the false impression that a person taking psychotropic medications for anxiety or depression needs to be on them for the long term. Nothing could be further from the truth.

FACT

It is not uncommon to hear someone say she's going to "double-up" on her antidepressants because of some depressing event. Don't do that. The research has indicated that beyond the maximum suggested dosage, these medications do not increase in effectiveness (if they are effective at all). Someone taking these medications should never alter the dosage unless instructed to do so by her physician.

CHAPTER 21

Panic Disorder and the Future

Suppose for a minute that you have undergone treatment and that the treatment has been successful in dealing with your panic attacks and panic disorder. What happens next? This chapter discusses some of the long-term ramifications of dealing with panic disorder in remission as a result of some type of effective intervention. The principles in this chapter are directed at individuals who have successfully dealt with panic attacks and panic disorder, but they can also be applied to someone currently in treatment for panic disorder. Often prevention is the best treatment, and being proactive is better than simply being reactive.

Moving Forward

Treatment has been successful. Are you cured of panic disorder? The notion of a cure comes from medical models of illness that are associated with eradicating diseases and conditions that are caused by external agents, such as viruses, bacteria, or other pathogens. When considering the treatment successes of psychological disorders such as panic disorder, the term *cure* is not an appropriate method to describe the outcome of the treatment. The reason for this is that even though a person may gain a sense of control over his situation, there are no external agents that have been eradicated leading to his sense of control. People still have their genetics; they still have their past experiences; they still are subject to situations that are associated with a risk for relapse; and their biology may have been altered in such a manner to leave them potentially more susceptible to anxiety compared to people who have not experienced panic attacks or panic disorder.

Psychological disorders are most likely never "cured" in anyone who undergoes successful treatment, but they are often managed. Nonetheless, the potential for a return to previous behaviors is always possible, and anyone undergoing treatment for any psychiatric disorder should be instructed regarding how to recognize and avoid future potential pitfalls that could lead to a relapse. One of the difficulties with the exclusive medical management of panic disorder is that it does not distinguish between a lapse and a relapse, whereas other treatments that do not rely solely on medications understand this difference. Understanding this difference is extremely important for people who have been treated for panic disorder or any other psychiatric disorder.

Lapse and Relapse

When living with a psychological disorder that is in remission, it is extremely important to understand the difference between the actual *relapse* of the disorder and the more common, but less serious, notion of a *lapse*. Understanding and recognizing the difference between these two is extremely important in dealing with future issues associated with past behaviors that have been dysfunctional.

A *lapse* is a relatively common urge or thought to return to former ways of behaving and/or thinking. Lapses are quite common in people who have been treated for psychiatric disorders, such as depression, anxiety disorders, substance abuse problems, etc. A lapse should be viewed as merely a temporary setback in one's thinking that is relatively common and offers the individual an opportunity to practice what he learned in treatment. The danger is to view a lapse as a sign that treatment did not work or that one is powerless against former ways of thinking and behaving. Nothing could be further from the truth. These types of thoughts or urges are quite common in many types of behaviors that people try to change, even behaviors that are not considered to be dysfunctional or harmful. You should treat lapses as an opportunity to practice your coping skills.

It might be beneficial to differentiate between a lapse and a slip. A lapse would be a returning thought, and a *slip* may occur as a result of a lapse. A slip is a very brief temporary return to past behaviors that is corrected before any potential damage can be realized. For example, someone on a diet may slip and eat a piece of cake once or twice, but then immediately go back on the diet, so the overall result is not detrimental. Slips can quickly result in relapses if not corrected. One should avoid slips by immediately recognizing lapses and having a plan to deal with lapses.

A *relapse* is more serious than a slip or a lapse. A relapse is an actual return to a sustained pattern of behaving or thinking that occurred in the past, but that one has previously changed. The key difference here is the phrase "*return to a sustained pattern*." Lapses that are unrecognized or unchecked can lead one to relapse.

With respect to panic disorder, a relapse would be a return to the fearful and avoidance behaviors that are associated with anticipating future panic attacks and/or the return of panic attacks in an individual who did not demonstrate these behaviors for significant periods of time. There are several steps one can take to avoid relapses:

1. Understand the difference between a lapse and a relapse. Take appropriate action during lapses.
2. Learn to identify situations that are high-risk for lapses and relapses.
3. Review what has been learned in treatment regarding high-risk situations and how to handle them.
4. Routinely practice the skills learned in treatment.

5. Schedule periodic "booster sessions" with a therapist in order to maintain good problem-solving skills.
6. Develop a coping card with written strategies and other information to outline steps in dealing with lapses.

FACT

If a person uses only psychotropic medications in the treatment of panic disorder, relapse prevention can only consist of having the medications prescribed again. For many who experience normal lapses, this means long-term use of medications with potentially disrupting side effects. It may be more productive to learn coping skills that can be used in the future as opposed to using only medical management techniques.

Living with Panic Disorder

Living with a devastating psychiatric disorder such as panic disorder is not easy. The very nature of the disorder is such that it affects a person's life on all levels. No person should have to live with the stress of having multiple unexpected panic attacks, constant worry as to when the next panic attack will come, and other associated behaviors that occur with panic disorder. Treatment outcomes for panic disorder are very positive. There are always some people who will not respond to even the best interventions; however, unless there are extenuating circumstances, anyone with panic disorder can receive relief from an empirically validated treatment approach. In some cases, such an approach may require the combination of two or more different treatment methods, but no one should be a prisoner of panic disorder.

If you have a psychiatric disorder, you should also learn the pitfalls of comparing your issues with the issues of others who either have the same or different disorders. While one can learn from the experiences of another, it is counterproductive to judge one's success in treatment compared to someone else. Everyone is an individual with differences, and not everyone will respond to the same treatment in the same manner. Some people respond more quickly than others; some people respond more slowly than others.

The only thing that should matter to an individual being treated for panic disorder is that *he is making progress.* It is important to remember that no one in treatment is in a competition or in a race with someone else to see who can get better more quickly. Remember to learn from the experiences of others, but do not judge your own experience by the experiences of others.

Life after Treatment

The empirical evidence strongly supports the notion that psychological treatment, such as CBT, for panic disorder results in significantly lower rates of relapse than the use of pharmacological-only or related types of treatments. Anxiety disorders are particularly relapse-prone disorders, as people will always experience varying levels of stress and anxiety in the course of their daily living. Moreover, everyone reading this book will experience very traumatic or stressful events in his or her lifetime, such as the death of a loved one, some serious medical diagnosis, car accidents, etc. Experiencing anxiety as a result of such events is normal and in many cases is unavoidable.

If you have panic disorder, it helps to recognize this. Just as you should develop a relapse-prevention strategy for normal lapses, you should also include a contingency plan for these types of situations. One very good contingency plan is to return to the therapist for a booster session. It should be stressed that having to return for a booster session is not an indication of failure in the individual, but instead a plan for success and avoiding a return to past dysfunctional behaviors. The majority of therapists who treat anxiety disorders recommend booster sessions for their clients and are quite sympathetic to the need for clients to periodically return for some extra support. The goal is to be proactive and not reactive.

ESSENTIAL

Coping with a psychiatric disorder is often a long-term process. Learning to deal with one's behaviors, change behavior, and be proactive is difficult. Over time, the process becomes routine and should become easier. However, a good treatment plan recognizes that there is always the potential for one to return to past behaviors and plans to avoid such a return.

You Are in Control

One of the most counterproductive beliefs a person can have is that she has no control over her life. Nothing could be further from the truth. The key factor in understanding notions of control is the understanding that one always has control over her reaction to the events that occur in her life. You have control over your panic.

The Story of Viktor Frankl

Viktor Frankl was a Jewish neurologist and psychiatrist who was a concentration camp prisoner of the Nazis during World War II. Dr. Frankl spent over three years in a work camp with other prisoners who had been ostracized from Germany. He went through some of the most severe hardships imaginable. For instance, he lost his home. He lost his wife and children who were also imprisoned and later assassinated. He lost his medical practice. He lost all contact with friends and family. He lost all of his possessions and every aspect of his life, although he never committed a crime. He lost all control over his life.

While a prisoner in the work camp, he was forced to endure near-death experiences every day; to work in harsh conditions such as severe winters with only rags as clothes and dilapidated socks or torn shoes to wear; was beaten often and constantly threatened with being killed by the guards; and was forced to endure these conditions while only eating a bowl of watery soup, a crust of stale bread, and an occasional small piece of sausage daily. The conditions he describes are much more harsh and severe than the vast majority of readers in this book will ever experience. Dr. Frankl had virtually no control over his life during this period of time. He was told exactly what to do, when to do it, and if he did not comply he was beaten and/or threatened with death. He saw many of his peers in the camps die as a result of the harsh conditions or be murdered by the Nazi guards. He had no hope of escape and he had no hope that he would ever leave.

It is no surprise that Victor Frankl struggled with his beliefs regarding free will and life's purpose during this period of time. He came to the remarkable conclusion that he was still in control of how he reacted to the severe circumstances which were forced on him. He could chose to give up, think of only himself, or endure and help others. He realized that he was not able to control the situation, the outcome of the war, the attitudes of the guards or other prisoners, or anything other than his own personal decision to react in a specific way to the events in his life. After the war he went on to become a leading psychiatrist, author, and developed his own brand of psychotherapy called logotherapy that is still practiced today.

Where Control Lies

The story of Dr. Frankl illustrates a basic fact of human existence. That fact is this: People often have little control over their external circumstances, but people are always able to choose how they will react to situations that confront them in their lives. As human beings, we may influence others, but we have very little control over them. We often have little control over the events in our lives. A person with panic disorder may feel that she has no control over her panic attacks or over the anticipatory worry that accompanies the disorder; however, every person with panic disorder can decide how she will react to her situation. You may not directly have control over your panic attacks, but you do have control over how you will react to having panic attacks. Even if you decide that you have absolutely no control over any aspect of your situation or how you respond, this decision is a willful one. Viktor Frankl realized this and made it his life's work to get this message to others.

Understanding that you have control over your reactions to the situations in your life also leads to the realization that one is responsible for how one reacts to the events in one's life. No matter what circumstances or events occur and shape your life, you alone are responsible for how you react, perceive, and interpret these events. To a person who understands and embraces this viewpoint, any obstacle can be confronted with the confidence that one can do something to affect one's situation. This means that despite how bad things may seem, one is never powerless.

This book has been about exercising one's control over her reaction to a devastating psychiatric disorder known as panic disorder. The first step in taking control of panic disorder is to take responsibility for one's self. When you realize you have control over your reactions, the task becomes far less daunting and life becomes far more optimistic. How you react to your panic disorder, or how you react to panic disorder occurring in a friend or loved one, is all up to you. *You* are in control.

Find Your Healthy Balance

Simply put, receiving treatment for some type of psychological problem or psychiatric disorder is one way for a person to find balance in his life. Stress, anxiety, nervousness, fear, etc., are all components of normal living. A person who has successfully dealt with his panic disorder will still experience all of these. The goal is to be able to balance the normal ups and downs of life such that the person can learn to function without letting these issues affect the quality of his life over the long run.

For a person with panic disorder, this can seem like quite a daunting task at first; however, once a person can gain control over his panic attacks, he can begin to balance his other issues. The key is to gain a sense of control over one's panic attacks and then to gain a sense of control over the rest of his issues, such as worry, behavioral issues, etc. Understanding this and being able to balance the relatively normal emotions associated with life allows one to gain a sense of control over life. Learn to recognize when things are out of balance, when stress levels are high, or when you are overdoing something, and then learn to pull back.

The key to maintaining balance is to remember the lessons learned in treatment. As stated earlier, practice what was learned often and never be too proud to ask for help if needed. Reviewing topics such as lapses and relapses, remembering the treatment goals one accomplished, and focusing on balancing stress, relaxation, and activity levels will go a long way in helping one maintain a sense of control over issues previously believed to be uncontrollable.

Conclusions

Life can be harsh. However, one can attribute meaning to existence and find purpose in life through three channels: the love of another or the love for another, one's life's work or life goals, and through enduring hardship and suffering. Many people have been successfully treated for panic disorder. At one time, these people believed they had no control over their panic attacks or over their lives. Treatment showed them the way and showed them that they can be strong. The safest path to follow in the treatment of any psychological disorder is to find an empirically validated treatment method that works for the particular individual in question. This book has been designed to help you understand panic disorder, understand the treatment options, and choose the best course of action.

No one should suffer with an anxiety disorder like panic disorder, and the treatment options are out there for the taking. Only you can control how you react to your panic disorder. Hopefully this book has shown you the way. Be well.

APPENDIX A

Glossary

Action-oriented psychotherapy
A group of therapies that focus on having the person actually do something to change a particular behavior.

Agoraphobia
An anxiety disorder where there is an intense fear or anxiety that is experienced in relation to being in a situation that one cannot escape.

Anxiety
A sense of apprehension due to some unrecognized or vague threat that is often accompanied by physical symptoms, such as perspiration, restlessness, feeling jittery, palpitations, headache, and other symptoms.

Anxiety disorder
A psychiatric disorder where the primary symptom is anxiety.

Anxiolytic drugs
Medications that are used to treat anxiety (most often benzodiazepines are given this title).

Benzodiazepine
Antianxiety medication that primarily affects the neurotransmitter GABA.

CBT (cognitive behavioral therapy)
A type of psychotherapy that combines behavioral principles and cognitive principles. Considered to be the best form of treatment for panic disorder (if used properly).

Comorbid/Comorbidity
Two or more disorders occurring in the same individual at the same time.

Complementary and alternative medicine (CAM)
A general class of interventions that are not considered mainstream treatments. These include herbs, diet, yoga, acupuncture, and many others.

DSM
The *Diagnostic and Statistical Manual of Mental Disorders* that is used to diagnose mental disorders in the United States. The current version is the DSM-5.

Empirical
To be acquired by observation. Empirical evidence or empirically based treatments are determined by strict, methodological procedures designed to eliminate bias and account for chance factors.

GABA
Gamma-aminobutyric acid is the major inhibitory neurotransmitter in the brain.

Group psychotherapy
Any psychological intervention that treats more than one person at the same time.

Iatrogenic symptoms
Symptoms created by a physician's treatment.

Insight-oriented psychotherapy
Psychotherapies that attempt to help people discover the nature or causes of their behaviors as the major mechanism of change.

Lapse
A relatively common urge or thought to return to former ways of behaving and/or thinking. Lapses are quite common.

Limbic system
A series of brain structures often considered to be critical for the experience of emotions.

NCS-R
The U.S. National Comorbidity Survey-Replication is a large study attempting to provide information about the demographic aspects of the disorders listed in the DSM.

Neurons
The nerve cells in the brain.

Neurotransmitters
Chemical messengers used by neurons to send signals in the brain.

Panic attacks
Intense periods of anxiety or fear that develop abruptly and often peak within ten minutes of onset.

PFPP
Panic-focused psychodynamic psychotherapy, for panic disorder.

Psychiatrist
A medical doctor who specializes in the treatment of mental illness. Psychiatrists typically prescribe medications and do not do psychotherapy.

Psychologist
A specially trained expert in human behavior. Clinical psychologists are trained to diagnose and treat psychological problems using psychotherapy. In most cases they cannot prescribe medication.

Psychotherapy
A contracted treatment between a trained professional and a person or group of people with the goal of solving a specific set of problems, lifestyle conditions, or the effects of some type of mental disorder.

Psychotropic medications
Medicines used for the treatment of psychiatric disorders.

RCT (randomized controlled trial)
A type of research method designed to specifically test some treatment or intervention on some particular issue. This is the most desirable form of research used to support treatments for mental disorders.

Relapse
An actual return to a sustained pattern of behaving or thinking that occurred in the past, but that one has previously changed.

Risk factor
Some element, biological or environmental, that increases the probability that someone will develop a disorder or disease.

Selective serotonin reuptake inhibitors (SSRIs)
SSRIs block the cellular reuptake of the neurotransmitter serotonin after it has been released in the synapse.

Stress
Experiences or perceptions that result in the stress response in a person.

Syndrome
A group of symptoms that hang together and define a specific type of abnormality, illness, disease, or disorder.

APPENDIX B

References

THE AMERICAN PSYCHOLOGICAL ASSOCIATION

The APA has a good series on panic disorder.
www.apa.org/topics/anxiety/panic-disorder.aspx

THE ANXIETY DISORDERS ASSOCIATION OF AMERICA

The ADAA offers a great deal of relevant information.
www.adaa.org/sites/default/files/panic_adaa.pdf

THE MAYO CLINIC

The Mayo Clinic offers some relevant information on panic disorder.
www.mayoclinic.com/health/panic-attacks/DS00338

THE NATIONAL INSTITUTE OF MENTAL HEALTH

NIMH has very good information on anxiety disorders and panic disorder.
www.nimh.nih.gov/health/topics/panic-disorder/index.shtml

PSYCHCENTRAL

This website offers the most comprehensive list of online resources for anxiety, anxiety disorders, and panic disorder.
http://psychcentral.com/resources/Anxiety_and_Panic/Support_Groups/

UNITED STATES NATIONAL SUICIDE & CRISIS HOTLINES

Offers numbers nationwide for people experiencing suicidal thoughts.
http://suicidehotlines.com/national.html

Books

There are several very good books that can be used to supplement much of the information in this book. Some are technical; others are a bit more aimed at lay readers.

American Psychiatric Association. (2013). *Diagnostic and Statistical Manual of Mental Disorders* (Fifth ed.). American Psychiatric Publishing.

Andrews, G., Charney, D. S., Regier, D. A., & Sirovatka, P. J. (Eds.). (2009). *Stress-Induced and Fear Circuitry Disorders: Refining the Research Agenda for DSM-V.* American Psychiatric Publishers.

Antony, M. M., & Stein, M. B. (Eds.). (2009). *Oxford Handbook of Anxiety and Related Disorders.* Oxford University Press.

Barlow, D. H. (2004). *Anxiety and Its Disorders: The Nature and Treatment of Anxiety and Panic.* Guilford Press.

Beck, J. (Ed.). (2010). *Interpersonal Processes in the Anxiety Disorders: Implications for Understanding Psychopathology and Treatment.* American Psychological Association.

Frankl, V. E. (1985). *Man's Search for Meaning.* Simon & Schuster.

Hatfield, R. C. (2013). *The Everything Guide to the Human Brain.* Adams Media.

Hinton, D., & Good, B. J. (Eds.). (2009). *Culture and Panic Disorder.* Stanford University Press.

Kirsch, I. (2010). *The Emperor's New Drugs: Exploding the Antidepressant Myth*. Basic Books.

Lazarus, R. S. (1966). *Psychological Stress and the Coping Process*. McGraw-Hill.

LeDoux, J. E. (1996). *The Emotional Brain: The Mysterious Underpinnings of Emotional Life*. Simon & Schuster.

Lilienfeld, S. O., Lynn, S. J., & Lohr, J. M. (Eds.). (2003). *Science and Pseudoscience in Clinical Psychology*. Guilford Press.

Nutt D., Feeney A., & Argyropolous, S. (2002). *Anxiety Disorders Comorbid with Depression: Panic Disorder and Agoraphobia*. Martin Dunitz Ltd.

Patten, M. L. (2007). *Understanding Research Methods: An Overview of the Essentials*. Pyrczak Publishing.

Root, B. A. (2000). *Understanding Panic and Other Anxiety Disorders*. University Press of Mississippi.

Rothschild, A. J. (2011). *The Evidence-Based Guide to Antidepressant Medications*. American Psychiatric Publishers.

Selye, H. (1976). *The Stress of Life*. McGraw-Hill.

Stein, D. J., Hollander, E., & Rothbaum, B. O. (Eds.). (2009). *Textbook of Anxiety Disorders*. American Psychiatric Publishers.

Szasz, T. S. (2011). *The Myth of Mental Illness: Foundations of a Theory of Personal Conduct*. HarperCollins.

Taylor, C. B. (Ed.). (2009). *How to Practice Evidence-Based Psychiatry: Basic Principles and Case Studies*. American Psychiatric Publishers.

Wells, A. (2013). *Cognitive Therapy of Anxiety Disorders: A Practice Manual and Conceptual Guide*. John Wiley & Sons.

Wolfe, B. E. (2005). *Understanding and Treating Anxiety Disorders: An Integrative Approach to Healing the Wounded Self*. American Psychological Association.

Treatment Assessment/ Which Treatment May Be Right for You?

The following questions can help guide you toward a treatment for panic disorder that you are most comfortable with. The questions are based on previous research regarding the personal variables that are sometimes associated with successful treatment outcomes. This brief survey is meant to be a guideline as to what treatment might best fit with one's needs and expectations. There are no surveys that can reliably predict treatment success, and no survey can identify which treatment will provide anyone with the best overall results. In addition, this survey is not designed to be used to make a decision regarding treatment. This survey is simply a guideline to assist one in choosing a treatment. If you have been treated for panic disorder previously, this survey will probably not offer any new information, but might still be useful. This survey has not been subjected to any form of empirical research to determine its reliability or validity. It is only offered as a guide for readers of this book.

Brief Survey

Instructions: Answer each question by circling the number that best matches your experience.

1. My panic attacks interfere with my ability to work.

   1   2   3   4   5
   Disagree Totally   Agree Completely

2. My panic attacks have been occurring for a long time.

   1   2   3   4   5
   Disagree Totally   Agree Completely

3. I generally trust the medical profession.

   1   2   3   4   5
   Disagree Totally   Agree Completely

4. I can explain the feelings and sensations that occur during my panic attacks.

   1   2   3   4   5
   Disagree Totally   Agree Completely

5. I am afraid to leave my house alone at times.

   1   2   3   4   5
   Disagree Totally   Agree Completely

6. I believe that I can get better.

   1   2   3   4   5
   Disagree Totally   Agree Completely

7. I sit around too much.

   1   2   3   4   5
   Disagree Totally   Agree Completely

8. I have discussed my panic attacks with others.

   1   2   3   4   5
   Disagree Totally   Agree Completely

9. I regularly take more than three prescription medications.

   1   2   3   4   5
   Disagree Totally   Agree Completely

10. I have more than three alcoholic drinks a week.

    1   2   3   4   5
    Disagree Totally   Agree Completely

11. I use nonprescription drugs on a regular basis.

    1   2   3   4   5
    Disagree Totally   Agree Completely

Using the Survey

People scoring a four or above on items 1 and 3 may find that medications may be beneficial to them or more suited for their expectations, especially faster-acting medications. However, someone also scoring above a three on items 10 and/or 11 may need close supervision, should disclose all medication substance use to his or her physician, and may need to combine medical treatment with psychotherapy. Someone scoring above a three on question 9 might need a complete medical review before treatment to decide the best course of action.

People scoring above a three on item 4, item 6, item 8, or any combination of the three may respond well to psychotherapy and perhaps to a CAM to accompany therapy or other primary treatment, such as hypnosis, biofeedback, meditation, etc. Someone scoring below a three on item 6 but higher on item 4 and/or item 8 may find a combination of medication and therapy to be helpful. Someone scoring a two or lower on these items may want to consider concentrating on medical treatments first and perhaps trying psychotherapy later.

If you score above a three on item 7, adding some approved (by your physician), supervised activity, such as yoga or some other exercise, may help your primary treatment.

Someone scoring above a three on item 2 might consider combining psychotherapy and medication.

Anyone scoring a two or below on item 3 might not be a prime candidate for medication as a standalone treatment and also may wish to incorporate some of the CAMs discussed in this book with psychotherapy (but only under the supervision of a physician, even though that seems a bit contradictory).

If someone scores three or higher on item 5, his or her treatment can be complicated, and some of the considerations discussed in the chapter on agoraphobia may be appropriate.

Use Discretion

Again, this survey is a guideline to help you make decisions. This survey does not guarantee any particular treatment outcome and makes no claims regarding the treatment of panic disorder in anyone. No one can offer guarantees regarding any individual treatment outcome. Any medications or the use of any other substances to treat panic disorder should be done under the care of a physician. Any formal therapy or complementary and alternative treatment should only be administered by trained, licensed individuals.

Index